SIR RICHARD BURTON

MICHAEL HASTINGS

Sir Richard Burton
a biography

Coward, McCann & Geoghegan, Inc.
New York

First American Edition 1978

Library of Congress Cataloging in Publication Data

Hastings, Michael, 1937-
  Sir Richard Burton.

  Bibliography: p.
  Includes index.
  1. Burton, Richard Francis, Sir, 1821-1890.
2. Adventure and adventurers—Biography. I. Title.
G246.B8H37 1978   910'.92'4 [B]   78-5486
ISBN 0-698-10936-8

Printed in the United States of America

For Victoria and George

Contents

Illustrations

ACKNOWLEDGMENTS

1 Royal Geographical Society
2 National Army Museum
3 The collection of Mrs Christopher Wood
4 Council of the London Borough of Richmond upon Thames
5 Royal Anthropological Institute
6 J. T. Bowden
7 Rodney Searight
Maps facing pages 91 and 117: Royal Geographical Society.

Acknowledgments

The author is indebted, for the kind help, research and patience, to the staff members of the Royal Geographical Society, Royal Asiatic Society, Royal Anthropological Institute (library section), British Museum (manuscripts division), National Army Museum (department of records), India Office Library and Records (commissioned ranks archives), Richmond Central Library (Orleans House), and the London Library. The author gratefully records the generous co-operation of the present descendants of the Agg family (Cheltenham), and the Mostyn-Price family (Staffordshire), and the Tyrwhitt-Drake family. Gratitude and thanks to J. L. Naimaster, D. Eaton, Ronald Pearsall, David Moss, John Brinton, Rodney Searight, Michael Plomer, R. E. Ablett, John Bowden, and Oswald Jones.

I

Years spent with the indifference of
tossed pennies by a wag swag father.

RICHARD FRANCIS BURTON WAS BORN MARCH 19, 1821, IN
Torquay, South Devon. His mother Martha and his father Lieutenant-Colonel Joseph Burton quickly moved back to Hertfordshire, to
Barham House, Elstree, where Martha's father Richard Baker lived.
Europe had suffered eighteen years of uninterrupted war in almost
every country. That year, at Trier, in Germany, Karl Marx celebrated
his third birthday. In Italy, from Ravenna, the same month as Burton's
birth, Byron was writing a letter to London on the prospect of money
and travel,

> Abroad, with a fair foreign education and a portion of five or six thousand
> pounds one might and may marry very respectably. In England, such a
> dowry is a pittance, while elsewhere it is a fortune.

And in West Hill, Long Island, New York, the child Walt Whitman
lay on a canvas frame cot on a bungalow verandah which fringed the
length of the wood building; he had just learned to walk and his
parents had warned him against climbing below the stoep.
Eighteen twenty-one in England, in terms of a living wage and a
happy working society, was not an encouraging year. A young man
in good health could aspire to the national average wage of seventeen

shillings a week, and out of twenty million inhabitants, less than fifty thousand earned more than £200 a year. And as for bought commissions in the army, a lieutenant-colonelcy could cost as much as £40,000. And such an officer could not expect more than £1,000 staff salary per annum from his investment in the commission. It was marginally better, in fact, to put his money into government 'blue chip' stock at three per cent. And clearly, Richard Burton's father, Joseph Netterville Burton, was by no means a poor man.

Richard's father possessed a peculiarly blunderbuss-like personality; he rarely succeeded in anything he set out to do and yet he always managed to make a large noise in all his endeavours. He was unusually unforthcoming about such things as his exact birth date, and his children never learned his correct age. He had been born into a share of many thousands of Irish acres in the last quarter of the 18th century. By all accounts he was the classic ne'er-do-well off-spring, none too bright but of a very presentable appearance, and it was thought best to shovel his carcass, like that of many a young dunderhead, into a uniform no matter what the commission cost, and send him away to war; any war would do. Joseph was attached to the 36th Foot Regiment at the age of seventeen. Strangely enough he was not alone the day he entered the barracks, he had persuaded a dozen of his tenant lads to accompany him into uniform. But as soon as they were ensconced in the fold of the 36th, most of these Irish lads fled home. Either the promise of pay he had made to them did not rise to expectations, or the youths decided that they had already served their roving teenage gent overlong.

Joseph was of a moderate height, according to his son, and had black hair and a sallow skin and what one might describe as a not overly ambitious nose—'high nose' is how Richard described it. Joseph had a piercing look in his eyes, a gleaming strength there, and wherever he went he was considered the handsomest man in the street.

Although the Burton family still possessed considerable estates in Ireland by 1815, they appeared an impoverished lot. For Joseph and his brothers and cousins a good marriage was the required order of the day. One cousin happily married into the comfortable Plunkett family, and another cousin struck yankee gold by marrying a Drax heiress.

In 1818, Joseph and his younger brother Francis came across a rather crusty English squire, Richard Baker, who possessed a frugal Scots wife, three daughters and an erstwhile spendthrift son nobody cared much for; the Baker family lived in a substantial house in Hertfordshire. It did not take the brothers long to find out that each Baker daughter was to inherit £30,000 on the father's death. In addition, the spendthrift son Richard Baker was to inherit the remainder of the estate, some £100,000. Joseph Burton wasted no time in attaching himself to the eldest daughter Martha. And Francis, his brother, not unexpectedly paid court to the second girl Sarah.

With characteristic disregard for Joseph's plans to enter the marriage market, his regiment the 36th required his services in Sicily, for a brief skirmish with the enemy, serving under his commander Sir John Moore. Having bought his way to a lieutenant-colonelcy, Joseph Netterville Burton got himself embroiled in some peculiar barrack incidents. When he was not fighting the enemy, he indulged in the chivalrous but arguably illegal hobby of duelling with long-barrelled pistols. On a choice occasion, one of his fellow officers found reason to insult Joseph, and in the ensuing shoot-out Joseph fired a good percussive blast and hit his opponent in the chest. Immediately, Joseph took charge of the wounded man and kept him under careful ministration in his own tent. All this concern could be put down to basic humanitarian impulses were it not for the fact that an officer could, at that time, lose his commission in the regiment for duelling. Within three months, the fellow officer took it upon himself to insult Joseph Burton once again. And Burton, never loath to rise, accepted the taunt and demanded a second duel. How both officers persuaded their seconds to witness this illegal event for a second time is unrecorded. Pistols were primed and each man took his turn with the percussive hammer beneath his forefinger. Joseph bowled over his opponent with an accurate shot to the chest, and once again rushed forward to lift the wounded man and drag him inside his own tent. Indeed, perhaps they surely would have found due cause to insult one another again but for Sir John Moore's decision to withdraw the regiment to England.

Joseph's preoccupations outside army duty were gambling and gun collecting. Like all other officers, he was not required to share the voyage home with his own troops in a foul, reeking cattle boat, and he chose to make his leisurely way through Italy and France. Although his British uniform was not exactly a welcome sight in these foreign parts, he nevertheless travelled as a representative of the conquering British nation. After all, to the eternal chagrin of all Republican citizens of Europe, it was Wellington and not Napoleon who ultimately represented the rule of right. But, on his travels home, Joseph Burton must have fallen in love with these foreign places. His first taste of Genoa, Pisa or Tours was very much to his liking. It was his 'European education'.

Joseph wasted no time, once he reached England, to seek out Martha Baker at Barham House, in Hertfordshire, and the romance blossomed beneath the wary gaze of the father, Richard Baker, and the suspicious temper of the profligate young Richard Baker. But Joseph's palpable intentions to claim Martha and her dowry for himself were about to be dashed by orders from the 36th Regiment to return to Genoa for a brief spell in the British garrison. Joseph acted promptly. He asked Richard Baker for the hand of his daughter. It was grudgingly given. Martha, a nervous girl with a sickly disposition, joyfully announced her engagement to the rest of the family. The happy couple wasted no time. Joseph persuaded Martha to marry him forthwith. In a few weeks he would be sailing for Genoa. Clearly, Joseph struck while the iron was hot. He did not want to give the Baker family the opportunity to dissuade Martha in his absence. They were wed immediately.

Joseph departed for Genoa alone. He promised Martha his speedy return. He had no idea at the time that his sense of duty to the army would almost cost him his rank and means of livelihood. During his stay in Genoa, the entire British garrison was embarrassed by the sudden arrival of Princess Caroline of Brunswick, with a small retinue. This embarrassment within the military camp was understandable. Caroline had been long separated from her husband the Prince of Wales. And his portly dandified self had spent almost ten years hounding her and insulting her throughout the British Isles. He searched endlessly for an excuse to annul the marriage, and this squandering toad, the 'fat friend' of George Brummell, was for ever trumping up charges of adultery against her, so that the poor woman was the target of every gutter press lampoon. Now he was hell bent on excluding her from his future coronation rituals. Unfortunately for Joseph, spies privy to the future George IV put him up as a possible witness against Caroline on the grounds of her supposed misconduct in Genoa.

On Joseph's return, he was ordered to stand prosecution witness against Caroline of Brunswick in a trumped up trial set in the House of Lords. The Prince of Wales was convinced of an affair between Caroline and her Italian courier, and he was literally weeks away from his own coronation. Parliament proposed a Bill of Pains and Penalties against Caroline, and she became the unlikely heroine of the more liberal element of British society. Colonel Burton decided not to give evidence against her, thereby virtually cutting his military throat. The Duke of Wellington ordered him to be placed on half-pay as punishment.

There had been some changes meanwhile at Barham House, in Hertfordshire. Joseph's young brother Francis was now engaged to the second girl Sarah Baker. And the old man Richard Baker had promptly rewritten the terms of Martha's inheritance now that she and Joseph were married. The inheritance was written out in such a way that, no matter what mischief Joseph got up to, he could not get his hands on Martha's money without prior permission. The speed with which this was done suggests that Richard Baker Senior took his son-in-law for a bungling and reckless heir to an Irish peat-bog, an assessment somewhat unfairly endorsed by the army's decision to abandon Joseph.

As for Caroline of Brunswick, events speedily reduced her to public disgrace. She was banned from entering the cathedral on the day of her husband's coronation and in no time at all the poor woman expired in misery. She had become a classic victim of British double-face: on the one hand liberal and sympathetic crowds rushed to see her coffin, and on the other the Tory wags of stiffening chauvinism raised their noses to her name as if it was a perfume which had turned into piss.

Richard Francis Burton was born a year after the marriage. Although he was born at Torquay, he was baptised at Elstree where, nearby, lived the Baker family. The child had bright red hair, dark piercing eyes and a strident yell. And no matter what old Baker thought of Joseph, he truly loved his grandson. This sudden passion almost made Richard Francis Burton a very wealthy child, but for his mother's interference. Martha was still deeply attached to her profligate brother, and defended him time and time again whenever he shamed the family. And yet, the more the old man saw of the infant Richard Burton – dark brat with unsmiling gaze pouring intelligence – the more he was determined to settle his son's inheritance on his grandson. For many months, Martha prevailed upon her father not to cut off her own brother. And it was Martha who, by creating this delay, robbed her son of a great fortune.

From all accounts, young Richard Baker was a madcap playboy who cared not a fig for his studies in law. But when it came to the gaming tables he was a proper sharp fellow indeed, and from Barham House it was an easy day's ride to a private gambling house in Curzon Street, Mayfair. Illegal as public gaming was, dandies and dullards, cash-knees and penny-punters would meet at either the Cocoa Tree, Watier's or the Italian Carbonari to arrange a table after dark. Young Richard could play faro or hazard, and discover glad girls from Highbury Barn or the Cremorne at his elbow. These bacchante dollies would queue on the steps of Watier's for the pleasure of the plastered swells as they fell out of their debts onto the morning pavement.

Richard Baker Senior had had enough of the rumours about his only son. He could see for himself the faro cards in the dandy's eyes. The old man made up his mind to drive to London to his lawyers and cut off his son altogether, leaving the bulk share of £100,000 to be divided between his elderly wife and his grandson. With an understandable ruefulness Richard Burton described his grandfather's fateful departure:

> My mother had a wild half-brother, Richard Baker, junior, a barrister-at-law, who refused a judgeship in Australia, and died a soap-boiler. To him she was madly attached, and delayed the signing of my grandfather's will as much as possible to the prejudice of her own babe. My grandfather Baker drove in his carriage to Messrs Dendy, his lawyers, with the object of signing the will, and dropped dead, on getting out of the carriage, of ossification of the heart; and the documents being unsigned, the property was divided. It would now be worth half a million pounds.

There is something persistently familiar about the grandfather's sudden demise on the steps of the lawyers' office. Those magnetic filings of ill-luck were already rubbing off from Joseph Burton to his son.

In all of Richard Burton's writings there is little reference to his mother Martha. This nervous young woman, fascinated by wildness in others, plain to look at but bearing with her a fine dowry, assumed a role in her son's life not unlike that of the split infinitive—utterly vexing, usually irrelevant to the issue, and merely a time filler out of convenience. But in her own right it ought to be said that she stood by her Irish officer husband who had a penchant for pistol fights, and eventually she gave birth to three spirited children.

Since 1803 all Europe had been in flames over the zealous territorial demands of the French Empire; by 1821, the major powers of Britain, Austria, and Prussia were keen to normalise the situation. There was to be a Restoration in France. And though Britain herself feared most the advent of a new Jacobinism in Europe, she had few territorial claims on the civilised continent. Britain's chief concern was to hold her pearl in the shape of India and thereby open up the Far East. Russia wanted the sea-lanes and happily acquired Finland.

Austria took back certain Italian states. Even the defeated French had enough Empire building strength left to claim Algeria. Slavery in the North Americas was soon to be abolished and the United States was marching already into Mexico. The Napoleonic Wars had temporarily slowed the great nations. France was impoverished.

Joseph Burton, now on half-pay and with no regiment to call his own, out of pocket and out of step with his fellow men, was determined to settle in France where he knew he could live cheaply. On his wife's £30,000 he was going to retire from life at an early age. He had not the courage to fight his way back into the army. And it would seem that all his horizons, all his future wakings would be confined to the more pleasurable pursuits – hunting and whoring, pistol-practising and swimming, watching the years observe him, and never questioning his own providence. Joseph suffered from chronic bronchials, and the French sunshine if not the boar hunting would do him a power of good, and the idea of taking up civilian employment simply did not occur to him.

Neither genes nor history will reveal just how Lieutenant-Colonel Joseph Netterville Burton came to father the fierce-eyed infant Richard, prodigy of a thousand energies.

II

Expatriate childhood and dungy
devilets a near marathon of burgher
niceties.

JOSEPH DECIDED TO SETTLE IN THE TOWN OF TOURS, IN
central France. It was the ancient capital of Touraine, with a population
of 60,000 people; it was the birthplace of Balzac, and of late had
become the principal burgh of the department of Indre-et-Loire. Tours
was, apart from being the venue of all Balzac's passion in his *Louis
Lambert* description of schooldays, quite a haven of retreat for a well-
to-do English military family.

Tours, then, was not unlike latter-day Gibraltar. Although, of
course, Gibraltar has remained a dominion of the United Kingdom,
British families were attracted there by a preferential exchange value of
their money. In the 1820s, not withstanding the Battle of Waterloo, the
crushing of France and its Republican schemes of a European Empire,
a town such as Tours was very popular with the British. The French
currency rate exchanged against the golden guinea with considerable
advantage for the British. In those early days of the restoration in
France and Italy, vast areas of land were liable to crop famine, and central
France in particular was often filled with migratory hordes of workers
moving from north to south in search of food and shelter. Before the industrial revolution could get under way many millions starved, and the
bankers of Europe had to come to London to find forms of reinvest-
ment to perpetuate the novel idea (first quoted in 1812) of a *middle class*.

Joseph Burton rented an old house on a river bank, the Château Beausejour; it stood close by the Loire and was surrounded by vineyards. The English community in Tours must have approached five hundred souls. At that time, catering for this community's needs, there was a chaplain, the Rev. Mr Way, a schoolmaster Mr Clough, and yet another schoolmaster Mr Gilchrist (who liked to chastise boys overmuch), a devoted doctor Mr Brettoneau, a certain the Honourable Martin Hawke who, it appears, filled his daily hours with sword-fencing and lessons in duelling, and a witsome Irishman called Mr Hume who led the Lieutenant-Colonel in numerous forays through Amboise Forest with loaded muskets in search of boars.

The Burtons, however, did not stay long at the château by the river. (Either it was too far out from the hubbub and gossip of town, or damp, or perhaps infested with rats.) They rented another house in a key street of Tours, the Rue de L'Archevêche. The Burtons liked to declare it was closer and more convenient for schools.

At intervals of twenty months Mrs Burton found herself pregnant, and returned with a single French maid to Barham House, in Hertfordshire, where her own mother still maintained a family home. When Richard was two Martha Burton gave birth to a girl—Maria Catherine Eliza. When Richard was four, once again Martha returned to England, and she bore a second boy—Edward Joseph Netterville.

In those 1820s, England was on the verge of the most unparalleled era of prosperity she had ever known; all of Russia and Prussia put together were no competition for England's trading system. England was the undisputed master of the world's trade. Even prevalent philosophic radicalism—such as the Benthamites, with their humane and healthy sounding doctrine of 'the greatest happiness of the greatest number'—paled beside the merciless machine of world expansion through trade, and merciless it was too when one realises how many captive and constrained markets England had carved out for herself from the West Indies to the shores of China. It was very nice for Martha Burton to wend her way back to Tours to her boar-hunting husband Joseph with another off-spring. Her government bonds in London were showing an all-time high in returns, and if certain importers were chafing at the imposition of new Corn Laws and Navigation Acts, as Martha reached the coast all around her on the docks she could see ample evidence of that supposed 'common good' the Liberals spoke of—for this tiny island had become both purse and spoon to the world's market place. It is remarkable that Martha never once remonstrated with her idle husband in Tours.

As Martha journeyed back and forth from Barham House with her babies, the world mourned the death of the greatest Englishman of the decade. Forty-seven coaches led Byron's funeral along Tottenham Court Road, in London. Eyeless and embalmed in a black pickle, this anachronistic *corsair* and flood fusion rhetorician for national liberty, rich English *Bolivar*, first international poet, whose own petty islandic community ostracised him—it was a thunderclap when his death was announced, and the club Watier's lowered its blinds and a teenage Alfred Tennyson scrawled on stone 'Byron is dead'.

As the children grew, young Richard took promptly to French and drawing, little Maria did everything quite so-so, and Edward the toddler played the piano very loudly. Joseph sent his children to an English Colony school in Tours. Richard Burton himself, in middle years, summed up the requirements of education, which suggests he found his own somewhat lacking:

To succeed in English life, boys must be brought up in a particular groove. From the Preparatory School, then Eton and Oxford, with an occasional excursion to France, Italy and Germany, to learn languages, not of Stratford-atte-Bowe, . . .

Burton considered his father to be a most moral and upright force, and yet, there is a certain sadness about the father's lack of control over these three children; for they were free, it seems, to become 'devilets', free to roist and charade away truant hours, meanwhile an ever-ending stream of belles, young and old, thin or bumpy, was hired for the evening chores, to supervise studies and supper and bedtime pranks. The Burton children were deft at lying on their backs and kicking out at the parlour maids and night nurses, and during the day Richard and Edward, aged eight and four, found trays of apple-puffs to steal from a gentle neighbour's windowsill and habitually sallied forth outside the French school to provoke what Burton later described as 'gutter boys and ruffians'.

It is a picture also of parental aloofness. There were Martha and Joseph, out each night with the other Britishers making plans to order beer by the barrel in Dieppe or select a decent (no Italians or Sicilians) elegant (Spanish staff best) hotel in St Malo, on the coast, for a summer holiday where they would bump into old English chums fresh from Dover.

Young Dick Burton had started his Latin at the age of four. In French and English he was bi-lingual by the time he was eight. He and his younger brother rode mules bareback along the best streets of the town, and one pleasant afternoon the schoolmaster announced he would take all the English boys and girls to watch a public execution. A woman poisoner was to be guillotined.

Nobody would cavil if this unlikely tale was part and parcel of a small boy's dreaming. After all, the Burton boys ran through forests imitating French kings and conquering new Aquitaines, they even stole muskets from their father's gun cupboard in the parlour to take out on their mules and pretend Belgian slaughter at famous Waterloo, but, it was a grown man who recounted this story of the public execution. It was not the boy. It was not even the boy within the man.

It is generally supposed that a middle-aged Burton dictated his only extant hundred and forty pages of autobiography to Isabel his wife while they were on ship together, in the 1870s. The story of the poor woman guillotined is decorated with a few remarks about heads leaning forward to study the impact of the blade upon the neck and the red pump of human blood so dreadfully loosed, but there it ends. It seems extremely unlikely that any schoolmaster would have taken the boys to such a spectacle. Does this anecdote spring from middle-aged bravura?

In France, in 1830, Charles X was dragged from his throne, and the entire populace of the country was in dread of an epidemic of cholera, which had broken out in the slum tenements of the larger towns. It could not have escaped Joseph Burton, in Tours, that a young family like this stood vulnerable to this crippling epidemic. One knows no other reason for this sudden return from Tours for the Burton family. No great aunt had died in England and left either Burton parent a small fortune. The children, quite happy in their schooling, had done nothing to deserve this peremptory decision.

Joseph ordered out the two coaches from their yard; the family put up most of their furnishings, carpets and curtains, lamps and kitchen ware, for auction on the premises. And what was considered valuable or indispensable was piled into the second coach with the family's three black labrador dogs. Martha Burton kept her silver cutlery and best china in a large wicker truck; the Lieutenant-Colonel had a number of bitumen-congealed family portraits inherited from Ireland, his pistols and his muskets, and two best pairs of riding boots and the long box of military swords of which he was so particularly fond. They had the three children and a maid in tow as well. In those times, certainly, domestic removals were complicated, but families had few possessions, they were not encumbered (as an average well-to-do late-Victorian family might have been) with unnecessary bric-à-brac; and when the Burton entourage—two coaches, six horses (third pair trotting behind), the family buried under knee rugs and drivers up aloft hoping for seventy miles every fifteen hours—set out for the north of France, it must have been a voyage undertaken with a great measure of trepidation. The postilion riders, who interchanged with the drivers, were responsible for arranging alternate horses, and if road halts were amenable it was possible to continue on all through the night; for there was nothing very pleasant about such travel, and those who undertook the adventure were constant prey to bad bowels, not a wink of sleep, draughts like pierced ears and muscle contortion from springless under-carriages. Not a yard out of one thousand was ever paved on the route and Burton himself remembered numerous stops when his parents unavailingly confronted landladies who plied them with absurdly steep demands for shelter and stable keep.

The journey broke Martha's health. They had to stop over at Chartres long enough to send word to her mother, Mrs Baker, to come and look after the family. It must have taken them two weeks to unite, even if Grandma Baker had moved with all speed. Eventually the family group moved on to Paris, Grandma Baker, the *garde-malade*, general dog's maid, and Martha Burton in a constant state of shock. More than likely this ridiculous journey came to a resounding head in the shape of a decent quarrel between the Burton parents. In fact, if there was any more expedient way in which to catch cholera, waterborne as we understand the epidemic to be, the blunderbuss Colonel Joseph had not found it.

They drove through the shanty suburbs of Paris and Grandma stuffed their mouths and noses with camphor tonic; they noticed the bullet holes on the walls of destroyed homes, and the coaches turned west down the interminable avenues of poplar sentinelled landscape, French and unmistakably none other, until they reached Dieppe.

The ten-year-old Richard stood on the fishermen's beach. This pretty cliff walled packet-steamer port was midway between Calais and Le Havre. England was an alien place. After Dieppe, he later recalled, it was 'a cold plunge into English life'.

He hadn't seen the country; his memory span did not reach back to Barham House in Hertfordshire. By all accounts, from the boy's point of view, his father lived a penurious life of boar hunting, just coin filled enough to avoid the pedestrian horror of actually having to earn his own living; and yet it must have been strange for young Richard— nothing really happened in their lives from day to day. His father had his boots nicely polished and his nervous mother equipped with a weak disposition occasionally had what we now might term a nervous breakdown. These breakdowns occurred with increasing frequency, and were not in any way helped by the curious lack of capability or simple sensitivity in the husband to do much to aid her in her misery.

Hardly likely was it that Burton Senior noticed much of the cultural landscape he had ridden his family so carelessly through; even less likely he knew anything about the France he was so abruptly leaving. it was a year in which Delacroix painted his novo romantic *To the Barricades* . . . and Pushkin had published the first part of *Eugène Onegin* in Paris.

The family was going to an islandic community bursting with commercial energy. Wars were—colonial matters aside—placed behind the new industrial society, and the immortal George Stephenson had spent a year fiddling with a steam-driven engine requiring steel runners to roll on called *The Rocket*.

Just what did Colonel Burton have in mind for himself when he returned to his mother-in-law's large house in Hertfordshire? Highly unlikely his old regiment would have him back on full pay, less likely he had kept up with any old friends for all these years, and it seems clear enough that he was as ill-equipped to return to England as he had been to leave the country ten years earlier.

The three Burton children followed their very 'Irish' father together with their mother and grandmother across country, closer to London, to a peculiar row of upright terrace houses, redbrick and somewhat plain, in a place called Maids of Honour Row, at Richmond, then a pretty Strand on a green on the outskirts of the metropolis. At this point Grandma Baker left the family, and it appears she took rooms in Park Street, Mayfair, behind Park Lane. Barham House was eventually closed up.

Naturally, the family's eyes and ears were on Joseph Burton to provide them with a sense of direction. Joseph banged his skull hard and came up with a thought—as he himself had attended neither Eton nor Oxford University, he decided this was the perfect course to set the two boys on. Little Maria, of course, as a girl, was required to stay at home and knit and collect the bills with a curtsey when they were presented at the door.

But where was the money to come from to pay for these expensive educations? Certainly not from Joseph. His military half-pay could manage the rent of the upright redbrick in Richmond, buy food and employ a staff of two daft maids, but that was the end of it. If Martha wanted new dresses she had to set to with young Maria, and cut and stitch out a decent enough copy from one of the drawings in the *Ladies' Journal.*

Joseph Burton, once he had announced his famous plan, waited for the formidable Grandma Baker, prudent Scottish woman though she was, to produce the necessary money to guarantee an Eton education for two violent lads who already hated the narrow walls and damp beds of their new British home. This guarantee was not forthcoming. He tried to pluck his wife's dowry of government bonds for this spendthrift scheme, but little came of that, either, and Martha accused Joseph of pilfering her inheritance.

No such luck. The ladies held tight to their bosom bonds and Lieutenant-Colonel Joseph Burton had to think yet again. A time consuming exercise he was pretty much unaccustomed to.

The Burton children were ten (Richard), eight (Maria) and six (Edward); not one of them had entered into English school society before this, and they were all quite shaken to their roots. The houses in Richmond were prim and mean, the entire field work of domestic architecture shrank pale and lifeless beside the poplar avenues and generous façades of Tours or Paris. Unlike the open uncluttered breadth of the French countryside this redbrick patch called Richmond Green was corseted with fences and obelised by 'public drinking houses' which disgorged warm flat ale. Burton recalled —

> We revolted against the coarse and half-cooked food, and, accustomed to the excellent Bordeaux of France, we found port, sherry, and beer like strong medicine; the bread, all crumb and crust, appeared to be half baked, and milk meant chalk and water.

For a year things were not going to get much better. The Colonel hung around impatiently for the money to send the boys to a decent Eton or Harrow. He waited in vain. Finally somebody, probably Grandma, had the boys packed off to a third-rate public school in the Old Town of Richmond at fees of £33 10s. a term.

Burton remembered the nicest of the school's nasties when he warned all those who might follow in his young footsteps to this class-provoking system of education, the private school.

> . . . What must have been our surprise at the food of an English school? Breakfast at 8 a.m. consisting of very blue milk and water, in chipped and broken-handled mugs of the same colour. The boys were allowed tea from home, but it was a perpetual battle to get a single drink of it. The substantials were a wedge of bread with a glazing of butter. The

epicures used to collect the glazing to the end of the slice in order to convert it into a final *bonne bouche*. The dinner at one o'clock began with stickjaw (pudding) and ended with meat . . . the latter was as badly cooked as possible, black out and blue inside, gristly and sinewy. The vegetables were potatoes which could serve for grapeshot, and the hateful carrot.

It does indeed sound like Dickens' Black Shop. The boys, though they could have boarded, returned home to Maids of Honour Row each night. This did little to encourage the other children to get to know the Burtons. An obvious wall was built up between those boarders who went to bed hungry and in tears, and the lucky lads who hit the pavement at five in the afternoon running at a wild sprint for a corner candy shop or their own mother's kitchen baking.

Their single year of English public-school life proved to be well-nigh intolerable. The Burton boys took extra packets of ham, polony or saveloys to school; they clearly paraded their superiority by producing a half-finished bottle of Bordeaux stolen from the Colonel's night before stupor (one of many such incidents which eventually prompted Joseph Burton to cry out in abandon 'the beasts in liquor!'); none of which much endeared them to their desk neighbours. It was fun for Richard and Edward to speak French so naturally, and at an instant, revert to the tongue of the country, and, though sadly obvious, it was not an unexpected reaction for the school to turn against these bragging Burtons with their frenchified ways and hold them sadistically down until the school bully administered a fair epistemological summation of the bruised-knuckles philosophy.

Richard Burton recollected an epidemic of measles which scourged the school in Richmond. And so severe was this outbreak that 'several of the boys died'. Nevertheless, for centuries English public schools have been racked with the measles and nobody (with the exception on the most rare occasions when a pulmonary infection developed) actually died from measles. Richard believed the fear of cholera hastened his father to leave France. Now, he claimed this epidemic of measles not only closed the school down, but persuaded the Colonel to take his family back to Europe post-haste. Either his father was a galloping hypochondriac or Richard's imaginings had already begun to run away with him.

For the next three years the Burtons stayed on the road. They hired Miss Ruxton, stout and of a red complexion, and a tutor, H. R. Du Pré, by all accounts a bulbous swell (a graduate son of a Rector) who was keen to travel on the Continent, especially with the aid of a modest stipend for being attached to a mad Irish colonel's noisy family and a weak wife constantly fading away behind smelling-salt kerchiefs.

They boarded a boat at Tower Wharf (in those days most passenger freight for Europe started up the Thames, in reach of central London town) and sailed for Boulogne. The boys danced and darted like hot-air wraiths on the decks, all hurrahs for France and howling hoots of deprecation for damp carrots and greens and flat brew rat beer England.

Joseph stopped in Paris to find comfortable rooms, but couldn't. He passed through Orléans and dallied just long enough to search for a country house on the fringe of the market centre. He failed. His yellow carriage headed for Blois, where its occupants found a small English colony perched on a rise just above the river bank, and the Colonel rented a villa for the rest of the year. The stout governess, Miss Ruxton, decided she had had enough of wandering and packed her bags home. The boys took up dancing and sword fencing, generally ignored Du Pré and his tutoring, but allowed him to teach them to swim. They learned the Gavotte and the Danse Chinoise, and Richard managed to pass his foil down Edward's throat 'nearly destroying the uvula'.

Their route took the carriages on from Blois to Lyons, to Avignon, through Provence to Marseilles, and there the family took the ferry boat across to Leghorn on the Italian coast, as it was then.

Once again Grandma Baker arrived from England to take care of the household: for it seemed that the Colonel was constantly falling prey to his old problem, asthma, and now Martha too was coming under the clutches of this fierce and nerve-wrought malady. Grandma Baker took it upon herself to accuse the Colonel of insanity (an accusation of some frequency throughout his life), and furthermore, of trying to kill off his entire family with this incessant ramble of horses, carriages, children, dogs, bad-tempered drivers and all through the ruins of Napoleon's Europe. What was it in aid of? Was he trying to put an end to poor Martha's weak heart? Was he determined to drive her soul into the dust of the road? And Grandma Baker had a knack of putting the knife in. She suddenly turned on Joseph one morning and accused him of wanting to meet up with a Sicilian girl he had known in Tours three years earlier. The suggestion, no doubt put in Grandma's most succinct tones, was that Joseph had had to use much of his pay to keep a pretty young Sicilian thing quiet back in those palmy pre-cholera days in Tours. To 'keep off claims' Richard Burton called it in later years; well, it can only have meant one of two things—either the girl was financially dependent on Joseph and his money and charms, or she was threatening blackmail. There is, assuredly, a feeling about the Colonel. A feeling that, when things got on top of him, he hastily reached for his wife's letter of credit, and without further ado, with not a word to anyone, they were all in flight again.

The family rolled on to Pisa. Things looked up here; the Colonel took rooms in a huge stone edifice on the wrong side of town, on the worst side of a river, facing a view which never received the sun. It took the Colonel the length of the summer to discover what a mistake he had made. During this time the boys studied Italian in the streets from the normal grammatically respectful intercourse of common epithets and various tomboy jackass punchups, and the Colonel's fancy was taken this time by a thunderous four-wheel trap which merely required an eighteen-hand high *equus caballus* equipped with the strength of a steam-roller. Joseph, delighting in this new equipage, acquired a titan quadruped called 'Dobbin' and sold off the second of his two coaches. All the family drove away from Pisa, the yellow coach leading, the Dobbin tonner on wheels a pace behind, and they made their way through Florence, to Siena, to Rome, and came to rest in Naples.

The boys studied with their tutor in the early morning; then they took four hours with a fencing master and another two hours secretly alone with pistol practice. Forbidden though it was, the father never once noticed the weapons missing from his much-treasured gun case and it is only to be assumed both Richard and Edward could load and fire as cunningly as they could clean and polish and return to the rightful case, these precious percussion pistols (most likely single-barrelled Mantons). We are not told how they paid for the shells, but it was not uncommon to refill a used case and cap it anew, even dilute the powder charge to share the number of shots, and the boys revelled in these pranks.

Behind their town house in Naples, the boys, aged fifteen and eleven, discovered a number of brothels. Richard and Edward telegraphed signs from their rooftop to a young prostitute, and she accorded them a measure of recognition, so much so, that, armed with knives both children wandered into the brothel one afternoon, albeit at the girl's request, and there set to in what Burton casually and much latter called a 'tremendous orgie'. Nothing was learnt about this, until, some time later, some of the girls exchanged letters with the handsome young British boys, and Martha Burton discovered these letters hidden in the boys' bedrooms. Uproar ensued. Years after Burton recollected the girls' letters expressed raving lewdness and vampish desire for their youthful English bodies, but we shall never know how much truth there was in the tale.

Between the age of fifteen and nineteen, the tutor Du Pré, hard as he found it, kept up with the likely lads Burton. The family returned to France to yet another small town filled with a snuff and whisky-taking colony of English. Burton makes a point that almost the entire population of any one of these colonies consisted of scruff gentry on the run from the law and retired Jamaican planters, having sold up, with nothing better to do than treat their servants like the slaves they had become accustomed to.

Joseph Burton had driven his wife Martha from town to town, colony to colony, for eighteen years; they had averaged a few months at each watering stop. Always the home was a rented establishment. New servants were employed, and the house linen unpacked. And all this time if she had complained much about it, nobody has recorded it for us. She took it all, the dreadful expatriate wandering, without any purpose or prospect of a future. Her grip on reality was, perhaps, her mother, who from time to time descended for a few weeks' verbal brawl with her son-in-law.

Joseph retreated to his gun case and his boar hunts. He had usually left any thrashings for Du Pré to deal with, and when on one occasion word filtered through to his distant brain that the boys had beaten Du Pré nearly senseless, Joseph even then decided not to press the horse-whip himself. His world was horizoned by the two carriages waiting in the stable yard, the new house rented, and the exigencies of bills to be met by courtesy of his wife's good humour and cheque-book. Martha must have withdrawn from them all.

As Joseph had failed to get his boys to Eton, he was more than ever determined to send them to university. They were not going to follow him into the army and its miserable half-pay stipends. Richard would go to Oxford, and Edward to Cambridge. That might keep the rogues apart for a while. After a decent theological course, they'd each take the Cloth. A living perhaps somewhere close by the sea, for Martha liked the sea. With a fine understanding of the boys' true natures, Joseph had done it again.

Richard and Edward arrived in England in 1840 with Du Pré. Grandma Baker fussed around them. Richard intensely disliked this damp and seedy little island kingdom; mean and small and pokey he found it, 'like a toy house'. Richard must have been looking at the redbrick shutterless terraces near Park Street, in Mayfair, where their grandmother had rooms; they reminded him of swallows' nests planted upon a palace wall.

That same year of 1840, twenty-seven-year-old David Livingstone, working on behalf of the London Missionary Society, set sail for Africa. From cushiony overstuffed Mayfair lodgings, Richard Burton waited out the long vacation to take rooms at Trinity College, Oxford. He was nineteen.

III

Dogsbottom scallycat sinner and canard Dick Byron roister goose who dare declare the family purse a clearance whip to harvest the Irish Famine?

THE YEAR 1840 WAS A TURNING POINT. QUEEN VICTORIA married Albert; Robert Peel became the new Prime Minister of England; the Whigs were the predominant party and they relied on the burgeoning middle classes to provide them with support. The period was one of slow reform. The Chartist Movement was strong. The Poor Law and the later Amendments took the workhouse away from the Church and provided it with a local area union administration. It was a period of steam-age promise as Britain entered into the industrial contracts of cheap labour, appalling working conditions in mines and factories. By 1840 even the conscience of the middle-class could be pricked with a sensational tabloid drawing of a fourteen-year-old girl, naked to the waist, hauling coal trolleys with leather chains and padlocks tied at her crutch, some two hundred feet below ground level, and for twenty pence a week.

England was in the throes of a great rail-building splurge. The country's trade was greater than the combined trade of France, Germany and Italy. The nation's wealth in terms of land and property was almost entirely in the hands of the Crown, the Church and the peerage. For a lad to go to university the parents needed the kind of resources which would support an ordinary middle-class family of six for a year. It was in the order of £150 a year to maintain each Burton son, Richard at Oxford, Edward at Cambridge; knowledge and good health, rank and possessions, freedom and comfort were the prerogative of that famed two per cent who owned ninety-one per cent of the nation's wealth. It is clear that something more than brightness or promise aided the Burton boys to university, and one assumes that Martha met the brunt of these costs.

It is said that the moment Burton entered Trinity College, Oxford, he heard another undergraduate giggling at his long moustache. Burton at once, according to his own legend, challenged the lad to a duel, demanding time, place, date and suitable weapons to exact honour. The bewildered student took flight. Nobody had seen a new boy wearing whiskers like that before—Mandarin style, inches below the corners of his mouth—and nobody had challenged anybody to a blood and guts duel in long memory at Trinity.

He grudgingly accepted a pair of dingy rooms on an upper floor, kept a lit fire with a red-hot poker deepthrust into the grate, and left his door provocatively open to offer any aggressive passerby a warm welcome indeed. Word soon got around.

According to his recollections, Burton had drinking bouts with Welsh students, and he inevitably left them all lying at his feet, drenched into darkness with good old flat beer, which he himself professed to loathe. Burton was dangled precipitately by a rope tethered to gargoyles on the roof, in order to plant sun flowers in a senior tutor's treasured border bed of shrubs. Burton, on his own admission, unable to afford horses, took to sculling, his beloved fencing, and to boxing. The latter sport suited his moody and magnificent reputation. When one considers he was almost six feet tall and weighed thirteen stone, and that what they called boxing was an endurance test across a chalked line, Burton must have found few adversaries. Burton made a firm friend of Alfred Bates Richards, of the same physique, the one man he could not master at the knuckle sport. Curiously though, a well-known pugilist, Mister Burke, or 'the Deaf'un' as he was known in sporting circles, allowed the students of Trinity to land any good punch they wished for a fee of 'half a crown' and Burton did not exclude himself from this challenge. Burton hurt his knuckles on the leathery countenance, as did the other students. Yet 'half a crown' was a week's wage to an urchin working a hundred hours down a pit shaft. Did the young student Burton exaggerate? Or was it the man Burton remembering an unlikely tale for his credulous listener?

Richard had the habit of smuggling cane guns into his rooms to shoot circling rooks. He hated the noise of the bells on the hour every day and plugged his nervous ears with cotton wool. He spoke Latin with an Italian everyday colloquialism. He wouldn't alter this at all and his tutors were exasperated. Taking Greek as a course, he boasted he could speak it, but could not write it down. Once more the tutors were in despair, for they recognised the quality of Burton, his quickness and authoritative fluency in tongues, but he would not confine himself to their curriculum for Honours in the Languages Course.

He called the place 'a hotbed of toadyism and flunkeyism', and if it was anybody's fault it was his father's — because as Burton thrashed wildly about at Trinity, positive that he was vastly superior to the other 'ignorant gentlemen' studying languages, he possessed no real understanding of group study. It had always been himself and Edward arguing with Mr Du Pré the tutor, or it had been Richard and Edward learning insults in the street and swapping punches with foreign boys.

His place in the Languages Course was taken by an inferior student who could, at least, render the Anglicised Latin the tutors demanded. Burton was aghast. This particular student Burton claimed 'had turned a chorus of Aeschylus into doggerel verse'. And young Richard had to bow out. He had been defeated by his own undoubted abilities. Though he could speak Italian, French, and a smattering of harbour-market Greek, when it came to the narrow strictures for exam graduation, his arrogance and impatience ruled him out of the race. It must have hurt. He understood the languages as well as the tutors. The tutors only wanted to procure their version of academic distinction. It was perhaps one of the earliest times in Richard's life when, though he remained so clearly the superior party, he had to take second place.

It taught him one thing, this language fiasco — he would never compete with others. All others were diminutive sparrows. He was filled with contumelious bile for them. And yet, much aware of his own inclination, he did not dismiss all languages from the daily tuition that was available to him.

At a dinner he met a Spanish Arabic scholar, Don Pascual de Gayangos y Arce, and, for no quite explained reason, except for that of wanting to appear exotic, Richard took up Arabic studies. The particular abstruse subject (although of course the Muslim Empire first translated for us all the principal scientific, historical and religious texts of the ancient world, and, in terms of international learning had stood supreme masters of bog arable medieval Europe), at once a calligraphy, a form of art, and a visual counterpoint, had two merits as far as Burton was concerned. To begin with there was hardly a handful of experts in Oxford to argue the subject with. And, far more satisfying to Richard, he could not see any other student on the horizon who shared this exotic interest. He was, once more, alone, and that was how he liked it. If instead he had taken up Mayan stelae and their hieroglyphics he could not have become more unique at Oxford.

How Richard Burton set about this new subject, with what self-propelled zeal, sheer delight in the innovative, the sheer exuberance of *firstness*, and his confirmed aloneness, is worth recording:

> I got a simple grammar and vocabulary, marked out the forms and the words which I knew were absolutely necessary, and learnt them by heart by carrying them in my pocket and looking over them at spare moments during the day. I never worked for more than a quarter of an hour at a time, for after that the brain lost its freshness. After learning some three hundred words, easily done in a week, I stumbled through some easy book-work (one of the Gospels is the most come-atable), and underlined every word that I wished to recollect, in order to read over my pencillings at least once a day. Having finished my volume, I then carefully worked up the grammar minutiae, and I then chose some other book whose subject most interested me. The neck of the language was now broken, and progress was rapid. If I came across a new sound like the Arabic *Ghayn*, I trained my tongue to it by repeating it so many thousand times a day. When I read, I invariably read out loud, so that the ear might aid memory. I was delighted with the most difficult characters, Chinese and Cuneiform, because I felt that they impressed themselves more strongly upon the eye than the eternal Roman letters. This, by-and-by, made me resolutely stand aloof from the hundred schemes for trans-literating Eastern languages, such as Arabic, Sanscrit, Hebrew, and Syriac, into Latin letters, and whenever I conversed with anybody in a language that I was learning, I took the trouble to repeat their words inaudibly after them, and so to learn the trick of pronunciation.

After two terms, the Colonel invited the Burton boys to holiday with the rest of the family in Germany. Martha and the obedient Maria lifted up the pair of reluctant students into a whirlwind of dances and summer steamer rides in Heidelberg. But for the Colonel it was all a bit of a shock, for he had no idea *what* Richard had been studying. The brothers must have discussed it in advance. When they confronted Joseph Burton it was a case of the unstoppable objects meeting the unmovable, but blinkered, subject.

Richard and Edward told their father that the intended but laughable career of parish parson was to be hurled out of the window with derision. Richard asked his father to withdraw them from the universities.

The Colonel would have none of this. Richard must stay. So must Edward, in his respective college. Country parsons they would damned well be.

Inexorable as the old man was, the Colonel strangely enough did not panic. He made no plans to hasten to England and drum sense into the renegade tutors. Instead, after a trip down the Rhine, a skirmish at fencing which made mockery of the German youths because both Burtons were clearly so much the superior duellists, Richard and Edward returned to, of all places, Ramsgate for a further holiday in a clifftop villa, overlooking the elegant little bathing resort of the period. The boys had not exactly had an open quarrel with the Colonel, it was more a matter of mutual embarrassment. Richard could not bring himself to call the old man mad for dreaming of a pair of country bumpkin parsons, and, in turn, Joseph Burton had no intention of flogging wearily back to England to be made mincemeat of by smarty breeched tutors or dons or the rest of those scallywag all-too-clevers. The Colonel knew which ground he felt safest upon.

At Ramsgate, the brothers made a pact. They laid a suitable plan. If they worked in unison, from either university town, it would be a *fait accompli* which the Colonel had no option to resist. Meanwhile, at Ramsgate, and at Broadstairs and Herne Bay adjacent, Richard and Edward chased pretty girls in summer hats along the beaches, in the warm evenings on the local esplanade terraces there was roulette and hazard, and somewhere the boys had met fellows who were leaving for India to enter the Bombay Army, for the British East India Company had lost many troops fighting in northern India and all Afghanistan was in danger from the British side. Official policy declared that British interests had to be maintained in northern India against the threat of Russian expansion. It fooled no one. The dream of John Bull was an expanded empire of eastern dominions. Even the icy slopes and steep-walled caverns of the Khyber, Kabul, Jalalabad ... even Jalalabad.

After the summer holidays, Richard said goodbye to his brother, who returned to Cambridge. For the first few days he settled back into Oxford regimen. He kept his plans to himself. All he waited for was a right moment, the spark to lever himself out from this nest of scholarly worms.

At university, the worst a student could do was to so degrade himself the authorities would be forced to send him down. The parents would be informed their son was held in disgrace. He could never return to his studies. The academic world had washed their hands of him. The not so bad alternative to being sent down was to be rusticated. There remained a careful distinction here. To be sent down was final. Rustication offered the possibility of return at a later time. If you were rusticated, well—you had been a bit of a bounder, but time would heal and the misdeed soon be forgotten.

Richard wrote nasty couplets about his tutors, and he gave beer and biscuit parties late into the night until the gate-keeper was forced to complain. He pasted cartoon caricatures of fellow students and seniors on the refectory walls, climbed up drainpipes to hang absurd items on roofs, disturbed flowerbeds, and tossed books out of his upper windows, and yet, it was not naughty enough. Most people shook their heads and murmured something about 'ruffian Dick Burton gone quite crazy', and if anything saw proof of the Governing Board's forbearance. These were the early weeks of the Michaelmas term.

It has seemed curious that Burton could not devise anything more shocking for the tutors at Trinity than throwing pies, drinking ale until the Welsh fellows collapsed, and hurling books. For wasn't this the Burton who, according to the legend, witnessed a public execution in order that he might watch the blood spurt, wasn't this the fellow who ravaged sirens in a Frenchy brothel until they begged for more?

Alas, all one has is a list of high jinks; mere nothing mayhems which would hardly have raised an eyebrow on Mr Du Pré, the old Burton tutor. Until, one day, word got around that a great and derring-do steeplechaser and point-to-point rider was coming to Oxford for a race. His name was Oliver the Irishman. For years it had been the general custom to ban students from gambling at Oxford, though little proof was that against private rooms; but, in particular, all students had always been warned off the race-track.

Such was the enthusiasm of so many of the fellows to play truant and watch Oliver compete in the race hurdle meeting, the very infection provided a cause for revolt against the powers that be. Apparently the tutors arranged a college lecture at the very same time as the race, and on learning of this Burton encouraged a dozen or so fellows from the various colleges, not his alone, to hire a tandem and drive out to the meet in style. It was port and champagne all the way there with a wave and a halloo to a couple of other absconding students who had already committed themselves to ride against the famous Oliver; by the time the race started all of Trinity had been told Dick Burton and the others were in open revolt. That night Oliver the Irishman was fêted from bottle to bottle, by all the young swells, punters and trainers, riders and ostlery yard workers, Burton amongst them, until the dawn raided their fragile sensibilities.

Those at Trinity were ordered first thing to a Green Room where the enormity of the offence was made known to them. To our ears it sounds like nothing of the kind, but it was considered then as an open rebellion, infectious and fostered by madcap jackanapes like Richard. They were told that if they misbehaved again they would all be rusticated for the remainder of that term. They might be invited to return the following term. At this stage in the proceedings Burton got the wind up, for he didn't want to return at any time. And that had been his secret promise to Edward on Ramsgate beach in the summer months. Burton wanted the authorities to go a step further. He stood up in the Green Room and announced firmly that the students could not be treated like children; if they wanted to attend an innocent steeplechase, in particular one of exceptional stature honoured with the presence of one such as Oliver the Irishman, then, so be it. They should be let loose and not connived against with orders to attend lectures which could easily be put off till the next day; he boldly reminded the seniors that 'trust begets trust', and further, 'they who trust us, elevate us'.

It suited Burton to be singled out. The brunt of authority was to come down on his neck. Perhaps at last they might send him down. He must have done a fair bit of mocking and tweaking of ancient whiskers to have stood out against his fellow students. But he knew he still had not won the day. He had enraged the elders with his hectoring, but he had to drive the wedge in deep to gain the condemnation he so badly needed.

Each parent at Trinity was not only obliged to pay the termly rate, but the university demanded a sum of money left as a deposit against loss of property or damage and as a down-payment on the rest of the scholastic year. Burton knew his parents had dutifully complied. He told the Board of Punition assembled in the Green Room that he had no intention of being rusticated unless the authorities rebated his parents this 'caution-money'. But he said it in such an unpleasant manner, and he put it in a phrase not far distant from 'unless the Board of Governors *honestly* rebate my parents with the caution-money deposited . . .', and that *was* the climax of the confrontation.

He had not only played miscreant and public revolt against the tutors, he was suggesting they sometimes dishonestly retained funds. Burton was told he must leave with a special recommendation not to return. He was delighted. He had been made the scapegoat, and a final insult on the dignitaries' heads did the trick.

He wrote in haste to his brother Edward at Cambridge. Edward had been complaining long and bitterly about the company of grocers his theological fellows had turned into and he reacted to his elder brother's exciting and dashing news. Edward, sparked with energy now, took it upon himself to lie in bed amorning until at least ten o'clock. It was the ritual of the theological class to attend Chapel at eight every morning. Within a matter of days, his tutor ordered Edward to explain himself. It was to be a severe reprimand, for this was no way to carve out a career devoted to the Cloth. My dear sir, Edward told the tutor with disarming candour, no party of pleasure ever gets me out of bed before ten o'clock, so do you *really* think that I am going to be in Chapel at eight o'clock? The tutor stared in disbelief. Are you joking, Burton? No, sir. Is that your mature decision? Edward looked up—my very ripest decision, he rejoindered.

Meanwhile Richard was packing the books he most wanted to keep, Arabic dictionaries, studies in Chinese and Greek, and to the astonishment of the seniors at college a large tandem was noisily brought round to the front of the building, led by a high-trotting shaft-horse. Burton called for his fellows to join him in a rousing exit from the yard. They piled high his baggage and a handful of them climbed atop. Burton took out a trumpet and the shock of its retort steered the horse and tandem over best flowerbeds and new-plantings until the gate-keeper howled with anger.

Burton dropped his jaunty pals on the Queen's Highway to London. A few waved their arms and cheered him. They would not see him again. Burton salvoed the trumpet and spirited the trotter out along the broad avenue of ruts and soft red earth in the direction of London. It was a fifty-five-mile drive, and he'd need at least one change of horse at the ostlers' yard, High Wycombe.

He had left behind him perhaps one friend, the muscular and redoubtable Alfred Bates Richards who eventually became a journalist and notable magazine editor. And he had left behind several acquaintances, contemporaries he seems to have had no time properly to investigate or compare himself with, like Benjamin Jowett who was to become one of the greatest moral teachers of his age, and Thomas Hughes, parliamentarian and founder of the Working Men's College, but later destined for fame with his novel *Tom Brown's School Days*.

It does indeed sound churlish; here was this youth who had barely begun to study anything, standing in the Green Room insulting the likes of J. H. Newman and Thomas Short, who were among the elders of the college, and then departing with a tin trumpet in high dudgeon and abandoned spirits, leaving his couplets, and his rhymes and his cartoons plastered on dining-room walls, and his last iambic arrow at the entire town—

> I leave thee, Oxford, and I loathe thee well,
> Thy saint, thy sinner, scholar, prig and swell.

He arrived in London to stay with aunts. He half expected to find Edward already there before him, similarly rusticated for good and all. He blithely informed his aunts he had left Oxford with 'a double-first with the highest honours'. The aunts hosannahed, and friends were invited to a little supper that following night. At the peak of the celebrations, Burton was somewhat miffed by a guest who instinctively knew the academic year was by no means over. The guest leant forward and raised his glass to Richard's. It was a toast for the brilliant student so successfully returned from Trinity College, Oxford. The friend gave a wink and a nod to the toast, and announced—

'Rusticated. Mmm? . . .'

The aunts froze and the dogsbottom scallycat had the honesty to blush like the evening sun.

Of all the chaps left behind at Trinity, it was Alfred Bates Richards, the mutton head puncher and fencing foe, all strength and a thunderous laugh in his belly, who echoed best the thoughts of those lesser mortals who did not roist and trumpet in high style back to town. Burton must have stood in the front of Richards' mind when he penned that young man's riddle—

> What will become of the boy? Who will turn out well? Who ill? Who will distinguish himself? Who will remain in obscurity? Who live? Who die?

IV

His observations on brothel boys and
the ten-inch oscoccygis on a man
creature serving two ladies one by
sodomy the other by succedaneum,
Dirty Dick . . .

THE COLONEL, JOSEPH BURTON, WAS ON A HIDING FOR
nothing. Furious sisters-in-law wrote to him from London. His two
boys were squandering their lives around town, careless and carefree,
rusticated from their colleges, and quite likely broke. First, the sisters-
in-law told him of the shame. Joseph flinched. Then they wrote and
informed him that both boys had no intention whatsoever of becoming
country parsons. Joseph must have given up that particular illusion by
then. Eventually word reached him that Richard and Edward had
made up their minds on future careers — they wanted to join the army.
Joseph did not take that very well. He sulked and fiddled in his wife's
garden, at the back of a pretty little Italian villa; and after considerable
thought he realised it was all more than he could bear to decide upon.
The boys had to go their own way. They were scoundrels and idiots,
with too much Irish blood in their veins, and it was clear their aunts in
London had no control over them. His sisters-in-law were screaming
at him to go to London and have it out with the young fools. His wife
Martha demanded he go to London right away. But Joseph held back;
he rattled the bore cartridges he always kept in his trouser pockets and
told himself there were better reasons why he should stay in Italy.
There were the length of the journey, the cost of it, the infernal
difficulties of changing horses at either side of the English Channel (oh,

but wasn't this the same man who kept his entire family on the move across civilised Europe for fifteen years? Who nearly brought his wife's health to ruin in his wake?) and what would he receive when he reached London? A slap in the face from the Baker family for staying away so long. A series of kicks from his mad erring sons. Worst of all, a demand to clear up their outstanding bills. The Colonel stuffed his pipe with the household favourite brand of *Standfast Virginia* tobacco, specially imported, eased his head into the truncated tarboosh skullcap the doctors recommended (smoking, it was believed, could damage the hair), and sat back in the warm sunshine. He had made up his mind. He was not going to London to see Richard and Edward on any pretext whatsoever.

The boys knew they had a father who was a disgrace to his own regiment. Joseph never relinquished the ignominy of perpetual half-pay, nor did he ever try to sell up the commission. It most probably suited him to be known in Europe, in those tiny British covens of renegade middle-class mores, as a lieutenant-colonel. What else had he to stand by? What credit could he gain without the title? Yet, it hurt. It was a centuries-old tradition for a father to introduce his sons to his own regiment; such a privileged scheme of things made it possible to buy a commission at a cut down fee. A splendid officer's name echoed once more down the ranks, and so forth. Joseph was not in any position to recommend his sons to his old regiment. And, although it remained unsaid, the boys' joint choice to enter the forces was a crude, but careful, brick at the Colonel's glass plate indolence.

In military circles there were two distinct grades, men of the Queen's Regiments and the Rest. The Rest was made up of a motley crowd attracted to the recruiting offices of the sacerdotal Directors of the East India Company. The company was originally founded for the purposes of trading with India and the East Indies. It received its original charter at the hands of Queen Elizabeth in 1600, and, during the course of the centuries, the Directors and the Company gained the power of a sovereign state within the framework of the British Empire. The Company built armadas and forts, raised garrisons of men and could claim sovereign possession over new-found lands, even appoint governor-generals from amongst its own ranks, all in the name of the Crown. And yet, those men employed in the ranks for the Company were known to receive less pay and greater chances of death in un-known foreign places than in any other department of the British Army. The Company's vast tentacles spread throughout the trading world; nevertheless it was generally considered to be a poor option to enlist in Indian Infantry Garrisons. Such men and officers were called 'indians' by the superior ranks of the Queen's Regiments. They were considered to be cannon fodder for foreign parts. If this snobbery had ceased, our old Empire control over far spread trading ports would indeed have changed overnight. The truth was, the richer swells in this time of effective peace cushioned their lives with social standing and a comfortable Whitehall career, whereas those fellows with less money but greater guts took the snub between their teeth and turned their backs on the home country. If anything, it was to our greater glory that this rougher element dominated British colonial aggression. They were the men who took careful notice of the sudden increase of wealth and provisions at home, the food, the clothes, the houses, the style of life—that famous 'quality' of life the middle classes always aspire to, and yet, these very men turned their backs on it. Fortune hunters on a miserable monthly pay packet though they were, nobody left England like this, for perhaps untold dangers, without a degree of bravura. The common soldier was promised little, certainly he could not afford good health in his own country, but wherever he was going to he knew no army surgeon would protect him from the indigenous ills. From cholera to typhoid, frostbite to rheumatic ophthalmia, there was only one good, reliable cure—luck.

The East India Company, for its own mystical purposes, assumed that the great warring Russian Bear wanted to sweep down on to all England's possessions in India. In 1839 Britain installed a puppet-king in Afghanistan. It was a perfect buffer-state, for on one side lay the quiescent Persian Empire, and to the north beyond the River Oxus lay the might of Russia. But this overlord occupation of the country of mountainous passes and sudden changes of temperature failed miserably.

The British officers could not contain the emergent leader of the Afghans, Akbar Khan, and the officers themselves appeared to be made up in the main of incompetent dolts, the likes of General W. G. K. Elphinstone, Sir William Macnaghten, and Lord William Bentinck. In London Lord Ellenborough, the minister who was responsible for the affairs of British India, supported his *Army of the Indus*. Meanwhile, the British East India Company had discovered a broad fluvial valley area called the Sind below Afghanistan which contained both the Indus and the Sutlej outflows to the sea in a vast basin of fertile land surrounding Hyderabad. The Company looked on little Sind with sovereign eyes.

Upstate, in Afghanistan, after three years of mad rule by the British troops who insisted on building fortresses on flat valley floors and handing out large sums of gold to any Afghan goat herder who had the wits to call himself an Amir, things got quite out of hand. Back home, the myth was that Afghanistan lay happily beneath the Queen's thumb. On the contrary, the British had no idea how to bribe, how to co-operate, how to rule such a remote mountain vastness, and so dreadful was the arrogance of these officer civil servants that they sent all their messages and provisions along valley floor routes where the bearers could be massacred by two guerrillas with muskets on a cliff ledge. The communications from Kabul, the capital, to the coast at Bombay were dreadful. Garrisons were left stranded in vulnerable lowland positions with token regiments; meanwhile those who could retire to the gentler coastal climate did so, taking with them their half-pay and their wives and mistresses.

In January 1842 the so-called Army of the Indus retreated from Kabul in disarray. The Afghan hordes struck again and again, until an entire army of 12,000 men, women, and children, and a further 4,000 camp workers were massacred in the bitter cold of the mountainous defiles which led to Jalalabad ninety miles east. When the news reached Bombay, the British could not at first believe it. When it reached London the government almost fell overnight. The defeat was pronounced a disaster as inexplicable as it was appalling. All that was left of an entire British Army of occupation amounted to 31 officers, 10 women, 11 children, 2 civilian clerks and 52 soldiers.

Outside the recruitment offices of the British East India Company a long line of men had formed. Though they could not read, they had heard that a great new British army of retribution and revenge was being called upon to come forward. Empty bellied boys from work-houses and incoherent lads who could no more take the killing drudge of Nottingham mines had heard this call to arms. It meant two meals a day. And it would give them a suit of clothing over their skinny frames. And a four-month cruise through warm waters in conditions which amounted to cattle stalls. And a monthly payment if one lasted that long in a strange place they called the northwest frontier of India. What had they to lose?

Richard Burton asked his father for a commission in the Bombay Infantry, a regiment attached to the East India Company. Edward, his younger brother, asked his father for a trainee surgeon's commission in the 36th Regiment, shortly going out to Ceylon; again the regiment was attached to the Company. Colonel Joseph was in no great hurry to reply to these requests. What the boys demanded would be very costly.

46

As so often is the case when the mention of money is brought up, a peculiar pall of silence fell. In later years all Richard Burton would say was 'my conviction is that the commission cost £500'. Nobody has the slightest clue who paid it, and to whom. For you could not directly acquire a commission from the East India Company; it was usually a title-deed, made out to a third party who perhaps merely bought out a certain officer and gentleman on his retirement from the army. Burton refers to it as a 'nomination', which had been handed over to a 'friend'. And the 'friend' sold the commission to the Burton family. It would seem this friend was in truth an old-fashioned agent, attached to the army hearsay, who made a living out of a small percentage gained from moving various nominations from person to person. Edward being the younger boy need not have cost so much. He had virtually decided on an apprenticeship in army surgery. A payment of £200 would cover all costs of a basic tutorial in a skill not too far removed at that time from an ordinary butcher's. Such new-fangled contrivances as hygiene, antiseptics and clean towelling had not as yet penetrated the surgeons' tents at army cantonments in foreign places.

Richard Burton spent the first few months of 1842 in London. He led an easy life. He had to find a tailor to measure him up for his red jacket and blue trousers with the vivid stripe. He needed a dress jacket for the evenings, various changes of tunic, and enough capes, boots, shirts and bed linen to accommodate him in all kinds of inclemencies. Tailors, it appears, were ever reasonable and helpful. If one paid a ten per cent deposit, opened a new account with a promise to pay, one walked hail-fellow-well-met out of the shop with stylistic aplomb.

It was an established fact of the age that the first mourner a woeful army widow might find at the graveside would be none other than the patient stitcher and padder himself whose long overdue account now ought to be settled. On the other hand, the boy conscripted as a common foot soldier had his pay deducted until his uniform and his boots were paid for, and if he should be so unwise as to lose his musket in action, that too became a steep deduction.

Richard bade his brother goodbye and spent some weeks in the Charing Cross Road area where a number of fencing salons and pugilistic stables were to be found. That part of London, now better known as Soho, before it became a haunt of brothels, heroin smuggling Chinamen, sailors and itinerant drunken artists, was famed for its sporting facilities. There were cock-fight emporiums and fields put aside for dog and hare coursing, and plenty of sidesmen to encourage a twenty-two-year-old six-footer to tape his knuckle joints and try as many as forty rounds if he liked against a bullyboy blackguard called Gypsy Jem or Dutch Sam, placed on the other side of a white pitch line or a drawn cotton thread. No matter who weighed what, all the crowd loved a game 'un. Most of these pugilistic camps taught a basic grammar of self-defence made up in the main of cheap homilies or crude devices such as pickling knuckles hard enough to crack a wood board. There were few rules to go by, any bet at any time was taken up, and an opponent could take as long as he liked to lift himself up from the floor.

During this time Richard had a sudden enthusiasm for astrology and he came under the influence of the artist John Varley, who had written a study of alchemy, *Zodiaca Physiognomy.*

Burton met a remarkable Scot in London. Duncan Forbes was a keen card-player, chessman, and a brilliant exponent of oriental languages. He fired Burton's enthusiasm for Hindustani, a language the young ensign would sorely need on the North West Frontier, and Forbes—a man who was virtually self-taught in the study of languages, who had spent three years in India—had the kind of unruly academic distinctions Burton best appreciated. All through his career Burton warmed towards renegade academics, brilliant wayward ones who appeared to belong to no uniform college of life.

Burton said goodbye to his aunts at the Gravesend dockside, when he departed on the barque *John Knox* on June 18, 1842, for India. Grandma Baker stayed at home in her rooms behind Park Lane. His parents remained in their Italian villa. The ensign carried books on Hindustani which Duncan Forbes had presented to him. In addition, he took umpteen wicker and satin-lined crates filled with white trousers and shirts, camp linen and mess-type crockery and condiments, various swords he liked to practise with, a collection of oddly assorted knives useful for all purposes from lethal throwing to best of beef carving, a brace of pistols, two saddles, ammunition, boots, a collapsible chair, piles of leather lengths, tins of polish, shaving soap, food medicaments, letters from his relatives. And to cap all these, he held a fat pink-lipped bull-terrier on a short leash.

The young ensign had shaved his head; he knew how the heat and the insects could play havoc with the skull, so it was best, he had reasoned, to cut it all off. He did, in consequence, appear a trifle strange. High cheekbones, fierce black eyes, a head filled with specks of stubble, and yet, a long moustache which rolled over his mouth corners. Hoping he might not frighten everybody off, he was sufficiently thoughtful of others to take with him an extra foible—a charmingly coiffured wig with which, at the mere whisper of a formal invitation, he might decorate his shiny skull.

Whatever might have been the apprehensions of officers like Richard on that summer's day in Gravesend they had not one iota of an idea of what it was like, this North West Frontier, a dream inspired by Whitehall military brass, a redoubt from which the Russian Bear could be repulsed. The other ensigns shared with Richard a belief in routing the Afghan hordes in retaliation, talk of rescuing beleaguered garrisons in mountain fastnesses, romantic notions that a quick charge with pistol and sword would send the senseless natives toppling in confusion over mountain walls. Even perhaps, if the right chance arrived, an ensign could relieve an entire town of Britishers on the brink of starvation and a grateful British Government back in London would newly appoint the young conqueror commander-in-chief of the entire cantonment. A colonelcy within hours. A commendation in the Dispatch Column of *The Times*.

The long voyage exhausted Burton of any further novelty. He boxed and fenced, he had shot musket at pigeons with cork bullets and a sniff of powder. He studied his books on Hindustani. And before his boat reached Bombay harbour, the emergency British troops had already returned through the Khyber Pass, and the avenging British Army was going to annexe an area of land from Afghanistan, now once again under British rule, to the territory known as the Sind, with more than 40,000 troops stationed from Kabul to Karachi to Bombay. Rumour had it that Lord Ellenborough was going to appoint Sir Charles Napier as Governor General responsible for the North West India Frontier and no guerrilla Amir was safe from Napier's iron determinism. Sir Charles Napier, born 1782, had purchased the rank of lieutenant at the age of twelve. A somewhat reckless and dishevelled figure, he had been a friend of Lord Byron, and his particular fascination lay in the ancient history of roads and trackways.

As for Ensign Burton, and the rest of the warrior hopefuls on board the *John Knox* — it looked as if war was out of the question. The cause, the vengeance, fluttered away in the hot wet wind which breezed the barque into port. The closer they got to the stone piers the more the wind and the tide abated, until an awful reeking heat possessed their nostrils. Their first impression was of a stinking bazaar, unclean and rotting; all the streets were open sewers and the buildings themselves, in Richard's words, were made 'splotched and corroded as if by gangrene'. It was a disenchantment for those troops disembarking. This was not the fabled East of romance.

Richard had no orders to muster immediately with his 18th Regiment. He took a low wood bungalow, unpacked, sniffed the air, and spent six weeks in this filthy port (as he liked to call it) adapting himself immediately to the demands a young officer gentleman must make on the community's labour force. No ensign could be seen without a full complement of staff. Richard, no doubt on a good word of advice, forbore to hire Hindus, and chose a dozen Portuguese-speaking Goan Indians. The servants, if they did not have a particular duty, squatted outside the doors waiting on the ensign's word; evidently they and their families treated this casual bondage, a virtual slavery, with a fine degree of good humour and tolerance. And they were made aware of the different calibre of their new master when he made up his mind to put aside the frivolous horse-riding in the early hours and the port and brandy billiards of the late afternoons, in order to seek out the finest language scholar in Bombay, a Parsee priest called Dosabhai Sohrabji, who was a renowned teacher, or *munshi*. Burton, equipped with his self-taught discipline of learning 300 words a week, studied the rudiments of Persian, Hindustani and Gujarati; he so impressed his *munshi*, the priest told him he could learn a language running on the spot. In fact, he owed his father all the Italian and French street slang he had picked up, and now, in Bombay for a few weeks, surrounded by servants fluent in Hindustani and Portuguese, the attraction of all these tongues struck him hard. He had no real evidence of his abilities yet, apart from the 300 word a week trick, but a far more serious mind emerged here. The billiard playing was to go by the board. He had just sufficient time to be introduced to Bombay society by the sister of the Captain of the *John Knox* barque. Burton later admitted he stood perfectly aghast in the presence of this society. Men, he added, whose parents were small tradesmen in England, or bailiffs in Scotland, found themselves ruling districts and commanding regiments, riding in carriages, and making more pounds (sterling) a month than their parents made in the year. It is easy to imagine the heady atmosphere of power to naive young officers newly arrived on the west Indian coast, but these colonial forces who cocked and strutted, rigged and oiled, trimmed out in red and blue and stiff sheen shatter polish high boots articulating a vocabulary of orders were at least not so idle they never dared leave that old Carlton Club Father's Land—gentle England. These were waifs with hair oil and high-pitched accents and venereal secrets.

Dick was ordered two hundred miles north to Baroda. There he joined the rest of his 18th Regiment. The cantonment was an affair of tents, occasional rows of wooden bungalows, army requisitioned, and various huts, if he had the stomach for it, in the native centre of Baroda. Drink and health were considerations which never stood far apart. Nobody was allowed to drink straight from a well; every army barracks had a manufacturing cell where a type of carbonic-gas was pumped into well-water which had been boiled. The richer lads, certainly all the junior officers, stuck to beer brewed by Bass and Allsopp. Few of the ordinary foot soldiers could have afforded the odd two pence or so a day for water free of contamination, but it has been a standby rule of the British Army that colour-sergeants encouraged their men to add lime or sulphur to water to avoid fever.

In Baroda, the young subaltern with his staff of twelve servants, his bull terrier and some new horses, a bungalow and a case of port and sherry and numerous tap barrels of carbonised water (now Burton loathes beer) was the normal picture of civilised behaviour. Unlike his fellow officers — who insisted on polished boots, and morning rides on well-groomed horses, and port with every meat dish, and billiards in the mountain cool evening light — Richard gave no further indication of having succumbed to the society of the time. He hated the company, and he buried himself in the three languages he had already begun under his *munshi* Dosabhai Sohrabji from Bombay. Five months later Burton applied to the Bombay office for an official examination. He was clear-headed enough to want a staff appointment as a translator, and he knew this was one of the most prized jobs for it meant continuous travel and confrontation with the various Indian Amirs, their lands, departments and customs. One dare not suggest the anthropologist in him emerged at this time, for all he wanted was the improved staff job with its attendant authority. It was, also, a means of coming into contact with the most senior officers of the British Indian Army.

Burton returned to Bombay and, along with twelve others, he took the language tests in Hindustani, under a remarkable linguist, General Vans-Kennedy. Burton came top of this examination, gained the General's respect, and was promptly made regimental interpreter for the 18th Company. He was sent back to Baroda where he astonished his servants by plunging into a study of the Gujarati language and, simultaneously, buying a number of monkeys for the bungalow and attempting a written study of sixty simian sounds. The establishment not only reverberated with this officer's painful self-driven zeal to recite out loud his test pieces, but, in all fairness to his fellow officers, the wood frame bungalow positively reeked of monkey excrement.

Within five months Burton was back again in Bombay taking another test, this time in Gujarati, which he passed with flying colours, well and truly defeating a young man called Lieutenant Christopher Palmer Rigby. Rigby, as it happened, was under the belief that he was the best linguist in the army. He had already taken tests in Hindustani, Somali and Amharic, and on this occasion he could hardly believe his bad luck when Ensign Burton squashed him. Their paths were to cross in years to come. Rigby was no inflated prig, he worked hard at his languages and was brilliant at them, but alas he and Burton never hit it off. Burton was ever the anti-scholar. He was proud of the fact he could learn a language from the inside skin of slang and street banter. Rigby, a genuine army career man, took to the official textbook; he was a slide-rule learner, a technique Burton derided. It was typical of Burton to approach a language through the backdoor, secretive and unseen.

In the years between 1842 and 1845, although Burton spent much of his time between Baroda and Bombay, with occasional missions to Karachi and to outlying army cantonments, there was no mistaking the indolence of this 18th Regiment. Sir Charles Napier, now at the age of sixty-three, and his other senior commanders had already done their duty. The Valley of the Sind and its Amirs were duly brought to toe the colonial line, and young British officers in blue trousers with the familiar red stripe in their white afternoon jackets spent months on end listening to the heat and the flies and watching the sand seep into the crevices of their polished nails. They lay out beside their wooden bungalows, some of them content to fry in the cruel light, others like Richard adopting local customs. He learnt to pour buckets of water over tenting or table linen, fold the wet material on a wigwam wicker stilt and lower his head beneath it. For a brief respite the heat faded, and the wet sun visor merrily steamed.

Burton tended to ignore the more trivial forms of amusement. He had no enthusiasm for tiger hunts or elephant baiting. Either the company was drab, or he did not shine enough at the particular sport. In the gymnasium he studied Indian swordsmanship and he dallied with the rudiments of Hindu wrestling. Not ennui, but a further underlining of a self-truth he learned to face: he could not take part.

He did not disguise the fact that he took to his bungalow in Baroda, alongside his talking monkeys and his dozen servants of Goan extraction, a young Hindu woman. Young officers freely enjoyed port and sherry and a variation of musical beds between married quarters, where senior men were often cuckolded. There were rooms in the native quarter of the cantonment where it was possible to meet a truant wife for a few hours, and where dandy lads were cueing billiards late into the night with absurd side-bets. Burton would have none of it. His Hindu girl was called a *bubu*. One of his servants made the formal arrangements with her family, Burton accepted her into his household and her duties were, she being compliant to an extreme, a cross between an unpaid prostitute and a floor sweep skivvy; it all depended on the affections of the white master, and his sensitivity in handling her relationship with the other servants. All *bubus* were well aware of this problem. A girl in his bed, unpaid, and with no prospect of marriage, was an object of contempt for the rest of the bungalow staff. She might gain a grip on the master's white emotions, but God aid her if she dared assume the rights of a common-law wife. A woman like Burton's *bubu*, half night-nanny half sexual go-fer was altogether an outcast from her own community.

Burton kept to his languages. In the evenings, in place of port and billiards and cheroots, he took the road out of the cantonment and spent long hours with the shanty shops and makeshift tenement village life which built up around the army barracks. There, well away from his regiment, Burton practised his Hindustani. He must have been supremely confident of his life in those native evenings. For there were no street lamps, only the dust rising and the danger of the shuffled footsteps of perhaps an angry indigenous, a shoulder of hate, that satanic knife in his grasp, a steel thrust at that British tunic and a soft-padded sprint into the well-mapped dark. The other lads in red and blue called him a 'white nigger' for his evening jaunts.

Burton, in these years, met three men who greatly influenced his life. Captain Walter Scott was a noble animal; a surveyor by profession, he had joined the Bombay Engineers, a likable and tough man, a loner to Burton's liking. Scott twice took the young ensign out on fact-finding surveys of the river valleys. Burton learned to map and survey, how to use the compass and the theodolite and the spirit-level. Scott had a burr in his tartan voice, a fierce independent way with him, a love of history and was a rough riding fancier of archaeological discoveries.

In Karachi, early in 1845, Burton met a curiously learned person, John Steinhaeuser; this man (he was a surgeon at the time attached to the hospital) shared Burton's and Scott's fascination with languages and orientalia, and Burton's interest in exotica began with Steinhaeuser. Burton, thirty years on, declared that Steinhaeuser first suggested various translation projects to him in the Sind. Steinhaeuser had a substantial collection of Hindu manuscripts, exotic, erotic, the kind of ephemera no British publisher would dare commit himself to for a translation. And in the future years, Steinhaeuser remained on the closest of terms with Burton; there remain few enough letters between them, but their obvious pleasure in each other's company was based on then little-known written works in many languages, works daring and mysterious to the delicate palate in the early years of Victoria's reign.

Both Scott and Steinhaeuser accompanied Burton on certain expeditions into those dark 'native quarters'; oft times it suited Burton's sense of humour to dress in strange costumes and try to pass himself off as a Persian or an illiterate Hindu with a mere smattering of the language.

The third great influence in Burton's career was his overall commander-in-chief, Sir Charles Napier. This tiger of a man had a reckless temper and an aggressive cut to his relations with other senior officers. Napier despised the traditional carpet-soldier in Whitehall; he was a restless, hard-driving fighter who had promised Sind to the British Government and delivered it, and made no apology for the frightful cruelties his men imposed on prisoners. It need hardly be lingered over, but those public executions – blowing men tied to cannon mouth into a cloud of blood, flesh and bone – were not the least of the many hideous brutalities the Bombay Regiments inflicted. Napier came into contact with the multi-lingual ensign soon after Burton arrived in Baroda. On a number of occasions Napier chose him to ride with the other senior soldiers, especially when a long day's trek ended with a difficult and tetchy Amir still unwilling to submit to the Crown of a little English lady six thousand miles distant. At times the young translator was positively facetious. He spoke curtly and confidently to the natives, and whatever Napier wanted said the ensign translated with a highly partial manner of authority. His abrasive manner fascinated the commander-in-chief, and it is a witty and clever young man's riposte to Napier when, on studying a newly built bridge across a river the commander asked Burton how many bricks he thought the bridge contained, and Richard replied, not batting an eyelid –

'Two hundred and twenty-nine thousand and ten, sir.'

Richard no doubt sensed the qualities shared between them; the loner instinct, and a talent for arousing enmity. Napier had received a personal government prize of £60,000 for his campaign in the Sind, he had even made steps to abolish slavery and accommodate the various amirs. Nevertheless, there were those other junior men in Bombay and Karachi, waiting their turn to put a knife into his back. The Bombay

Government, under Whitehall's thumb, merely tolerated Napier's outspoken ways. Napier, now close on a pension, was blunt enough to call a 'touch' a bribe, and a *bubu* woman a whore. He saw life clearly in black and white.

In Karachi in 1845 as well as his white friends such as John Steinhaeuser and Walter Scott, Richard was in the habit of taking a *munshi*, and an Indian merchant friend, and a servant, Allahdad, into the native quarters, the bazaars and the market halls. This mania to be identified as a 'white nigger' cut him off from the rest of his regiment. It certainly improved his Sindi language, and it also enabled him to dabble in theatrical disguise. But this skulduggery was not done in the name of a youthful anthropologist; Burton was in fact a fully-fledged spy for Napier. The Governor-General had to know what the teeming under-life was saying. That quirky underground of gossip amongst the circumcision feasts, the weddings and the funerals was the stuffing of truth. Napier could not rely on an Indian sepoy soldier to bring him these curious titbits.

Karachi was a village of a town, with perhaps two thousand inhabitants within, and a floating population of twice that from week to week; the army cantonments were a mile distant from the market place, and soldiers were not encouraged to loiter at night. There is no indication that anything Burton spied upon put him in much mortal danger; it was a useful little trick, and Burton always reported back to the old soldier in person, and this surely was an example of Napier's respect for the multi-lingual ensign.

Unexpectedly, Napier took umbrage at a finding of Burton's. The ensign casually accounted for the normal variety of brothels in Karachi, and Napier was content to accept the fact that seven such houses were the inevitable result of having a British Army Force of up to six thousand men in the area. Then, Richard Burton dropped a bomb on Napier's toes. He told him that there were at least three brothels which catered for all forms of homosexuality. The young officer might have been truly surprised by Napier's response. The upright elderly soldier was shocked. Though syphilis was a common matter in the ordinary brothels which did not bother him at all, he was sharply pained by the idea of his troops 'succumbing' to beastly foreign habits. He asked Burton to make out a full report on these *lupanars* as the male brothels were called, and hand it to him under the proviso it would not go beyond Napier's eyes. Either Napier or Burton realised the risks involved if such a report reached the Bombay Government, and yet nobody gave a thought to the very real danger of harbouring such an offensive file. It was certainly not the case of a senior officer requiring written fodder for his secret peccadilloes. It was a measure of his faith in Burton that Napier never considered the added risk of blackmail. It was a shaky arrangement to have a report written up, filed, and never acted upon, on the condition that it was never to be presented to the Bombay Government. Of course, military reports are in the habit of being filed away in a sea of official memorandums, but in the case of pederastic brothels, the subject was electric enough to endanger any military career.

Richard rubbed the henna back into his jowls, dressed himself as an Iranian merchant and duly investigated three male brothels. The hosts in these establishments were in the main a mixture of eunuchs on parole from their harem duties, and young boys, who were obviously the principal attraction. Burton visited all the porneia available, with that curious relish of his for the most obscure detail; he observed the clothes, the prices charged, the customers and their predilections, and made his assessments of the separate entertainments such houses might offer a lonely soldier; he discovered it was not just the Bombay Infantry who came to these places, it appeared that the local Amirs were themselves customers and landlords of the brothels. At the time the more run-of-the-mill heterosexual prostitutes were very keen on routing the colourful eunuchs and boys because they were losing hard-earned clientele. Either the boys were charging too much and offering better service or the girls were losing their charms and jaded amirate palates yearned behind their backs for something more exotic.

Burton handed in all the details and, according to a mention in William Napier's four-volume study, *Sir Charles Napier* (1857), taken from the Governor's diaries, the brothels were closed down overnight. The diary notes do not make absolutely clear that the cloak-and-dagger inquiry annihilated the catamite foundations in Karachi. Napier kept the report intact, albeit locked away in his private files. Yet what was the point of keeping this report when he had, according to thin diary notes (thin on the ground that is in proven veracity), finally dealt with these houses of peculiar trade? Surely the report, with the danger of others reading it and the risk which might be attached to the ensign's name, should have gone the way of the brothels, into oblivion? Staff officers would have ridiculed the ensign's amazing sorties and the make-up and the disguise which he used to penetrate these houses. And there was worse still to come, for in no time at all the supposed sanctity of Napier's files was intruded upon by a successor.

Napier, after his retirement from the army, made no mention of

Richard by name in the diaries. As for Burton, it took him almost forty-two years before he could describe again those theatrical voyages into brothels filled with boys and eunuchs, fat and greedy Amirs and tempted Bombay infantrymen.

It was not until 1886 that Burton described his nocturnal adventures in Karachi under the orders of Sir Charles Napier. From his notes he was clearly fascinated by the demands the boys made on their clients. In certain cases they demanded twice what a mere eunuch could offer in services. He wrote about these boys of special delight to their buggering clients; 'the scrotum of the unmutilated boy could be used as a kind of bridle for directing the movements of the animal'. Curious though it may seem, Richard enjoyed throwing this titbit out as an aside, with not the least explanation of how he came by it. Interspersed in the paragraphs on pederasty are references to his memories of Karachi; and it is obvious that most of these notes made up the report he handed to Napier. He wrote of boys 'prepared with extreme care by diet, baths, depilation, unguents and a host of artists in cosmetics'. Then Richard abandons the subject, until he brings himself to a meeting with a Persian whom he invited to expand on the art of buggering an unwilling victim. The Persian responded without hesitation – 'Ah, we Persians know a trick to get over that; we apply a sharpened tent-peg to the crupper-bone (coccyx plate) and knock till he opens.' Evidently Bombay marines were plied with drink until they lost consciousness. Then they were stripped and peppercorns were inserted in their anuses. Their nostrils were stuffed with cayenne until they sneezed and/or farted so violently the peppercorns were 'fired' from the rear to the delight of the observers, who took bets on the distances achieved by the peppers. And then, again, there comes a fruity concoction about a high-caste Indian who for months had maintained a love affair with a common soldier. The Indian believed it was his privilege to be the bugger, the *al-fa'il*; it was beneath his dignity to be the passive agent in their relationship. One day the common soldier became tired of his permanent role as the *al-maful*, the object of all this doing, and he requested a change in the roles played. The snooty Indian Brahman loaded his musket and shot the passive paramour dead . . . Then, in an orgy of barely connected ephemera, Burton wrote of 18th-century Jesuits who brought a tailed man to Europe from the Americas whose oscoccygis measured anything from seven to ten inches, and who enjoyed a form of group stimulus using one lady in front of him and serving a second lady behind him simultaneously, thereby, one assumes, achieving a Jesuitical double in sinfulness—simple sodomy on the one hand and penetration by a form of succedaneum, on the other.

From these occasional references back into the Karachi past, it is as if he is trying to remember just enough of the report he made to Napier to make one understand what a verbal nest of horrors he had written up, and yet could not bring himself to enlarge upon that mysteriously vanished report.

Richard lingered three more years on the Indian coast. After Napier was recalled, he fell ill with rheumatic ophthalmia and spent some weeks recuperating on the Portuguese-owned Island of Goa. He managed to avoid a plague of cholera, he twice attempted to attach himself to the Sikh Wars which had broken out, and he wrote at least three technical papers on the Sindians and their languages. We have his word, and his only, for a ludicrous adventure on the Goan Island with his servant. He appears to have 'fallen in love' with a beautiful nun. She, we are led to believe, was prepared to run away with him for ever, and on the night of the romantic tryst Burton and his servant broke into the convent. Richard, on losing his way through unfamiliar passages, entered the sub-prioress's room and promptly carried the amazed good lady over a wall and down to a waiting boat. The astonishing tale includes two guards who had been carefully drugged, and no end of long daggers in fat sleeves and dark lanterns swaying in the erratic night air. The sub-prioress, according to Burton, was an *ugly* creature with a fat mouth and a dreadful mien, and this farce reels obscurely to an end filled with sounds off of mayhem and alarum exeunts and howls of execration. Clearly, if not intended for the supper table, such nonsense was made for the Bombay infantry gallery glee boys, with half a bottle of port for a stage.

It was 1847. By now, Napier had departed for Britain and a quite astounding piece of skulduggery occurred. The report filed in Napier's papers which Burton made on the male brothels had not only been left behind in Karachi, but somebody had leaked it to the Government Offices in Bombay. According to Burton he was in very serious trouble, and the authorities threatened to cashier him overnight. Hard as it may be to look back now and find fault with a junior officer who was merely doing his duty at Napier's request, there lingered a bad smell around the 'white nigger'. It was rumoured he had enjoyed the trade found in these brothels, or how else could he glean all that information? But, mind you, we only have Burton's word for this. At the time he had applied for a job as an interpreter to travel with the troops in the Second Sikh War, and he had been rudely turned down.

The post went to a fellow officer who knew a sixth of Burton's languages. It was a bitter blow. And Burton had to blame it on somebody —

I applied in almost suppliant terms to accompany the force as interpreter. I had passed examinations in six native languages, beside studying others, Multani included, and yet General Auchmuty's secretary wrote to me that this would not be, as he had chosen for the post Lieutenant XYZ who had passed in Hindustani. This last misfortune broke my heart. I had been seven years in India, working like a horse, volunteering for every bit of service, and qualifying myself for all contingencies. Rheumatic ophthalmia, which had almost left me when in hopes of marching northward, came on with redoubled force, and no longer had I any hope of curing it except by a change in Europe. Sick, sorry, and almost in tears of rage, I bade adieu to my friends and comrades in Sind. At Bombay there was no difficulty in passing the Medical Board and I embarked at Bombay for a passage round the Cape, as the Austral winter was approaching, in a sixty-year-old teak-built craft, the brig *Eliza*; my career in India had been in my eyes a failure, and by no fault of my own; the dwarfish demon called 'Interest' had fought against me, and as usual had won the fight.

In more rational terms, it is not unlikely that the army took one look at his painful eye condition and passed Burton over for the time being. And, in truth, it remains a queer account of events to place all the blacking of his name on this Napier Report on male brothels, then three years old. The whole charade has every particle in it of Burton's bizarre relationship with fact.

In May, 1849, the twenty-nine-year-old Bombay infantry interpreter took with him one servant, Allahdad, boarded the barque *Eliza* and sailed for Europe. It would take him four months to reach England. He was already engulfed by sickness, the death of an aunt, and the quick rumours about his homosexuality.

The country he was returning to after being abroad for seven years was on the crest of the 'thirty years' peace'. Agriculture was still its largest national industry. The Factory Acts had done much to ameliorate the shocking conditions of women and children employees. The Great Reform Bill had cut away the power of the Chartist Movement, and in London J. M. W. Turner commenced work on an enigmatic and final painting, *The Visit to the Tomb*. Chopin had died that year of 1849. Dostoevski was arrested in Russia and sentenced to death for revolutionary activities. In America, the novelist Herman Melville had already set sail for his *Moby Dick*. In Germany, Rhineland middle-class representatives invited the young radical journalist Karl Marx to take over the editorship of the *Neue Rheinische Zeitung*. In universities throughout Europe academics were discussing a 'republican brotherhood', and in Windsor Castle the rotund little Queen Victoria had been told of a bunch of suffragettes from Manchester. According to the report they were *a shrieking sisterhood*, and the little lady was so upset she wrote out an appeal to all her friends to enlist support against this mad wicked folly of women's rights which was certain to ravage every sense of womanly feeling and propriety in the female breast. The first Divorce Act was eight years hence.

As the *Eliza* sailed away from the Indian coast, a twenty-two-year-old subaltern named John Hanning Speke joined his regiment in Multan to serve under Lord Gough in the Sikh Campaign. With him he had a friend, James Grant.

V

Victim himself of that peculiarly
British classification – 'too clever
by half' – and at war with British
understatement.

IN VIEWING BURTON'S LIFE, IT IS A CONSTANT PROBLEM THAT
from 1849 onwards, from the age of twenty-nine to his death in his
seventieth year, almost everything we can learn about the man is seen
through the eyes of Isabel Burton. We are entirely in Isabel's hands,
because only she had access to what biographical notes he left behind,
and all of this was ground into her own two-volume monument,
published after his death. There is a very good example of her attitude
in the first sentence which takes over from his personal narrative. As
far as Burton was concerned he boarded the *Eliza*, bound for Europe,
half sick, blind, reeling with guilt at having gained nothing in seven
years' foreign service, and filled with anger that he had left behind him
the slur of a rumour that this 'white nigger' was a sodomite who
roamed male brothels in search of nether exotica. What does Isabel
write with her first breath?

> When Richard came home, he first ran down full of joy to visit all his
> relations and friends. He then went to Oxford with half a mind to take
> his degree.

To be exact, he had one aunt in London who would put him up
temporarily, for the rest of his family was abroad; his brother Edward

had sustained a crippling brain injury in Ceylon after an elephant hunt where some Ceylonese took it upon themselves to give him a hideous thrashing; the ever kind Grandma Baker had been dead for three years; Burton had no friends left in London; and he never visited Oxford to discuss taking a degree with his old college for the simple reason that the college had long ago wiped their hands clean of 'dirty Dick' when they sent him down. Furthermore, if anything was to put him into low spirits, let alone prevent from 'running around full of joy', it was the inevitable cut and thrust of being hounded by creditors with a very long memory. Richard quickly joined his family in Pisa.

Not long after he and Allahdad arrived, the household—that is, his mother and father, his sister Maria (now married to a Lieutenant-General Stisted and the mother of two daughters), and an Italian cook Sabbatino—took fierce umbrage at Allahdad's behaviour. Evidently the Indian grew lonely and depressed, and finally he mustered all his pent-up anger in one remarkable scene in the kitchens below when he tried to roast the cook Sabbatino over a charcoal stove. Joseph was in what has been described as his 'usual excellent state of poor health'. Maria Stisted took it upon herself to smooth out the troubled waters. For Richard had become a raving madman with fevers, boils, the pain still in his eyes, and he insisted on sporting various exotic shirts and balloon cotton bloomers with tight puttees above gold gondolier sandals. Joseph Burton had soon had enough of this. His son had become a lunatic. He talked incessant gibberish with the nigger servant who had a fancy to roast the cook, and something must be done about it. Burton had now taught his servant to recite, parrot fashion, the phrase 'God damn Italy!' over and over, and this quite naturally did not endear Allahdad to the restless natives of Pisa. Maria Stisted, as her husband was far abroad and at war for his Queen, hastily packed all her luggage and took one of her father's coaches. She bundled Richard and Allahdad and her two daughters inside and drove back to the French coast. She persuaded Richard he needed her medical guidance and care, and she strongly endorsed her father's request that this lunatic Allahdad be posted straight back to wherever it was he came from. Richard was defeated. He was too ill to bother putting up a fight and simply gave in to his sister's remonstrations; at best, he could only have showed callow class motives for keeping Allahdad anyway, and he knew there was little more Hindu he could learn from the servant. It was essential, Maria affirmed, to present himself to his senior officers at the East India Company, explain the degree of his ill health, and come to some terms with his regiment.

Burton and Maria ordered new horses at Dover and made for London, back to one of those long-suffering aunts. Poor Allahdad was bundled on a ship bound for Bombay.

Richard laid up at his aunt's home with his sister for a few weeks to survey his situation. Nothing looked particularly bright on his horizon. He had just enough fever, boils and poor sight to justify sick-pay from the East India Company. An echo of his father's early troubles with the army did not escape Burton. On the surface of things, it looked as if he were bound to emulate the old Colonel himself. As Richard approached the offices of his commander-in-chief Sir James Hogg to explain his erratic toings and froings from India on to Pisa and back home again, he knew he was about to make a copybook facsimile of Joseph Burton's relationship with the army. Richard did not find it difficult to convince the army surgeons of his bad health. As for Hogg, he wasn't going to grumble at the temporary loss of this young officer from his ranks. Hadn't Lieutenant Burton got an unseemly regimental smell about him? Something about being a common bugger and haunting 'backgammon' (military slang for sodomy) parlours in Karachi?

Sick leave from his regiment meant, in the case of an officer, that he must report back to his seniors within a reasonable time; meanwhile, unless the army decided otherwise, he could retain full pay. The one redeeming feature in Richard's favour is that this sick leave pay and general freedom would provide him with all the time in the world to set about the two most pressing problems he knew lay ahead. First, it was necessary to marry a girl of wealth from his own class. Secondly, he was going to write. He had brought back with him from India twenty volumes of diaries and notes, observations and records of his language studies. Above all, he was not going to extend repetition of Father's behaviour by allowing the years to consume him. He was going to fill his hours in as honourable a manner as any gentleman of his class; and what better convalescence than a term of sick-pay devoted to rich girls and the art of letters, beneficently paid for by the East India Company?

Burton chose Boulogne for very much the same reason his father had chosen Naples, Florence, and all the others. Joseph was an inveterate expatriate. His wounds would not allow him to settle in the old country. As for Richard, well—it was significant to be a pretty exotic fish in a small pool like Boulogne; the bantam with his six obscure languages could strut the promenade with ease. Who could contradict him?

Isabel recorded that Boulogne was merely a home for the stranger who had done something wrong. She might have been thinking of Richard at the time. But more likely she remembered those shady odds and sods who arrive by stealth and depart with speed. Such towns are always filled with derring-do expatriates. The gambler who sold his grandmother in a last card throw. A divorced woman who believed London gossip did not reach so far across the channel. Or an officer from the Bombay Infantry who had a bad scratch from the past. In these glum little resorts, servants were cheap, and fixed incomes from the London City spread the good social butter life quite fatly.

His mother hated the idea of him living on his own. She took this as a fair enough excuse to leave her husband, and she wrote to her daughter Maria to meet her in Boulogne as well. In no time at all Martha Burton rented a small terraced house, once again furnished with few of her own chattels, and Richard had to succumb to her frivolous ministerings. He had no choice. His mother made the meals. His sister hunted about town for prospective brides. And he hid himself in an upstairs room to write. He wrote some two thousand pages based on notes from the Indian years; his diaries and his vivid memory gave birth to *Scinde: or the Unhappy Valley, Goa and the Blue Mountains, Sindh and the Races that Inhabit the Valley of the Indus*, and a fourth manuscript—*Falconry in the Valley of the Indus*.

For many months he had recurring physical ailments, from liver pains to inflammation of the bladder, and the year of 1851 gave him little respite from the daily grind of his writing, except for a sitting for a portrait painter, François Jacquand, a friend of Maria Stisted, who in fact arranged this commission; and the occasional visits to a gymnasium to demonstrate his Indian sabre techniques to a capable instructor, M. Constantin. On one visit Richard took up swords with a French Hussar wearing only a shirt and breeches with his neck and chin bared, and he struck the other man's hilt with such force that seven times in succession the Hussar was barely able to make a single stroke. The Hussar retreated with a pained if not severely strained wrist, and the audience in the gym were startled by the brute strength of this burly young Englishman who, by all accounts, was unconcerned with the niceties of style, he simply wanted to disarm his opponent. Richard enjoyed the astonishment of the French audience inside the gymnasium that afternoon. For he could fence in the more formal French manner, had he chosen to, with speed and acumen the equal of any Hussar in Boulogne.

Burton found a publisher for his first manuscript, *Goa and the Blue*

Mountains: or Six Months of Sick Leave — the firm of Richard Bentley, well-known to the armed forces as a military publishing house. Bentley accepted the second manuscript before the first book reached the shops; it was *Scinde; or the Unhappy Valley*. It is best to look at these books side by side, for they betray many of the failings one could discover in Burton as a youth. *Goa and the Blue Mountains* makes no pretence whatsoever at fine writing. It amounts to almost a hundred and twenty thousand words compiled from furious diary jottings made when that painful retreat from good health sick with rheumatic ophthalmia in 1846 took him to the Portuguese colony. In the first place, so much haste was he in to slap it all down, the pages reek of notes copied ad nauseum from diaries he could hardly disguise, and there is an element of impatience and exasperation in his own *feel* towards the material. For an operative writer, someone working from field-study diaries, he makes no attempt to meld the notes into a common prose sensibility. The chapters have a patched quality, of hefty unevenness, as if he did not care too much to reach for a style only to fill the pages and the time with undoubted energy. He could spend pages on the subject of proper military use of the bayonet, or the Todas people, mountain dwellers, who practised a form of poly-andry, even pour out from his gossiping heart his own malevolent little prejudices — niggers, Jews, freemasons — but all the while the reader can find no justifiable explanation for the stay in Goa, or indeed for the publication of this book. It was something an author of definite promise ought to have filed away in a bottom drawer. When the *Athenaeum Magazine* reviewer cautioned Lieutenant Burton for not 'obtaining some competent opinion on the merits of the book before he printed it' and suggested to the new author that a good friend might have advised at least a third of the piece tossed out of the window, Burton and his publishers Richard Bentley & Co paid no heed whatsoever. Within a short time the second book was issued, *Scinde; or the Unhappy Valley*, and again these two-fold faults emerged: the sheer impatience of the writer with his material, his notes and data, and the exuberant disinterest in compiling a prose surface with any degree of order. The writing, jammed with addenda and quite fascinating pieces of marginalia, never moulded itself into a fluid narrative. The work bounces like a jellybean, in the main a travel narrative based on his surveying expeditions with his old friend Walter Scott, it is acutely marked with a disdain for the common reader. It is as if the author despises us for not having taken part in the same travels, the reader feels he is held in contempt for his topographical ignorance, and, at a time when such travel writing was indeed a popular art form, this did not go down well with the book-buying public in London or Edinburgh. It was a mixture of undue haste and arrogance which filled these two books. Describing a cow in the book, Burton adds the kind of footnote he clearly could not resist —

> The Panjagaviya, as the Hindoos call them; if you want to know what they are, consult a Hindustanee dictionary.

It wasn't until he came to a parting of the ways with his publishers, and he was obliged to approach William H. Allen & Co with a third manuscript — *Sindh, and the Races that Inhabit the Valley of the Indus*, that Burton accidentally came upon the style of letters his name would evermore be associated with: now, his scramble for notes and addenda had become a mania, certain chapters of five thousand words were encased by marginalia of an equal amount of words. In effect, he was writing two books in every single volume. The notes and detailed observations, singled out of context, chapter and paragraph, made up the most fascinating material. They were the bones of insight and imagination, and they were the very elements of good writing, that as an anthropologist, as an ethnologist of pioneering stature, he ought to have expanded upon. The narratives were concerned with the trivialities. The notes were concerned with the major issues. He put all the routine stuff of when and what time in the pages, and kept all his insight and acute observation to the marginalia and addenda.

Most reviewers were reluctant to admit what an anthropologist they had in their midst. For Burton had crossed crudely over the narrow bridge of good taste and travelling tales to something a little nastier; his arrogance showed, and with it he seemed determined to filibuster the reader. Here were books jammed with Portuguese, Persian, Sanscrit, Hindustani and Arabic, detail upon detail about Jat people, Belochi families, Pathans, Sindians, their rites, moral contracts, their beliefs, their drugs, pets and income tax: until it becomes apparent that the writer urgently needed a person to say, stop here, turn about, infuse the narrative with the notes, for these are the blood of the prose. Alas, nobody was suitable for the job. The Lieutenant, somewhat enraged at the paltry criticisms of his books, turned in a fourth manu-script, *Falconry in the Valley of the Indus*. In it he took a freewheeling stab at the critics; once again he was forced to change publishers. William H. Allen, like his predecessors, Richard Bentley & Co, could not unload these books on to a public which had lost interest after a dull press. Burton's four books did not sell. He himself made no effort to come to London or Edinburgh to advance their sales. It was common practice for writers of travel and adventure to follow up the publication with a score of lectures. But Burton hid himself in Boulogne. As far as he was concerned, he was right and everybody else was wrong. All it had required was the good intentions of an honourable critic to recognise that this new writer was capable of making the most colossal mistakes and yet producing a stunningly original composition. Burton made no pretence at literature or art. But his energies, and the incredible variety, the vast canvas of curious and bewildering data from gypsies to incest, from bayonet drill to Islam, in half a dozen languages, made it plain enough that the man was a protean Gibbon, of analytic ethnology, uniquely gifted with a sense of inquiry into so many studies. All it required was a lead, a word of direction, or a chance to develop and unify the extravagant energies. Born in Germany, he would have been hailed as an heir apparent to a combination of the brothers Humboldt, one a philologist, the more famous other a naturalist. Born in England, adrift on sick pay, tucked away intransigently in tea-table tattle Boulogne, Burton was a victim of that notorious countermand of the understatement, he was in effect 'too clever by half'.

Falconry in the Valley of the Indus was more of an extended essay, forty thousand words long; its notations were filled with a kind of aggrieved polemic against those earlier English critics who did not appreciate the breadth of his talent. He was right in his insinuations, but wrong in demonstrating his arrogant assumptions. Of the four books now in print, Burton learned that more than half the copies were still on the shelves. But, in those days publishers carefully preserved all unsold copies, because invariably author and publisher had shared the cost of the edition.

VI

These years in Boulogne he spoke twice
and danced once with a plump teenage
girl who insisted upon staring. English
village community as congested as
Fortnum & Mason's fruit-crush counter
on a Friday afternoon.

SHE WAS NINETEEN. WALKING ALONG THE BOULOGNE RAM-
parts with her sister. A warm September day in 1850. Isabel Arundell
was a tall young woman with blue eyes and a rather square jaw. She
had thin lips which smiled warmly, and thick brown hair flowed
beneath her hat. She had been educated for six years in an Essex
convent; now she had joined the rest of her family in Boulogne,
ostensibly to learn French. It was a good watering place for impoverished expatriates to find husbands for their daughters. The
Arundell family was Roman Catholic. And, although much has been
made of Isabel's stern devotion to her faith, it was no fall from grace to
fall in love with the tall strange figure on the ramparts, it was more a
mark of her independence, some spark of determination which in
itself proved more formidable than her family's Church. She was
immediately struck by the sight of Richard Burton striding along with
a cane over his shoulder like a rifle, wearing a short jacket made of
black tufted wool. His hair was smoothed back across a dark forehead,
and his moustache drooped on either end of his lips with a mandarin
thickness quite unusual for the fashion of the day. His eyes wore a
satanic expression, flashing and cruel, they seemed both melancholic
and obsessively contemptuous of all they surveyed. She believed he
could read her mind. He was Miss Brontë's Rochester to the life. She

gasped to her sister once they had hurried on, 'That man will marry *me*'; and the next day she made sure she saw him again on the same promenade.

At that time Burton was deep in his writing, and all his diaries and notebooks were laid out across plank shelves upstairs in his bedroom, and still racked with fever, it is difficult to believe he took much notice of young Isabel that September day. They bumped into one another with contrived nicety the next day on the ramparts at Boulogne. This time, we are led to believe, he not only 'followed us' but he paused long enough to scribble against a wall 'May I speak to you?'. Leaving the chalk there, he stood aside for Isabel to chalk reply, 'No, Mother will be angry.'

Like many other recollections of Isabel, there always remains a hint of fable. There was no reason why they could not talk. But at nineteen and self-involved to an extreme, her determined dreams must have taken the form of reality until she was convinced of nothing else. As for Richard . . . he had two years of writing before him, and an acknowledged fascination with two very pretty cousins in his own family. There was a simple explanation for his repeated enthusiasms for his female cousins – they were the progeny of those Baker aunts who held keys to quite substantial dowries. Why should he waste time on Isabel, who had none?

Isabel was the eldest daughter of Henry Arundell who ran a wine counter in central London with some success. The name Arundell carried with it high regard amongst other Catholic families, and Arundell had prevailed upon a leading Catholic, Lord Arundell, to become Isabel's godfather. The Arundell family had lived rather well in England before they came out to Boulogne. Lord Arundell of Wardour proved kindly and though there was no direct hereditary link with Isabel's family, there remained a sympathetic association between these families. Isabel's mother came from a family equipped with a minor baronetcy, and Henry Arundell rented a manor house in Essex to bring up his extravagantly large family. Isabel's mother was the second wife to Arundell. His first wife produced a son and heir to the wine counter, and the second wife dutifully bore him eleven further children. It really does appear as if the wine trader had strong social ambitions, for he married not once and well, but twice and very well. Isabel's mother commanded a natural entrance into most of the more illustrious Catholic families of the time, even to the point of supplying Isabel, her first child, with a coming-out ball at Almack's Club under the benevolent eye of the most senior Catholic in England, the Duke of Norfolk. Anyway, Isabel moved to Boulogne with her cricket team of younger brothers and sisters, and a degree of desperation must have struck the Arundell mother. For Isabel's chances of making a good marriage, in other words catching a young fellow with at least half a title and a foot in the door to a reasonable country estate, were pretty minimal. Few Catholics as staunch as these Arundells expected any great entrance into the prevailing Protestant ruling class.

It looks as if that coming-out ball at Almack's the year earlier was something of a disaster. No male had leant forward with a proposal of marriage. The majority of girls at this time were wed before their nineteenth birthday. Not surprising this, at all, when their life expectancy did not stretch much beyond forty. Isabel's family had one need of Boulogne, and that was its cheapness. A colossal family, twelve children, and a number of servants, could just about scrape along in France; it would cost them three times that on a country estate in Essex. Isabel once listed the suitable Catholic families in Boulogne, the Seymours, the Dundases, the Chichesters, the Jerninghams, the Bedingfields, the Cliffords, and the Molyneux-Seels, and all in all they did not offer her a great choice.

As for Burton, no one could be convinced this three-year sojourn in France was a series of cockrobin preambles along the ramparts, white stuffed shirts and lily clean hands, gossip afeather-flirt behind ebony and satin fans. If the town had indeed been jammed with fillies one would have expected Joseph Burton to have blundered himself there in a trice, 'asthma' notwithstanding. Dick and Boulogne were not an easy combination.

Burton's old ally from the Sind days, John Steinhaeuser, joined him in Boulogne for a stay. By this time Richard was considered something of an eccentric. This dark frowning esoteric young man had become noted. People now referred to Burton as that 'awfully clever soldier'. Isabel's ears pricked up. Mothers with pretty daughters had had a sniff of a rumour about him. Something about too intimate behaviour with 'niggers' in Bombay. He had a stigma attached to his name. Difficult for them to pin down. But spoken in hushed tones behind sash-curtain drawing rooms, the rumours became a mannered cause of exclusion from this English colony. Now, he had become an author. It bore him little prestige amongst the mothers in Boulogne. A penurious author as a future son-in-law was nought out of ten in the dance-card pecking order of marital matters.

Burton and Steinhaeuser savoured the few invitations they could cull. But Maria found it difficult to persuade the nicer girls to visit her gruff and spiky brother, let alone Steinhaeuser. Richard was rather delighted by this public exclusion. He turned his charms to find the racier skirts around the town. He was attracted to Isabel's older cousin, Louisa; she was a girl with a quick and clever tongue which suited Burton very well. The mother was a dragon, it seems. She had wind of Burton's nefarious meetings with Louisa and she summoned him to her. In later years, Isabel dramatised the confrontation—

'I sent for you, Lieutenant Burton, because I think it my dooty to ask what your intentions are with regard to my daughter?'

'Your dooty, madam . . .!'

'Yes, sir.'

'Alas, madam! Strictly dishonourable!'

'—!—'

'I regret to say, strictly dishonourable!' he repeated. And Richard strode out of the room with the intention of tracking down the filly subject of all this fuss. Eventually he found her—

'Look here young woman,' he began, 'if I talk to you, you must arrange that I do not have "mamma's dooty" flung at my head any more.'

'The old fool!' his friend blurted out, 'how like her!'

Meanwhile, Isabel's secret devotion was kept in abeyance. But she had been deeply affected by a remarkable prophecy which she had received from a gypsy woman when she had attended a convent school in England, a few years before. The gypsy's name was Hagar Burton. She told Isabel—

You will cross the sea, and be in the same town with your Destiny, and know it not. Every obstacle will rise up against you, and such a combination of circumstances, that it will require all your courage and energy and intelligence to meet them. Your life will be like one always swimming against big waves, but God will always be with you, so you will always win. You will fix your eye on your polar star, and you will go for that without looking right or left. *You will bear the name of our tribe,* and be right proud of it. You will be as we are, but far greater than we. Your life is all wandering, change, and adventure. One soul in two bodies, in life or death; never long apart.

Isabel could not put this memory aside. She repeated it to herself so often it assumed all the proportions of romantic destiny. It was to be an irrevocable tryst. That is, if she could persuade the object of all her aspirations. Isabel's account of this episode is as good an explanation as any of her strangely detached, but determined, character. All her life, it seems, she was one of these people who are dogged by omens. Though she did indeed moon from one party to another yearning for this dark man who had the brow of a god and the jaw of a devil, she was supported by an immense reservoir of belief in her own fate. And Dick did indeed possess the name Burton. It was an ancient Romany family sobriquet, and about as common as the Smith travellers in Northumberland, or the Brown family of gypsies in north Wales.

Her mother gave her a novel, *Tancred, or the New Crusade*, by Disraeli. It had all the ingredients Isabel so yearned for. A handsome young earl leaves England for the East where he falls in love with a beautiful Jewess. In part the novel, one of a trio, was a political guide to Whig Reform; in commercial terms the beautiful Jewess of the East, who was doomed to never marry the hero, was a best-selling concept. Isabel of course dreamed of Gypsy Lore, Arab encampments, slaver caravans, earls and beauties, and whatever other trivia was grouped beneath the misnomer of the Forbidden East. Perfect diet for a young girl in Boulogne, eldest of eleven, with the impending weight of marital stakes on her shoulders.

Richard was in despair about his book sales. And his arrogant public truculence did not help matters. A book like *Tancred* sold edition after edition. It was such an easily consumable glossed veneer of Eastern Promise. To be 'Byronic' now that the millionaire republican freedom fighter for Greece was some twenty years in his grave had, at last, been reduced to a bland and modish design. The style, and not the essence of the great poet, had become a commodity. The original *dare* in Byron's nature, his angered idealism, the torn heart of rapture would be blended down to pap fodder for the new-found genteel art of recreational reading.

Richard may indeed have scribbled in chalk 'may we meet again soon?', on a wall beside the ramparts for young Isabel, but he certainly did not pursue the lass in 1852, or for that matter 1853. Only her dreams and infatuation (she had read his books on the North West Frontier and she felt her heart thump a little harder behind her corselette with its grosgrain-ribbon busk at the mention of his name, and it was not too difficult to feel faint with all that ribbing across her crushed lungs) only her dreams raced away with this beau-ideal. For he had hardly ever spoken to her at parties, a glance occasionally across a tea table, the odd smell of his breath when he once asked her to dance, port and black cheroot odour from this devilish type. On that occasion she locked her sash and gloves away in a drawer never to wear again for he, that special prince of hers, had touched the items with his own gloved hand.

Richard never gave up on his fencing. His afternoon workouts in the gymnasium became a regular break from his mother, his sister and their efforts to find him a wife. He much preferred the heavier blade of the sabre, and accordingly invented two new strokes: a certain *une-deux* and a sequential strike the *manchette*. The gymnasium freely allowed Richard the title *Maître d'Armes*, an acknowledged honour, but the novelty in his fighting lay in his peculiar brand of rough-house footwork. The average Frenchman employed a frontal stance at foil play, and developed this style into the broadsword events. Burton supplied a new element. His sabre could cut and thrust, and the strength of his arm allowed him numerous extra points according to the ancient 'touch' system, because his touches had the efficacy of a blunt hammer. In fact, quite accidentally Burton heralded the newer basket-handled sabres which were to become so popular in German universities; they were equipped with the added novelty of a 'secret cutting edge', eight inches of sharpened steel on the concave edge above the tip. The concept of the sabre as a hacking instrument which can, nevertheless, be used with skill according to the strength of your fore-arm, was to speed up in Germany and England the outlawing of the more notorious blood duels, the like of which Karl Marx indulged in at his home university. With new life preserving laws, fencing in Europe turned to the art of épée.

This love of fencing brought him round inevitably to the use of the sword point in battle, and, quite naturally, he sat down and wrote out a fifteen-thousand-word manual *A Complete System of Bayonet Exercise*. Richard had never quite accepted the appalling tactics the common infantryman used when on a forward march. The British foot soldiers had been taught to empty their musket, and from then on to use the musket like a bludgeon at close quarters. Although the bayonet was a fixed companion of a soldier's belt, he never had any training in hand-to-hand sword-thrust combat. Another printer, William Clowes & Co Ltd, brought the pamphlet out in London. The publication coincided with Richard's first voyage back to England for almost a year. His mother had persuaded Joseph Burton to take a cottage at Bath, in Somerset; there was some trifling plan to 'take the waters'. Maria Stisted was to join them, and Richard did not appear to show much enthusiasm for that. The Boulogne house was closed. Once in England there is no indication whatsoever that Richard made contact with his father. There was a division of guilt and mistrust and filial disappointment.

As soon as Richard arrived in England, his brigade commander, Colonel William Sykes, took umbrage at the Clowes publication of the bayonet pamphlet. It was an offence, Sykes indicated, to encourage foot soldiers to meddle with bayonet drill on a charge forward against heavy fire. Clearly Sykes didn't trust the British soldier to run and load a bayonet at the same time. Burton's pamphlet, it was maintained in official army circles close to Sykes, did nothing but add confusion to the common soldier's drill. This was despite the fact that the American and German and French armies had already added bayonet drill under charge conditions into their normal barracks training.

Richard was a thirty-two-year-old officer of a lowly regiment, possessor of a bargain-basement commission; for all these months he had been 'out of action' writing books about India nobody was in a great stampede to buy; he was held in bad odour by the Chairman of the Court of Directors of the East India Company, and he had caused his immediate superior commanding officer to whinny at the sight of the bayonet essay. Hardly a success at anything, in his thirties, with a life expectancy short of fifty years, and what was he to do? It was either an act of financial suicide, a sudden trick of bravura he worked up in a bottle of port with his friend John Steinhaeuser, or a decision which would have him retired from the army, with parallels of patrimonial infelicity. He made up his mind to travel in disguise to the holy Muslim shrine of Mecca, a town for pilgrims of Mohammad, fiercely forbidden to the infidel explorer, let alone an itinerant British army officer.

It was not possible to extend his 'sick leave' into a fourth year. If he was going to write again he knew he had to travel. Returning to the army fold at this stage in his life was an intolerable prospect. He was unlikely to be posted to anywhere of his own choosing. His brigade commander Colonel Sykes would be more inclined to shove Richard across to the Burma coast or the southern tip of Siam.

Richard went about his scheme with a degree of cunning. He enlisted the aid of Roderick Murchison, President of the Royal Geographical Society, who had already warmly received Burton's complimentary copies of his Indian books. Murchison had taken over the reins of the Society just at a time when truly ambitious individual exploration was about to become a cult. The age of highly paid *I was there and I saw it* popular journalism had already started in America and in France.

In 1853, Livingstone commenced his great march from coast to coast, across Africa, from Quilimane on the east to Loanda on the west and the shores of the Atlantic. The Society under Murchison was financing various expeditions, ever mindful of their cartographic and commercial opportunities in opening up new paths, but yet determined to keep a dignified distance from the run-of-the-mill empire-building in which the principal countries of Europe were about to indulge.

Murchison arranged for Burton a personal interview with James Hogg, Chairman to the Board of Directors of the East India Company, and, along with Colonel Sykes, Colonel Yorke, both from the Bombay Infantry, and General Monteith, Richard achieved his aim. Hogg at first refused to help Burton in what seemed like a madcap adventure crossing the Arabian peninsula merely 'for the purpose of removing that opprobrium to modern adventure, the huge white blot which in our maps still notes the Eastern and Central regions of Arabia'. And Richard bold as brass also asked for two years' leave for this risky voyage. Hogg did not take to the young man. But in view of the limited number of wars there were to fight there was certainly some decent propaganda to be gained from a young officer setting out to study Arabic 'in lands where the language is best learned' and perhaps reporting back to the Company on opening a market for stud horses to be trained in India, and further obtaining some information on the vast and unknown desert of the Rub al Khali. Hogg was not prepared to put up a penny for an insane journey to the forbidden city of Mecca, but Richard could have a year away to polish his languages. Later, Richard appealed to Murchison to make up this loss of cash, and quite rightly, Murchison was more than willing to underwrite an attempt to enter Mecca. It was the kind of jewel in the stakes of achievement which the Society stood for.

VII

Too easy for the unbeliever fabulist
exorciser to enter Mecca in his disguise,
too hard to arrive at the gates with
belief alone.

BEFORE RICHARD, IT IS SAID A BRITISH SAILOR WAS CARRIED
into Mecca as a slave in the 17th century. But the most famous secret
entry was made by the great Swiss traveller John Burckhardt who
entered Mecca disguised as a Syrian merchant in 1814. Burckhardt was
a brilliant linguist, and before he dared risk his life trying to enter the
Holy City he spent four years in the Arabian desert, and so word
perfect did he become, and such an authority on the Koran text, he was
able to pass himself off as a travelling doctor of Islamic law.

Undoubtedly Richard had some of Burckhardt's accomplishments.
His Arabic was not quite so adequate. His appearance, shading six foot,
with a heavy square head, his broad hands and feet quite unused to
desert life, seemed bound to give him away instantly; and risk there
was, for certain. There have been a number of recorded instances of
French and Russian travellers silly enough to get inside the walls of
Mecca. Their deaths were speedily brought about. They were, most
often, simply taken some distance beyond the thousands who camped
on the outskirts of the city on their progress to Mecca, and decapitated.
Their bodies were wrapped in sheets and placed in unmarked sand
graves, along with any possessions they had brought with them.

From time to time there has been some pretty silly speculation about
Burton and circumcision during his five-month preparation in London

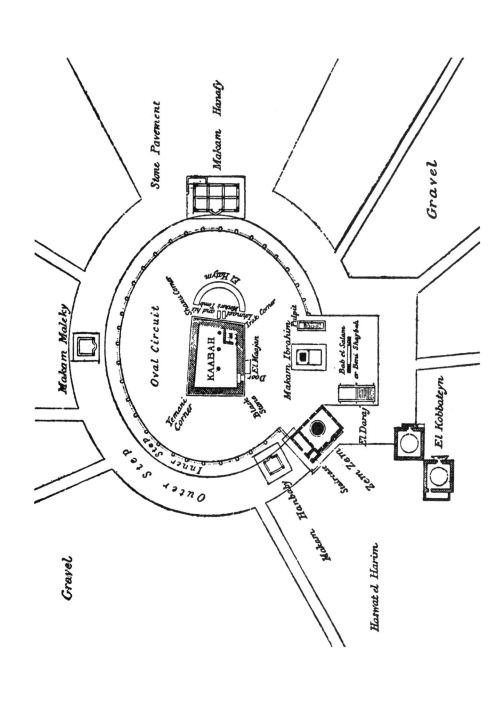

Stone Pavement

Makam Hanafy

Makam Maleky

Gravel

Gravel

Oval Circuit

El Hagm

Shami Corner

Latimed and his Mother's Tomb

Irak Corner

KAABAH

El Magan

Door

Yemani Corner

Black Stone

Inner Step

Outer Step

Makam Ibrahim

Pulpit

Bab el Salam or Beni Shaybeh

El Daraj

Makam Hanbaly

Zem Zem

Sakkas

El Kobbateyn

Hasvat el Harim

for the voyage to Mecca. At least one biographer, supplying a quote from a Burton text of a few years earlier when he was in Boulogne, has openly suggested Burton sought medical advice and underwent the necessary surgery; less mindboggling stands the more obvious solution, and that is that the man, being the son of an army officer, might indeed have had the operation at birth on fairly routine grounds of health and common hygiene. Circumcision is not at all an unusual procedure for army families who might at any given moment be required in far distant places lacking in every kind of sanitation. For centuries families in France and England have been aware of the bizarre, and often quite painful, situations young Louis fifteenths have had with dangling loose integuments which can turn the act of coition into an embarrassing disaster. Circumcision has never been an unusual subject to fetch up in a study of Burton. Almost all of his own books give an inordinate amount of marginalia over to the subject, for he was fascinated with all forms of this surgery. He had decided to adopt the role of a part Arab part Persian traveller; he'd be known as Mirza Abdullah with the assistance of some walnut juice, and he'd leave England wearing Arab costume. In retrospect, there are humorous shades in all this of Duncan Grant and Virginia Woolf dressing up as sheikhs to persuade an Admiral of the Fleet to give them an official tour of various warships in a British harbour; but there were great risks involved, and Richard had only five months in which to prepare a language and a general knowledge of Arabic custom on a par with Burckhardt who took all of four years to achieve this.

His mother and his sister stayed in a house at Bath during the summer of 1853; his father was elsewhere, perhaps sitting it out in yet another French provincial community, or back in Italy pinching fat girls' bottoms; Richard took a course in shoeing horses and even went so far as to work alongside a blacksmith. Again, in the past, others have inferred from this sudden and brief apprenticeship that he must have been making plans to acquaint himself with every last Arabic custom. On the contrary, if he was going to travel with horse dealers for the Company, it was a wise thing to know the rudiments of the smithy's art. And Burton had proposed to Hogg at the East India Company that he might open up a healthy trade in unbroken horses to the British army-maintained ports in India.

There were no goodbyes. He hated to waste his sentiment on tearful farewells. On a morning at his mother's house in Bath, he rose early, left two short notes on his bedside table, and rode up to London in a mail coach. His family would refer to him later as their 'Arabian

Knight'. Meanwhile, his mother wrote a full report to his father, and more than one aunt in London must have shed a lonely tear. In Boulogne, a twenty-four-year-old Isabel Arundell, with her parents in near despair at her inability to clinch any kind of marriage, continued with her annual round of tea parties, muffins and hot butter, straw-berry jelly spoonsfuls and lemon tea, and an uneventful parade of garden waltzes and warm sea weather promenades. In her diary she claims she prayed for this hero, though he was still a virtual stranger to her, every night; Burton, nevertheless, wrote to nobody besides his intimate family, and if he made any prayers on his ever-present Koran, it was highly unlikely they were proffered up with a thought to that winsome gel in Boulogne. He intended to sail from Southampton on April 3, 1853.

Certainly, Richard had his dates right; for the anniversary of Mohammad's famous flight from Mecca to Medina in AD 622 fell in July. And July was the month most of the great pilgrimages set out for Mecca and Medina in accord with their religious practices. The flight from Mecca to Medina was called the *hegira* of Mohammad and his small band of disciples. All those who undertook the long voyage to the fabled city of Mecca to kiss the shrine undertook a *haj*, and they rightfully became known as the *haji*, or, one who has made the pilgrimage.

Richard reached Alexandria in a *kafan* shroud, carrying his assorted baggage in a variety of containers, and making certain no trunk or leather bag had European markings attached. He took with him a collection of usefuls any daringly disguised pilgrim might need for the voyage—Persian rug, goat-skin waterbags, saddle-bags, a copy of the Koran and enough writing and drawing papers and pen and ink; all of which, quite rightly, might sum up the *haj* of his character as played out in the guise of one Abdullah. For an instant the casual reader is willing to be fobbed off with the romance of the account. And accord-ing to all previous legend, this 'Mr Abdullah', *kafan* shrouded, with henna facial make-up, slip-slop sandals and a star sapphire brooch in the upper *kafan*, attired thus, and with at least four fluent languages at his command, is about to achieve the impossible—to enter Mecca as a true convert of Islam.

But when one explores a little more deeply below the surface, the whole performance becomes more oafish, almost bordering on school-boy comic jape territory. Richard carried, and did not consider it strange to be discovered with them, at least twenty-five gold sovereigns, each one stamped with a royal British warranty from the

Mint, each one weighing the normal 123 grains troy; furthermore, he took with him a large medicine chest and a sextant in a fold-out cherry wood box, plus a brace of fine pistols made in France.

To make matters even more confusing, Richard applied at the embassy in Alexandria for a passport in the name of Abdullah, which placed him under British protection, and which was countersigned by an Alexandria police official. It sounds glib, this sudden new lawfully recognised character Mirza Abdullah, but it is difficult to deny that these kind of instant formalities could be undergone with the aid of a half gold sovereign or so.

Richard and his servant Nur went on to Cairo where he changed a few sovereigns into less identifiable currency. He bought donkeys and camels, small provisions, and joined a vast caravan from Damascus which was to cross the lonely Nejd Desert. Hundreds of irregular Muslim cavalry, the bashi-bazooks, guarded the trail to Medina by night, and a curious young Arab called Mohammed attached himself to Richard's small unit.

Usually, Richard had always got away with the natural flair for languages he undoubtedly possessed; but his disguise was not quite as foolproof as it has been made out to be. His Persian and his Arabic were by no means perfect tools; he could not, and he knew this only too well, convince an Arab like Mohammed that he was anything but a Hindu-speaking Pathan from Northern India. This made life a lot easier for him. He could stumble as much as he liked in Arabic, for neither Nur nor Mohammed knew much Hindustani. And it made sense of them, albeit temporarily. At least on two occasions, friends he talked to suspected Richard of being an infidel. His bags were ransacked, but all they found was the sextant (a mysterious westernised affair it must have appeared) and his French-made pistols. Richard discreetly hid the remainder of the sovereigns on his body; as for the passport putting 'Mirza Abdullah' under *British* protection, God knows what he did with that; if he had been caught with it, the entire *haj* would have been ruined, and he would have been lucky to escape with his life.

The medicine chest, it is said, was meant to be convincing proof of Abdullah's claims to be a home-grown physician. It can scarcely be believed though; Richard had a smattering of medical knowledge, but nobody came forth to be cured of anything particularly serious, and in retrospect, the idea of Abdullah being a doctor seems an unnecessary complication.

In July the Damascus caravan arrived at Medina. Richard, or Mirza

Abdullah, constantly aroused the curious eyes of his extra servant young Mohammed; and yet Richard felt confident enough to linger at Medina several weeks. It was during this time he must have retraced his steps and covertly made illustrations of the walled town from an outlying hillside which he later used in his three-volume edition *Personal Narrative of a Pilgrimage to El-Medinah & Meccah*.

Unlikely though it seems, Richard did indeed find the time to make detailed maps of the city, visit the tombs of the Prophet's family, complete a number of sketches of fellow pilgrims, despite the danger of these tasks, and the Islamic distaste for naturalistic likenesses. In his volumes on the pilgrimage he gives no clue as to how he set about this. For the Muslims were still pouring into the town at all hours, there was no particular moment throughout any day when all was quiet and serene, and artists and cartographers could walk about undetected. One can only assume that Burton sketched and measured, took sightings and drew accurate plans of mosques and tombs to the nearest 420th foot without the least suspicion falling upon him. In truth, it was either a much less dangerous job for an inquisitive 'Pathan doctor called Abdullah' to set about Medina like a quantity surveyor gone berserk, sextant in one hand, tape measure in the other, or Richard had actual measurements taken by Nur or Mohammed, the young servants.

On the 31st of August, Richard and his new friends joined the caravan again, heading south to the fabled Mecca. It was to take twelve days. The entire caravan travelled best by night; the nocturnal cool made the 250-mile ride easier, and the robbers, vagrant tribal pariahs and flintlock rats of the desert, eager for a fat Turkish carcass, had less chance to attack. Nothing was safer than a moving target in the darkness.

On the 9th of September, a day's ride from Mecca, the pilgrims in Richard's section of the winding caravan came to a halt. It was time for the ceremony of *Al-Ihram*. Each pilgrim had to undergo a mutual round of inspection by the others. All finger-nails and toe-nails had to be shortened. Each person washed himself in the water-hole and covered his skin with oil afterwards. Richard was instructed in prayer facing across the desert towards Mecca by the young servant Mohammed. Nur, the boy, prepared Richard's tunic — an *Ihram*; a toga-length cotton strip made up of two lengths which were wound tightly around his midriff, and fastened with his belts.

In the morning light, those pilgrims at the head of the column, which in itself numbered ten thousand heads, strained their eyes for the first sight of the holy venue: a thrilled murmur spread through the onlookers as the upper storeys of the buildings came into sight at the end of the Pass of Death the caravan rode through. And for those who had travelled six months enduring hardship to reach here it was the soul's exhilaration to suddenly come upon this small town of Mecca. In the 7th century it was a village of heathen Arabs, who were well satisfied with their lot, until the young Prophet Mohammad rose up to declare that the former shrine must be a place of worship to his version of inevitable monotheism – there is no god but Allah, and Mohammad is the prophet of Allah.

Mecca grew to nothing more than a township of fifty thousand inhabitants, made up of sandstone houses and a mile square forecourt where the Ka'aba stands. The Ka'aba, a black cloth draped square temple, is the ancient (but often rebuilt) receptacle for the mysterious Black Stone which lies fixed into a wall-face inside the building. The Stone is a dark lava-base piece of a meteorite which fell to earth 1,500 years ago. A black bolt from heaven which always assumed, in Arab eyes, a grave and awesome omen.

The servants led Richard, among many other new arrivals, at nightfall, into the gates of the town; the boy Mohammed took the 'Pathan doctor' straight to his mother's house where he was invited to rest until early in the day when the first of many duties had to be performed. Richard was required to perform the *Tawaf al-Kudam*, or 'circumambulation of Arrival'. In essence, this meant that he, along with many other thousands of pilgrims, must squeeze himself into the teeming hot and dusty court where the Ka'aba stands. He had to walk around the windowless square shape, touch it, look upon it with dutiful awe, and Richard has remarked upon the Arab joke which finds a dull-witted pilgrim who has all his life prayed facing towards Mecca looking around at the other pilgrims in the court of the Ka'aba and enquiring in what direction must he pray now? Faced with the throng outside the black draped monument, he was to recall –

There at last it lay, the bourn of my long and weary Pilgrimage, realising the plans and hopes of many and many a year. The mirage medium of Fancy invested the huge catafalque and its gloomy pall with peculiar charms. There were no giant fragments of hoar antiquity as in Egypt, no remains of graceful and harmonious beauty as in Greece and Italy, no barbarous gorgeousness as in the buildings of India; yet the view was strange, unique – and how few have looked upon the celebrated shrine! I may truly say that, of all the worshippers who clung weeping to the curtain, or who pressed their beating hearts to the stone, none felt for the moment a deeper emotion than did the *Haji* from the far-north. It was as if the poetical legends of the Arab spoke truth, and that the waving wings of the angels, not the sweet breeze of morning, were agitating and swelling the black coverings of the shrine. But, to confess humbling truth, theirs was the high feeling of religious enthusiasm, mine was the ecstasy of gratified pride.

Richard walked around the shrine seven times, chanting out loud the required prayers. Beside him near-dead pilgrims were carried on stretchers, shrieking and wailing Turkish and African Muslims lined the walls of the shrine, tugging and cutting away snippets of the black cloth as discreetly as they could. Richard's pilgrimage may have come to a high point, but his duties were far from finished. The boy Mohammed led him with the other pilgrims in a horrendously complicated series of utterances, each one a hurdle of a prayer, said in order that he might, at the last, bend to kiss the holy stone set in the wall. Afterwards he gave no indication of his fears for his own safety, nevertheless he was acutely conscious, as indeed were the other pilgrims, of the searching stares from the servants and guides who prodded the pilgrims round and round the shrine, and even, at last, into the very portals.

Outside the wall, by the single small door Richard chanted 'O Allah I do this in Thy Belief and in Verification of Thy Book and in Faithfulness to Thy Covenant, and in Perseverance of the Example of the Apostle Mohammad—may Allah bless Him and preserve!' One step more, and the guides prodded the pilgrims again, and those close to Richard joined him in unison with 'O Allah, Thou hast Rights, so pardon my transgressing them!' Standing at the open door to the shrine, in the crush of faces, Richard was compelled to add 'O Allah very the House is Thy House, and the Sanctuary of Thy Sanctuary, and the Safeguard Thy Safeguard, and this is the Place of him who flies to Thee from Fire!' Gradually the pilgrims in the front including Richard were shovelled ungraciously into the porch, or Makam Ibrahim, their heads beneath the sacred roof, and young Mohammed the servant invited Richard to recite—'O Allah, verily this is the Place of Abraham, who took Refuge with and fled to Thee from the Fire—O deny my Flesh and Blood, my Skin and Bones to the eternal Flames!' Now the guides and servants were pushing the pilgrims around the inner curve of the Ka'aba wall. If anyone did not respond with alacrity to the next prayer they were pinched and pummelled, no matter the intense heat inside the shrine or the lack of air—'O Allah, verily I take Refuge with Thee from Polytheism, and Disobedience, and Hypocrisy, and Evil Conversation, and Evil Thoughts concerning Family, and Property, and Progeny!' It would seem to the

84

weary traveller that there was no end to this chanting ritual. The guides took an almost sadistic pleasure in shoving and wheeling these Inebriates of the One Faith from one end of the shrine to the other. Here was the Shrine's water spout, or small well-spring. The pilgrims surged forward, and again another chant started up, 'O Allah verily I beg of Thee Faith which shall not decline . . .', and by now many of these pilgrims had already taken up prostrate positions close by the walls and yet the herding feet almost stamped upon them, and at the west corner of the shrine young Mohammed jerked Richard alert to a further utterance, commencing 'O Allah make it an acceptable Pilgrimage . . .', until at last the Black Stone in its corner emplacement hove into view. Guides and servants held the faithful head as he bent to kiss the famous meteorite, and just as his lips would brush the stone, once more the guides invited the supplicant to join them with a chorus of the prayer commencing 'O Allah verily I take Refuge with Thee from Infidelity . . .'

The ordeal was over. The servant called for a dozen other stalwart guides to lead Richard out safely from the sweating pot of flesh inside the Shrine. All the way back, in the retreat past exhausted pilgrims yet to reach the Black Stone, young Mohammed swore and kicked and cursed at one he imagined to be a Persian. For, in legend, it is said that a Persian Infidel found his way to the Stone and publicly defiled this great relic of Islam. The boy kept on repeating to all and sundry 'O hog and brother of a hoggess!' Quaint and curious though this may seem, it indeed produced an effect. And the perspiration-clad Burton stumbled out through the tiny doorway into the relative cool of the day.

Few since Af, night shadow of the Egyptian Sun God who only traversed half the world in the dark hours but one who was doomed never to take up the true mantel of great Ra, have travelled so far to tell such a pack of lies at the top of his voice in a box-like windowless shrine deep in the Arabian desert, as did Dick Burton.

In later months, Richard referred back to the servant Mohammed's fiery insults in the intense atmosphere of the shrine at Mecca: but Richard is not really fooling any reader when he suggests, as he does in his *Personal Narrative of a Pilgrimage to El-Medinah & Meccah*, that it was the Arab boy who interspersed his abuse to all and sundry with such phrases as 'Ave Maria purissima, — arrah, don't ye be letting the pig at the pot — sanctissima, and so forth'. He obviously treated the procession of prayers in the shrine with a carelessness, a levity, even with a total disregard for his own safety, and throughout his writings he often places his own words in other men's mouths.

There is a strangely facetious element about Burton's daring entry into Mecca. Only he could quote dotty Irish pidgin inside the shrine, and only he could boast that he drew sketches of the interior on the inside cloth of his white *Ihram*, without being detected. Of course, as with most matters Burtonesque, belief must be suspended somewhere along the line. In terms more relevant to this century, Burton cast himself perfectly in the role of a man encasing himself in a natural standpoint, as the phenomenologist Husserl would have it, and from this vantage point, his adventure made absolute sense to him, it was all part of *a world without* which had been so successfully deceived. And, like the gambler who has tossed his first full house of dice, it was this very firstness, a phenomenal instinct, which mattered most to Richard.

He stayed long enough in Mecca to make the holy walk to Mount Ararat, where Adam learned to pray. Richard camped for nights in the great forecourt of the shrine; he walked everywhere, took measurements, made sketches in the cool of twilight; he visited the tomb of the Prophet's mother, and he toured the holy cemetery of Mecca.

After almost a fortnight in the city, he packed his servant Nur, now *Haji* Nur, off to Jidda with his heavier steel trunks; in due course, Richard hired two further camels and young Mohammed followed him across the desert for the seventeen-hour ride to Jidda, to meet up with Nur. Obviously he was in a great hurry to leave, for to be caught out now, after the shrine had been penetrated, would have been foolhardy in the extreme. As soon as he arrived, he dumped the two servants outside the Vice-Consulate at Jidda, raced up the steps of the white building, and though still dressed as the Pathan doctor from the 'far-north', he bullied his way into the presence of Vice-Consul Charles Cole, and shoved a piece of paper under the bewildered man's nose which read, 'Don't recognise me; I am Dick Burton, but I am not safe yet. Give me some money which will be returned from London and don't take any notice of me.' Mr Cole was rather nonplussed. So must we be. Surely, it would have been no more dangerous to whisper in clear English his name and rank to a fellow Britisher than it was to utter Irish doggerel inside the Ka'aba?

Meanwhile, outside the Consulate, Nur and Mohammed waited for their master; he had money which he owed them, and Nur had placed all his trunks in an hotel near to the port-side. Richard bought an expensively decorated costume and, for the few days he remained at Jidda waiting for a boat bound for Suez, he gradually allowed his mask to fall away. It is surprising that the Arab boy Mohammed found Burton at all credible by now. When the Suez boat *Dwarka* docked,

Burton ordered first-class accommodation for the return trip, and young Mohammed simply cracked. He had discovered Burton inside his cabin emptying out the trunks with gusto, and the Arab boy saw something, perhaps a very western article, a toiletry, that passport, and the boy ran to Nur and exclaimed, 'Now I understand. Your master is a *sahib* from India. He hath laughed in our beards.' And with that, Mohammed disappeared along the jetty.

VIII

To Harar with guns, calabashes, burnouses, donkeys, guides and saddlesores, with Jack Speke speechless atop a camel as incognito as a Christmas tree fairy on an Isfahan minaret.

RICHARD SPENT SEVERAL WEEKS IN CAIRO, AT SHEPHEARD'S Hotel, in the company of many young officers; yet he insisted on wearing his burnous and his henna make-up. He stepped too close to a Briton on a verandah in his somewhat clumsy disguise (hardly likely is it he registered himself in to the desk clerk as the coloured Pathan doctor Abdullah) —

'Damn that nigger's impudence! If he does that again I'll kick him!'

'Well, damn it, Hawkins,' Richard looked out from his masked head-dress, 'that's a nice way to welcome a fellow after two years' absence!'

'By God, it's Ruffian Dick,' the Britisher exploded.

It does sound like a jolly good smoking-room story. Perhaps, many years ago, one officer did confront another fellow in a comic disguise like that. So common is such an anecdote, that sixty years on and into the present century the equally quixotic and elusive Thomas Edward Lawrence spread an identical tale about himself in Shepheard's.

In due course Richard packed his bags again and took a boat for the long passage to Bombay. On board he met a convenient ally, James Lumsden, then a very senior member of the Bombay Council, and somebody who could certainly help Richard at a time like this.

To start with he had to find six months to sit down and put together all his Mecca notes into a three-volume *Personal Narrative of a Pilgrimage*

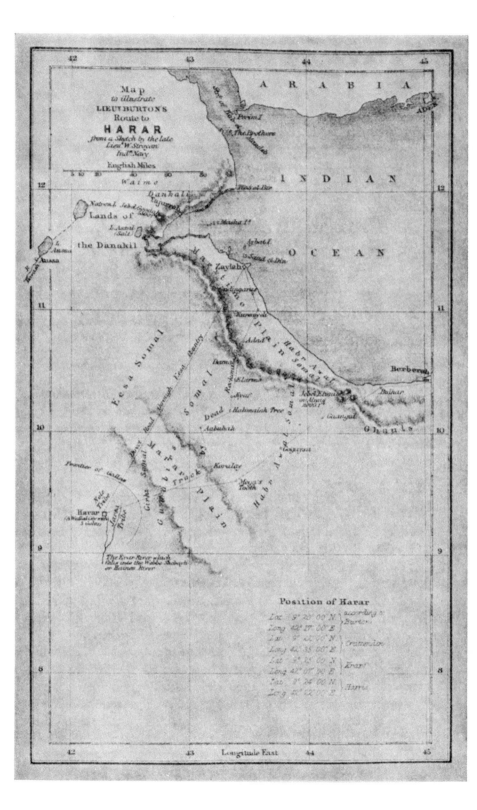

Map
to illustrate
LIEUT.BURTON'S
Route to
HARAR
from a Sketch by the late
Lieut. W. Stroyan
Ind.l Navy

English Miles

ARABIA

INDIAN

OCEAN

Aden

Lands of
the Danakil

Eesa Somal

Somal

Berbera

Ghauis

Harar

Position of Harar

		according to
Lat. 9° 20' 00" N.	Long. 42° 17' 00" E.	Burton
Lat. 9° 42' 00" N.	Long. 41° 35' 00" E.	Crutenden
Lat. 9° 35' 00" N.	Long. 42° 07' 00" E.	Krapf
Lat. 9° 24' 00" N.	Long. 42° 02' 00" E.	Harris

Longitude East

to El-Medinah and Meccah. He still had half a year's leave accorded to him by James Hogg, chairman of the board of the East India Company, and that is why Dick Burton did not set sail immediately for England after the close of the unique adventure in the desert. If he had wanted, he could have sailed home, and for a few months he might have been hailed as a daring officer of prankish adventure, a noble asset to the Bombay regiments. But he had not put all his notes in order, and he was keen to make an honourable profit out of all this, and messing about basking in salon London sunshine would merely waste away the final months of his leave. James Lumsden was a godsend.

Richard charmed the man. He stayed six months at Lumsden's home in Bombay, where he wrote with great speed the long narrative which contained so many of his remarkable asides; his footnotes alone amounted to some fifty thousand words, almost a quarter of the entire book.

Within a short time the British newspapers made much of his disguised entry into the city walls of Mecca. It did not take Richard long to acquaint himself with a reputable house of publishers, this time Longman Green, in London, and secure the firm promise of a three-volume publication of his manuscript over a period of six months. The public had an appetite for volumes in sequence, and Richard was the ideal hero and author of an account which was to become known as a classic of exploration.

On the surface, it was a strange decision to remain in Bombay just when the first volume of the epic narrative was brought out in London. He had every opportunity to milk success and fame to its fill. Instead, he stayed on at Lumsden's home and made deliberate plans for another expedition. It may be that he had the strongest possible motives of self-interest to stay in India. At the hour of his highly praised publication in London, England was in the throes of the Crimean War, and it might indeed have looked inappropriate if this officer on seemingly endless leave was seen to preen and strut with literary fame.

Richard's furlough was fast running out. Weeks wasted taking a boat back to England would not help him in his plans. He persuaded Lumsden to introduce him to the Governor of Bombay, Mountstuart Elphinstone, whereupon he assiduously acquired Elphinstone's patronage and above all used his newly gained prestige to put a fair distance between himself and his duties as a junior officer at the Bombay garrison.

In Bombay his legend had stuck in the military throat and would not easily dislodge, but other young officers and gentlemen revered him. If anything, he was an asset to the East India Company and troop morale, and Richard cleverly weighed this up long before he decided to forgo London literary fame. He had freedom here in India, the Directors of the Company were willing to listen to him, and he knew they would be stupid to refuse him another leave of absence loosely based around an expedition.

Harar, in Somalia, East Africa, was another forbidden Muslim city. Walled, and said to be protected by a genocidal Amir, Harar was a centre for East African slave trading. For years now, the British, in the shape of the East India Company, had held an interest in Somalia. Here was a country ripe for colonial exploitation. The usual British hypocrisy was to denounce the awful trade in bodies in Somalia, paint the local Amir the colour of Ghengis Khan, point out half a dozen British and French missionaries rash enough to lose their heads in Somalia soil, and one was but a hair's breadth from self-righteous 19th-century crusading in the name of Christianity, and the annexation of the entire region.

The Directors of the East India Company were keen to penetrate Somalia under any guise, although they remained ostensibly in friendly rivalry with the French for control of this splendidly placed strategic site on the Gulf of Aden; in particular, the Directors wanted to place a tame sheikh, the Sheikh Shamarkay of Zaylia, as kept governor of either Harar or the other major city Berbera. The plans had been kept on ice for five years, until Richard arrived in Bombay and discovered the Company was not unwilling to promote an expedition into Somalia to explore commercial channels. Britain's policy of divide and rule bore every hallmark of carefully nurtured schemes. The only problem was to find the willing explorer first.

During these writing weeks in Bombay, under the comfortable social umbrella of James Lumsden, Richard made one or two new friends, who were to last a lifetime, in particular, a twenty-one-year-old Bombay-born scholar and one-time employee in the Civil Service — Foster Fitzgerald Arbuthnot. Foster and Richard acquired a joint fascination with Hindi and Sanskrit editions of a number of love manuals. It is important to note this friendship here, because within a few weeks, Richard was to renew contact with that other friend and literary compatriot, John Steinhaeuser in Aden, who shared equally with Arbuthnot a lurid interest in erotica.

In years to come Isabel Burton was to note her husband's companionship with Arbuthnot. In one breath she would manage to recall a certain 'Frederick Arbuthnot' who was also, to the best of her selective recall, 'a friend of many years of mine'. These figures, Steinhaeuser and Arbuthnot, are but shadows at the moment; it cannot be assessed just how much influence they possessed over Richard in Bombay and in Aden. They remain part and parcel of that enormous area of secret darkness in Burton's life it has always been difficult to penetrate. They were the kind of friends who had no place in Isabel's picture of life with Burton.

Richard persuaded the Directors of the East India Company to grant him a further furlough, enough equipment and provisions, and the right to select his own team, for an expedition based on official goodwill and general reconnaissance of the commercial opportunities inside deepest Somalia. To begin with, Richard recruited three old friends from the Bombay Infantry—Lieutenant G. E. Herne, Assistant Surgeon J. E. Stocks and Lieutenant W. Stroyan. As a junior officer in the Indian Navy Stroyan had travelled before with Richard on a survey in Sind. Unfortunately, just before the officers set sail for Aden, which was to be their provisioning venue, young Stocks dropped dead, and Richard had scant time to look for anyone else.

In Aden, Richard learnt that the Royal Geographical Society had also chipped in £1,000 for what, on the surface of things, seemed nothing but an adventurous jaunt; but along with the good news came the bad: Colonel James Outram was the Political Resident in Aden, and he resolutely opposed this feebly justified expedition. For some days now he himself had been badgered by another young officer, a Lieutenant Speke, for permission to go hunting alone in Somalia! Now three other lieutenants plus £1,000 from the RGS had also arrived to collect equipment and stores. Outram gives the impression today of having been one of those minor officials ever dreaming of a soft administrative post on the Mediterranean.

Now there was this rather upright officer named John Hanning Speke battering on Outram's door, carrying numerous rifles and hunting trophies from his ten years' service in the Indian Army, and Outram therefore with no little cunning advised Speke to apply to Burton if he wanted to go 'hunting' in Somalia. It was a very strained and strange meeting, that first confrontation between Speke and Burton in Aden. Here was Richard, already an author and an explorer and established linguist, and in through the door marched a six-foot huntsman, crack shot, 'nigger'-damner and small-arms enthusiast, who had not bothered to learn the rudiments of Hindu in all his ten years in the country.

Outram thoroughly enjoyed himself. It was a perfect case of trying to put mustard and jam on the same sandwich. Furthermore, Outram made it clear to Burton that if he wanted to travel then Speke must go with him. There was, surprisingly enough, no explosion of temperament when Speke and Burton first collided. A youngster of twenty-six, six years Burton's junior, prattling away about killing things animal, human or any other kind his brilliant shooting could bag, son of a West Country landed farmer, educated at a minor Public School, born a prig and a cold fish and bred to live out comfortable days hunting in Somerset—Speke certainly was not Burton's cup of tea. But Richard was a patient and remarkable realist at this stage. He discovered that Speke had almost £400 on him, and he promptly invited the huntsman to pay for his own porterage; it was a form of blackmail Speke had to accept. When one reflects on the numerous accounts of Speke's natural parsimony and general unforthcomingness when it came to money, this final request from Burton the leader must have niggled deep. Speke nevertheless impressed Richard with his willingness to work, his apparent openhearted exuberance and his evident determination to take part and to take orders; Richard later recalled a

> lithe, spare form, about six feet tall, blue-eyed, tawny-maned; the old Scandinavian type, full of energy and life, with a highly nervous temperament, a token of endurance, and long, wiry, but not muscular limbs, that could cover the ground at a swinging pace, he became an excellent mountaineer.

Richard gave Speke for his assignment the job of exploring the Wadi Nogal in Somalia, once they had crossed the bay to Zeila. He ordered Herne and Stroyan to explore Berbera, follow the slave routes and make a general study of the commerce. For himself Richard reserved the jewel of the entire trip—the approach and entry into the inland city of Harar. Burton, Stroyan and Herne were to meet up again, three months hence, at Berbera. Speke was to join them at Aden. The last Outram saw of this fascinating quartet of Britishness was, to his way of thinking, the last he'd see of them. For Richard had infused a kind of madcap them-and-us secret agenting about the entire voyage to Somalia. Once they were in port, each man sorted out his camels, servants and various guides. It is not known what disguise Herne and Stroyan effected, but we do have sketches of Richard and John. Richard once again employed his Mecca ruse, the *Haji* Abdullah, pious Muslim and itinerant carpet vendor. Richard could speak Somali with flair and he was quick to attach his servants to a migrating tribe that was headed inland. By contrast, John Speke's performance was absurd. This tall, blond and blue-eyed figure incongruously supplied himself with an Arab costume from head to sandal, perched himself aloft his camel, gripping on to half-dozen cases of London manufactured shotguns and rifles, and made it perfectly clear to his servants he could speak not one word of Somali.

It took Richard, his nine camels and his servants nigh ten weeks to get within twenty miles of Harar. At this juncture his servants warned him that his face made him a danger to them all and that was just about as far as they dared go with him. He looked like a Turk, the servants declared, and the Amir of Harar had a hitherto not widely reported predilection for castrating Turks, and their entourages. Richard heeded this advice. He relinquished his Abdullah character, climbed on to a brown donkey, and made up his mind to enter the city with humility, and not the foolhardy pomp he had promised himself.

With two nervous servants he rode his animal through the gates of mysterious Harar. He insisted on keeping a cutlass in his belt, and though challenged about his other weapons, he prevailed somehow, and rode on into the mile square fortified town, equipped with a pair of unimposing minarets and 8,000 souls who spoke a highly individual tongue of Harari.

He found the infamous Amir, this mad-dog sultan, to be a pimply skinny fellow of his own age. Burton promptly prostrated himself before the Amir and offered him a polished six-barrelled revolver. The Amir and his Vizier, and the rest of the court at Harar, were not amused at this act of colonial bonhomie. They had had word every day for a month on this white man's progress towards the city in the desert. They had heard about his servants leaving him. They had watched him change his image from Abdullah to a minor staff officer obliged to sit on a donkey. The Amir must have marvelled at these eccentric approaches to his capital. Essentially, Harar was a desert retreat for Muslim missionaries. Quite understandably, this walled monastery did not take kindly to men armed to the teeth with hunting rifles and sabres. At Harar, the Koran was memorised and taken out to the surrounding tribal areas and preached.

The Vizier, Richard discovered, suffered from chronic bronchitis, and he offered to send back medicine for this when he returned to the coast. The Amir, by no means the fool Burton would have us believe, invited him to provide a document to explain his presence in Harar. Richard procrastinated awhile, then returned with a forged article. He composed an ingenuous letter purportedly from the Political Agent in Aden, James Outram, introducing Burton to the Amir as an officer and gentleman intent on promoting good relations between Harar and the Crown. The Amir received this simple note and invited Richard to translate it for him. Richard described himself in glowing terms. It was a performance which totally nonplussed the Amir and his court. The young Amir invited Burton to rest for a while in the town. Richard spent several days collecting a thousand words of Harari. He also noted that every step he took in the town he was closely spied upon. The Amir sent his speedy outriders back across the desert towards Berbera, not only to check up on Burton's tracks, but to discover how many other Britons there were lingering in the vicinity for no apparent reason. Before ten days had passed, word came back that other white men were making peculiar forays by water courses and trade routes (Speke, Stroyan and Herne). The Amir did not question Burton about these men. He maintained an aloof calm, and allowed Richard to sweat out another couple of days under constant surveillance. On the tenth day of this incarceration he was allowed to leave. Later Richard claimed that he outwitted and outplayed the murderous Amir. He maintained he finally escaped the city by warning the Amir that his other white soldier friends would inform the highest authorities should he not return unharmed. Yet the Amir had his sights on Burton before he was within twenty miles of Harar, and the gloomy sight of Speke and his fair features atop a camel, decked up in a kaftan, could hardly have cast fear into the Amir's soul. More likely mirth.

Richard hastily left the gates of Harar and with his few servants and donkeys decided on a direct route across desert towards Berbera. He was late, he knew, to meet up with the others; and speed was all important. He met his old retinue of camels and servants twenty miles beyond the city walls, ordered them the normal route back over the Harar prairie; and for himself, he chose an arduous five-day desert hike through murderous heat to Berbera. At one stage all four of his group went without water for thirty-six hours in heat approaching 120 degrees. Richard, with skill and sense, at last found a water-hole from the flight of a desert form of grouse, a katta, which circled around a desperately needed oasis.

Richard fell into Stroyan's arms at Berbera. He had almost killed himself and his three servants on this five-day march. His excuse for such a risk was that he had not dared to approach villages in the Habr Awal country, he believed they were as vengeful and murderous by nature towards white strangers as the Amir was reputed to be in Harar. Considering the Amir's forbearance, it ill-became Burton to call any Muslim village a hive of killers.

RICHARD BURTON and his sister LADY MARIA SISTED, painted in
Boulogne by François Jacquand, 1851.

RICHARD BURTON in 1854, believed
to have been taken in Aden.

RICHARD BURTON in 1855. He has
wrapped his *jubbah* around himself. It is a
long outer garment, made of cloth,
usually black or brown, which identifies
a member of a learned profession on the
pilgrimage to Mecca.

GENERAL SIR CHARLES JAMES NAPIER (1782–1853). A
pen-sketch of Burton's Commander-in-Chief in Sind in 1846.

GENERAL SIR CHARLES NAPIER, OF SIND, CALLED BY THE NATIVES "SHAYTÁN KÁ BHÁI."

NAPIER again, of whom
Burton said: 'Napier did
not care a fig how many
enemies he made and his
tongue was like a scorpion's
sting'.

GENERAL WILLIAM F.
BEATSON (1804–1872).
Beatson, in the Crimea,
was a brawling raki-
slugging skirmisher.

GENERAL CHRISTO-
PHER PALMER RIGBY
(1820–1885). This photo-
graph shows him as
Colonel Rigby, H.M.
Consul at Zanzibar, 1858.

RICHARD BURTON in 1863, a portrait taken by Ernest Edwards entitled 'Capt. Burton, Traveller'. In the early 60s Edwards invented one of the first pocket-size folding cameras using collodio-emulsion dry plates not exceeding 3¼ inches square, with a walking-stick tripod.

RICHARD and ISABEL BURTON
in 1861. These portraits by Louis
Desanges were a wedding gift from
the artist.

RICHARD BURTON in West Africa, 1862

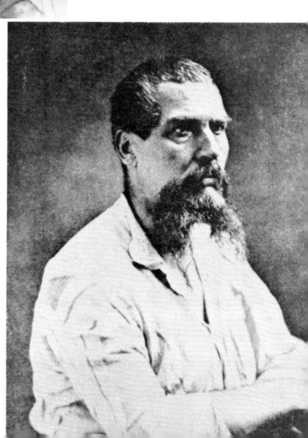

RICHARD BURTON in
1864, a London studio portrait
sometimes referred to as
'Burton in his Spanish shirt'.

SIR RODERICK
MURCHISON (1792–1871),
President of the Royal
Geographical Society.

COLONEL JAMES AUGUSTUS GRANT
(1827–1892).

JOHN HANNING SPEKE
(1827–1864) at the age of
thirty-four.

HENRY MORTON
STANLEY (1841–1904) and
his wife Dorothy in the
Engadine, 1890.

EDWARD HENRY
PALMER (1840–1882),
explorer and oriental scholar.

CHARLES TYRWHITT-
DRAKE (1846–1874),
amateur magician, enthusiast
archaeologist and linguist.

CAPTAIN VERNEY
LOVETT CAMERON
(1844–1894), African explorer.

RICHARD BURTON in
1865, the year he set sail for
Brazil.

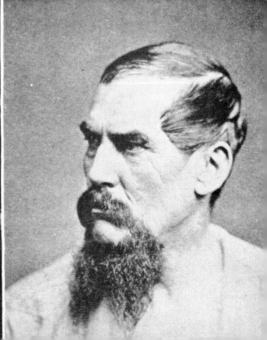

ISABEL BURTON in 1869,
at the age of forty.

RICHARD BURTON in 1872.
This is a copy of the famous
portrait which Sir Frederick
Leighton completed by May
1972 (now in the National
Portrait Gallery, London).
It has been variously attributed.
The anonymous artist has
reconstructed a more hollowed
and a drawn study.

A maquette for the large portrait of Burton in fencing clothes by Albert Letchford.

ALBERT LETCHFORD (1866–1905) at work in the Trieste house, 1889.
This portrait stands over ten feet high and was commissioned by Isabel.

THE BURTONS with ALBERT LETCHFORD in Trieste, 1890.

FOSTER FITZGERALD
ARBUTHNOT (1833–1901),
civil servant, linguist and arts patron.

RICHARD BURTON in
1883, with his hair dyed black.
An Elliot and Fry studio portrait.

LEONARD CHARLES
SMITHERS (1861–1907),
printer *sub rosa*, aesthete,
pornographer.

RICHARD BURTON in
1888, in failing health.

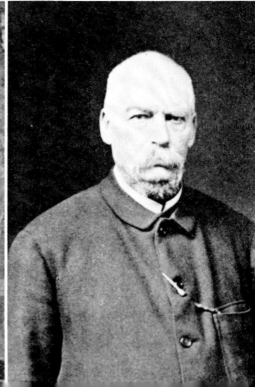

Top: THE BURTONS with F. GRENFELL BAKER in a Folkestone garden,
October 1888. Portrait by G. N. Miller.
(The mnemonic designed by Oswald Jones).

Bottom: the 'Laocoon' group. 2nd-century BC Rhodian sculptors Polydorus,
Agessander and Athenodorus.

RICHARD BURTON in the Trieste garden, 1890, three weeks before his death.

'Breakfast scene', a portrait by F. Grenfell Baker in 1890, from the Burton album. The wall behind is covered with Letchford paintings of the interior and exterior of the Trieste house.

ISABEL BURTON, 1890, in her own
room in the Trieste house. Portrait by
F. Grenfell Baker.

Isabel's chapel corner in one of the rooms
in Trieste, by Grenfell Baker, 1889.

ISABEL BURTON in London, 1892. A
studio portrait of the widow, wearing
her customary 'Mary Tudor' clothes.

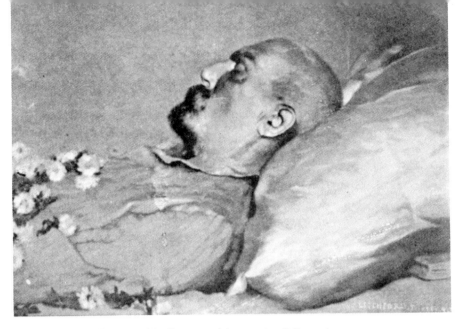

Albert Letchford's memorial portrait of Burton's corpse,
commissioned by Isabel, 1891.

On Isabel's recommendation, Grenfell
Baker assisted Albert Letchford to make
a death-mask, and to wax body-mould-
ings of Burton's left hand and foot.

Isabel Burton's mausoleum for her husband in the Catholic cemetery at
Mortlake.

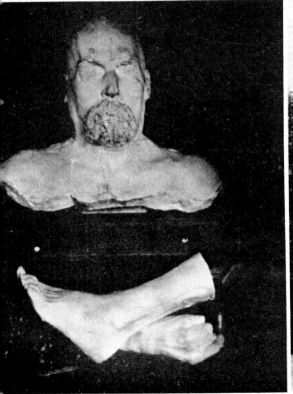

Back in Aden, the three friends, Stroyan, Herne and **Burton**, exchanged notes. They filled out a decent enough report for the surprised Outram. They opened their mail and waited for Lieutenant Speke who was already a fortnight late. Burton had very bad news at Aden. Letters informed of his mother's sudden death, on her way to yet another rented home in Bath, Somerset; but this painful information did not check his eagerness to fill a journal with all aspects of the Harar adventure, and certainly he did not consider returning to England to share his father's grief.

At last, John Speke arrived by dhow at Aden with dozens of sewn sacks and piled wicker baskets of dead trophies. The deck was awash with his shooting talents. He had apparently bagged everything from an Egyptian goose to wildebeest and antelope. It was a killing array. Less impressive was the official outcome of Speke's twelve weeks of wandering among the Somali in search of an oasis called the Wady Nogal. The unpalatable truth both Speke and Burton had to acknowledge when they met again was that Jack had not been able to find this wady. His *abban*, or guide, had deceived him, robbed him, and treated his ignorance of the Somali language and customs with considerable contempt. Speke had little else to offer in defence. He had cantered through the land shooting at anything that moved, and Burton was dismayed. He announced his disappointment in thinly disguised terms. John Speke could only reiterate the unalterable fact — it was Richard in the first place who appointed the useless beggarly guide. Richard should have chosen a native much more in tune with Speke's linguistic deficiencies. Both men treated the incident with curt but comradely interest. It was not possible to have a blazing row in front of the resident Political Agent at Aden, it would do no good to British morale. Richard vented his anger on the poor guide. The man was prosecuted and fined a punitive sum of rupees, plus a couple of months in prison. In addition, the benighted fellow was banished from the Aden colony with his wife and children, in a formal court of justice.

It is not too difficult to imagine the repercussions to all this amongst the Somali and the Hindustani. The news of this spiteful trial spread quickly in north Somalia. A day of reckoning was to be had. Few natives grasped what these Britons intended as they stumbled along the coast in their ineffectual disguises; sport and politics made erratic bed fellows.

Richard's journal had now taken the shape of another long narrative, *First Footsteps in East Africa*, and when it appeared in London eighteen months later, Richard made only too plain his resentment at Speke's failure:

> . . . savages cannot believe that a man wastes his rice and cloth to collect dead beasts and to ascertain the direction of streams. He was known to be a Christian; he is ignorant of the Moslem faith; and, most fatal to his enterprise, he was limited in time.

Richard made careful mockery of John Speke in public, in London in 1856, and included a bowdlerised version of Speke's own diary in his book. It was to be a wound of a lasting nature.

Nowhere in his book does Richard put up a case for Speke, though there clearly was one. Richard was the commander of this expedition. Responsible for staff and servants alike. It was neither here nor there that Jack Speke paid wages out of his own pocket. Richard fudged the issues up with a certain animosity towards a junior officer less equipped with the language. Finally, it was Richard himself who instigated the prosecution of the hapless guide. At this stage of the rivalry between the two men, Speke had much on his side to justify himself. He had come for the sport, after all. He misinterpreted his leader's romanticisms for *laissez-faire* orders: and had paid for it out of his own pocket.

Richard wrote up what he could of the Harar expedition, and all four officers stayed on in Aden for a couple of months. In retrospect, Burton described the restlessness he endured in Aden —

> If I had 'let well alone', I should have done well; but I wanted to make a new expedition Nile-wards, *via* Harar, on a larger and more imposing scale . . .

Although he had time on his hands with this long furlough, Burton knew there would come a day when Outram in Aden, or Lumsden in Bombay, on behalf of the East India Company's Bombay Army, must declare 'back to camp'. The war in Crimea was a national debating issue. Richard felt some personal turmoil, too. He was the eldest child, and he had made no effort to return to England to share his family's sadness over the loss of his mother. Leave would have been easily granted had he intended to go back. Instead, he applied to Outram for a further year's leave of absence for exploration. With Speke, still by no means an enemy, more a wary junior to Burton's black moods, he offered up a concoction to the authorities. They would take a large expedition into East Africa, via Harar, turning from the west to the south-east towards Zanzibar in an attempt to detail the slave routes between Berbera and Zanzibar in the south. This official plea was but half the true plan in their minds. Richard and John had already suggested to each other the great pearl, dream and desire of all African travellers—the discovery of the source of the Nile, and together they planned this secondary goal which Outram need not hear about. It was, after all, a novel matter to go for the great blue riband of exploration honours from east to west, when the most common approach for the 'coy fountains' of this great river, the supposed 'twin mountains of the moon', was always the approach south from the Egyptian basin.

Both Burton and Speke have laid their claims as to who thought of this expedition first. It seems that Burton was the creator of the scheme. There was a little-known tale of a Greek merchant, Diogenes, of the 1st century AD who had made a northbound overland journey for twenty-five days starting above Zanzibar. Diogenes claimed that within this short period he had come upon two great lakes and a snowy range of mountains which fed the Nile with a double source of water. This was the kind of footnote which fascinated Richard, and Speke was not familiar with Diogenes. Moreover it was not Speke's job to approach Burton or Outram with plans of any kind. He was there in Aden courtesy of Outram's random benevolence, and as all he wanted to do was shoot and hunt, his best bet was to cling to Burton's kaftan.

Who knows what the adventurous Diogenes had come across? Perhaps he'd seen, within the space of that short period, the mounts of both Kenya and Kilimanjaro. Fable and centuries had turned these into the fountains of legendary promise. It aroused Richard's curiosity, to think he might strike out overland, and within perhaps these same twenty-five days the possible goal of a lifetime ambition might be his. Yet what would he have done? Continued west beyond Harar to what is now Lake Baringo? Cheated Outram, and continued north-west towards Gondar and Lake Tana? This was surely self-delusion on Richard's part. How could he explain to the East India Company why he was marching some thousand miles north by north-west of Zanzibar? A happy miscalculation?

The clue lies in the twenty-five-day span Greek Diogenes took. Richard imagined that a six-month outward-bound expedition would take in, and more, the tracks of Diogenes; doubling back to Mogadishu would be no problem. Outram's largesse is inexplicable. Yes, he said, take a year's leave, and take Jack Speke with you, and come back with a solid report on the slavers. The best that can be said for Outram is that he chose these men to act as spies and he acted with cloak-and-dagger Whitehall high jinks. The worst that can be said is that he was simply glad to get Burton and Speke out of his sight, perhaps never to return.

The money was provided. Sixty camels and forty men were recruited. Guides, cooks, carriers, donkeys, guns and Rowtie tents. In April 1855 Richard delayed the expedition while he waited for further mail and provisions from London. This delay proved fatal. He had assured Outram that for a guarantee of safe conduct, he'd travel alongside a vast five-hundred-camel-strong caravan returning to Harar, and now he had missed this train.

Richard camped outside Berbera on the start of the westward march; the tents lay close by the sea. He placed two men on guard duty for the night. The tribal chiefs in the vicinity were instantly angered. They had been led to believe the Burton camp would travel with the Harar caravan. Now they were convinced these Britons were spies. In addition, no one had forgotten the trial of Speke's guide. It was a humiliation which yet rankled.

On the night of April 19, Richard acted as host to a small ship's crew and their friendly captain who had anchored close by the camp's shoreline, and many crewmen stayed the night. At about two a.m. the camp was ripped apart by Somali tribesmen who attacked the tents with stones and javelins. The Britons together with those sailors who had not returned to their bunks that night, were hurled out of their tents. Stroyan, Burton, Speke and Herne, half-naked, reaching for their revolvers in the dark, stones flying at their heads, the heady effect of a night's boozing upon them, were suddenly fighting for their lives. Speke always insisted on his alacrity, 'I bounced out of bed, with pistol and dirk in hand, and ran across to the central tent to know what was the matter. Richard, half in and half out of nightshirt roared, "Be sharp, and arm to defend the camp!" ' Speke, like Burton, hardly able to see anything, felt the tenting collapse around his head. Massive stones were smashing into the framework. Speke tried to step out into the dark. A jagged stone smashed into his knee and he fell back inside. Richard, quick to be unthinking, curtly called, 'Don't step back, or they will think we are retiring!' Speke's pride got the better of him and he ran outside, blindly charging at shadows and emptying his revolver. When his Deane-Adams five-shooter jammed on him, he was rolled to the ground with a club to his chest with, as he later put it —

a dozen Somali on the top of me. The man I had endeavoured to shoot wrenched the pistol out of my hand, and the way the scoundrel handled me sent a creeping shudder all over me. I felt as if my hair stood on end; and, not knowing who my opponents were, I feared that they belonged to a tribe called Eesa, who are notorious, not only for their ferocity in fighting, but for the unmanly mutilations they delight in. Indescribable was my relief when I found that my most dreadful fears were without foundation. The men were in reality feeling whether, after an Arab fashion, I was carrying a dagger between my legs, to rip up a foe after the victim was supposed to be powerless.

Speke was trussed like a chicken and sat upon by a taunting Somali. But at least he hadn't lost his manhood. As for Richard, within moments of Speke's tumble, the leader of this encampment was about to kill one of his own servants when the boy shouted out. Richard held his sabre back, and in the shocked instant a javelin entered his cheek, pierced the lower jaw, carrying teeth and bone with it to emerge the other side of his face.

Burton was rescued and carried off towards the ship at anchor by members of the crew. Speke was tortured with a spear point as he lay on the ground; one spear gashed through his thigh, yet he managed out of blind panic to reach the shore-line and the safety of a crew man's boat. He found later he had received a dozen spear thrusts.

Herne came out of the fray with deep bruises; but poor Stroyan was knifed through the heart, and a Somali slit open his stomach and mutilated the corpse still further. Of the enemy perhaps five had been dispatched. The stores had lost guns, food, tobacco, clothing, and the entire expedition was called to a halt. Burton and Speke and Herne limped back to Aden.

John Speke had lost the sum of £510, Herne and Stroyan and Burton were ransacked of all their valuables. It is a minor point, but Speke's loss underlines the lengths he felt willing to go to pay his own way on this expedition. Burton treated his companion like a rich marksman out for the spoils of the chase. It is easy to understand, even sympathise with Speke's unfortunate position in this first footstep towards the Nile. Speke had acquired the role of whipping boy. In time he'd learn to regret such a humiliating 'bit part'. He deserved better from Richard.

The British authorities in Aden used this outrage as an excuse to attack the slave trade at Berbera. The British Navy blockaded the coast of Somaliland until Stroyan's killer was brought to justice. Within three weeks Burton was packed off to England to face a military Court of Inquiry into the attack. Rightly so, the Inquiry found Burton at grave fault. He had commanded badly. He had delegated night duty with appalling carelessness. Speke had already raced halfway across the camp to get Richard's orders, and all Burton could do was to suggest the fellow officer was trying to hide. It was John Speke who had shown the anger and the bravery. It was Richard who, as commander of the expedition, had almost hacked down one of his own men before an enemy's javelin struck him poised at his own indecision. One cannot make too much of Burton's rashness. But, adding it all together, moment by moment, who shrank from decision?

Not Speke.

IX

Blood as discovered horror to be avoided like laughter, the outside a better place to explore seen through a perspective; always the frame rather than the canvas.

THE CRIMEAN WAR OF 1853 TO 1856 WAS, FUNDAMENTALLY, an attempt by the Russian Czar Nicholas I to seize Turkey. The Czar had visions of a Russian empire embracing the whole of South-Eastern Europe, and was determined to gain that 'key to the Russian house', Constantinople. The battles which raged around Sebastopol, between the Russians on one side and the allied French and British on the other, the fame of the military hospitals in the Dardanelles and the redoubtable Miss Nightingale, were the topic of all London newspapers.

It was folly on the Russians' part to attempt to envelop Turkey. Thousands on either side had died from cholera and malnutrition. The inept Lord Raglan and the overzealous Czar Nicholas had also lost their lives. Nothing was achieved by this war; apart from a formal agreement in 1856 to allow the Danube traffic to flow freely.

John Speke followed Richard back to London and acquired a commission in the Horse Guards and was swiftly promoted to Captain. He sailed out to Constantinople with his hunting guns and cases of bullets. Richard spent a month with his brain-damaged brother Edward and his father and paid a visit to his mother's grave, yet though he applied to four regiments for a posting to the Crimea he was turned down each time. Eventually an old commander of his, General

W. Beatson, accepted Richard for a troop of irregulars, Indian and Bombay conscripts, which were labelled the 'Bashi Bazouks'; within a short time Beatson took such a liking to Richard he made him his Chief of Staff. Although Richard had been a captain for some years now, no elevation of rank was offered. It must have stung. Four times he had been rejected, four times Richard had been told he was merely an *Indian*, a regimental title hardly worth more than a bugle's toot in an earl's infantry. But, if this was the truth why was Speke promoted so quickly? Speke was just as much an *Indian* officer. Clearly, when Speke presented himself to General Vivian, his future commander, he gave as good an account as was possible of an officer and a hunting gent from Somerset. In other words he fitted in well. He was back to his old bland exterior. If Vivian had inquired about events in Somalia when an expedition camp had been virtually annihilated, Speke need only have mentioned the madcap Captain Burton and his silly night defences.

Dick's new commander William Beatson was something of a howling gale of a man. Rowdy, uncontrollable, with flashing blue eyes he was in his middle fifties and had already served thirty-five years in the Bengal Army. On one occasion Burton had to rewrite Beatson's official dispatch to Constantinople to mitigate the candour. Apparently Beatson's violent language was akin to – in Dick's description – 'pistols for two and coffee for one'. Dick believed that Beatson was on a par with Charles Napier, who once demanded that a fine soldier must ride 'eternally on horseback, with a sword in his hand, eating, sleeping and drinking in the saddle'.

For four months, between July and October 1855, Burton witnessed the Crimean horror. He travelled between Balaclava, Constantinople and the Dardanelles. He acquired a gaudy blue and gold uniform of a somewhat independent design, and made himself quickly acquainted with all of Beatson's staff and officers. In numbers, these wild and woolly Irregulars and 'Bashi Bazouks' amounted to more than 4,000 men. Dick took exception to some of the roughneck Irish and Moroccans, not to mention the occasional Sicilian, who were closest to Beatson in the General's Staff, though he himself spent more time under Beatson's tent than he did with the fightin' an' feudin' 'Bashi Bazouks' camped out on the plains. But he did try to advance the cause of this cut-throat four thousand.

Under British and French command the fortress garrison of Kars housed 15,000 loyal Turkish soldiers. Kars was besieged by the full weight of the Russian troops and was threatened with famine. It seemed as if the British Ambassador in Constantinople, Lord Stratford, might indeed accept the theory that Kars ought to be relieved by the 'Bashi Bazouks'. Richard presented the Ambassador with a scheme to march '2640 sabres in perfect readiness' on Kars. To Burton's amazement, Stratford turned red in the face and shouted the young officer out of his room – 'You are the most impudent man in the Bombay Army, Sir!'

In a sense Stratford was a prisoner of the Whitehall mentality. He knew full well that Beatson's Irregulars were foaming at the bit with impatience to relieve Kars. He knew, too, that Whitehall was not in favour of thousands of Turkish Irregulars coming to the aid of the 15,000 Turks locked within Kars. The eventual fall of Kars was to be taken into account politically. Kars, as far as Whitehall was concerned, was only of value as a military sacrifice. Whitehall was glad of the number of Russians encircling the starving garrison. The real military front was to be Sebastopol. Lord Stratford could at least see this for himself. Perhaps Kars had always been doomed, but the British design to hold back the 'Bashi Bazooks' was a clumsy and unwarrantable example of warfare via diplomatic *haute politique*. Burton observed the rage in the frustrated mettle of his Irregulars. These 'Bashi Bazouks' felt ashamed. The British had lost both Kars and the loyalty of these men of 'Beatson's Horse'.

Inevitably, so much restlessness amongst the men brought matters to a head. The 'Bashi Bazouks' stationed in the Dardanelles erupted. By the time Burton returned to his camp he found the entire place in a state of siege. Certain Irregulars had been in hand-to-hand combat with French and Turkish soldiers. Infantry and cavalry surrounded Beatson's tents, and these Turkish Regulars were prepared to fire on the 'Bashi Bazouks'. On September 28 Beatson was replaced by Major-General Richard Smith.

General Beatson and his Chief of Staff were summarily ordered to return home. Officers' tents were filled with rumours: Beatson and Burton had conspired with other officers to usurp General Vivian's authority, Beatson and Burton could not control this rabble of 4,000, etc. By October 12, both men set sail for England, beneath a cloud of disgrace. General Beatson found energy to issue a writ for slander against the Dardanelles Vice-consul who had filed a Whitehall report virtually calling Beatson a brigand. It was not a very happy leave-taking for Richard. Once again he had fallen foul of senior British Army policy. And however well-intentioned he had been in his efforts to relieve Kars, however hard he had worked for the good of those 'Bashi Bazouks', somehow he had misinterpreted the overall British policy. As for Captain Jack Speke, he had merrily stationed himself at Kertch, in the Crimea, and found himself able to concentrate on the available fauna.

It is a curious fact that Dick wrote only a twenty-three-page account of his Crimean experiences. In later years Isabel inserted this material into her own biography of Burton. And his account of these months is a very slight thing indeed. For a while he had placed himself amongst some of the worst carnage and mutilation any battlefield had ever witnessed, and yet he could not bring himself to describe these horrors. Here was a man who could detail all the blood pangs of Indian circumcision and exotic anal porneia, but was quite incapable of mentioning those notorious asylums of mutilation – the Crimean Hospital Tents. The young officer Leo Tolstoy, on the battle-plains of Sebastopol, alerted his instincts with the pared-back nerve of a hare's retina –

> On the uneven ground, ploughed up by new explosions, lay everywhere twisted gun-carriages, jamming down the corpses of Russian and French soldiers; heavy cast-iron cannon, for ever silenced and by a tremendous force hurled down into ditches and half-covered with dirt, bombs, shells; again corpses, ditches, splinters of beams, of blindages, and again silent corpses . . .

Dick's shyness itself records volumes. Writing on Louis-Ferdinand Céline, Trotsky remarked that 'either the artist will make his peace with the darkness, or he will perceive the dawn'. Richard could not make his peace with the Crimean horrors. He returned to England with the permanent markings of a child-man. The images of untold bodies were too great a reality. Mecca and Harar were dreams to be entered into. And distance creates longing, and proximity closes horizons. And, Richard Burton would dream.

X

Not proposing marriage fishing, not
asking love suggesting, not demanding
funds from Speke inviting, not leaving
with a kiss with a letter, not promising
to return positively avoiding it, not a
form of verisimilitude in his actions
more the options of a quick brown fox.

THE PEARL OF ALL EXPLORATION IN 1856, 'THE GREATEST
geographical secret after the discovery of America', was the 'unveiling
of Isis', the search for the source of the Nile. Geographers and hydro-
graphers naturally felt curious about this river which, for a thousand
miles or more, flowed through one of the driest basin areas of the
world. Why had it never dried up? What vast reservoir fed this great
stream, and how could this source be explained? Besides, in the middle
of the 19th century almost all exploration was a means of gaining
ground upon other nations.

In the 1st century AD the great astronomer Ptolemy designed a map
which showed the source of the Nile in the form of two great lakes,
bound by a mountain range, thereafter dubbed the Mountains of the
Moon. Four hundred years later, Herodotus ascended the Nile until
cataracts and impossible falls sent him back. Nero is said to have sent
soldiers up the Nile only to lose them in an impenetrable bog. In the
18th century the indefatigable Scots traveller, James Bruce, traced the
source of the shorter Blue Nile from the feed-in rivers to the Wad
Medani and on to Khartoum. But this clearly was not the source for
the main thrust of a great river which was yet over a thousand miles
from the Mediterranean. Somewhere in the wreathed mists of water,
scud and swamp, and insect-infested terrain, a White Nile roared north

from a heart of liquid deep in the centre of East Africa. Few explorers looked for the source beyond the early cataracts below El Ais. More sensible souls argued there had to be a way due west from Somaliland to these fabled lakes. The crucial question was: if Mount Kenya and Kilimanjaro were not the Mountains of the Moon, what vast scape of flood and heights still lay in the centre of the continent?

The cause of the Nile, a romantic cry of bravery, its true source, was surely the most exciting scheme Richard could realise. He had partially tried when he started off with John Speke and the others. It was still very much in his mind. Furthermore, it was the only gem of exploration which could guarantee backing from philanthropists. If an explorer wanted to go for the mysteries of ancient cultures in far-off Mexico, nobody would have offered a shilling. But all colonial eyes were on the trade routes around Africa, the promise of minerals and gold, and certainly to British political eyes the 'black continent' was the focal point for a country determined to stay the largest sea trader in history. Richard certainly had credentials for the attempt. Twice before the Royal Geographical Society had come to his aid. Roderick Murchison, then President of the Society and a good friend of Richard's, was more than willing to vouch for him. Socially and culturally he remained a gentleman, one of them, a bit of a vagabond, but committed to no other Empire but his country's own, and politically sound. Chaps like this either came to sticky ends or they made fortunes in strange ports where the gun and the white face reigned.

Murchison, aligning the RGS with the resources of the Treasury, produced another £1,000 for such a trip. Richard would make an attempt on the source of the Nile from the east, from Zanzibar. It would take up to three years. He promptly invited most of his friends, including John Steinhaeuser, to accompany him. Politely they refused. Richard nervously approached the East India Company with another of his half-pay schemes. Could they treat the whole enterprise as a means of gaining greater glory for his regiment? For a few weeks it looked as if the Company was indeed prepared to cough up a further £1,000 to meet the RGS donation. It was a false hope. His old commanding officer Colonel W. H. Sykes had put the evidence of Burton's more hazardous exploits together, from Harar to the Crimea, and Sykes promptly withdrew his financial backing. He did not withdraw the generous decision on behalf of the Company to grant another long furlough. If Burton achieved the impossible and brought back the Mountains of the Moon and all their mysteries the East India Company would still to some degree, share in the glory.

Burton did not waste time. He needed the type of person who was hungry for travel and sport and solitude, who was yet willing to produce the best part of £800 towards the expedition. Within a matter of days Richard wrote to John Hanning Speke. Speke accepted with alacrity. There was something servile about Jack Speke here. Richard had insulted him, yet he came back for more. Speke once wrote to a friend, Robert Playfair '. . . I am a great loser by reputation as well as by pocket . . .' and one's heart reaches out towards this awkward fellow, brazen and yet insipid, dull but curiously sensitive, quick to wound yet twice as eager to be wounded again, a tall good-looking charmer unable to dance with a pretty girl, an arrogant shot with a rifle but a hopeless linguist. He must have seen through to Richard's merciless logic. Speke equalled money. Money meant trip was on.

Richard had been in London for six months, making plans for the expedition. During this time Isabel's cousin Louisa Segrave, who had recently married, reappeared in his life. She was a beauty, an old flame, and the kind of bright breezing filly he might well have wed.

We only have Isabel's account of how events led Burton back to herself.

As she was riding through the crowds at Ascot Day races, the gypsy Hagar Burton caught up with the carriage. Years earlier, Hagar had told Isabel she would choose a man called Burton. Now the gypsy reached the carriage door and shouted out —

'Are you Daisy Burton yet?'

'Would to God I were!' Isabel blurted back.

'Patience,' cried the gypsy, 'it is just coming.'

During August, apparently Richard took Louisa through the Royal Botanical Gardens at Kew one afternoon. There they encountered three women — Isabel, her sister Blanche and a girlfriend. What would appear to be a perfectly normal group of five souls on a warm afternoon beneath the Chinese Pagoda became, forty years on in Isabel's heated prose, a glass-house inquisition:

'We immediately stopped and shook hands, and asked each other a thousand questions of the four intervening years, and all the old Boulogne memories and feelings which had lain dormant, but not extinct, returned to me.'

One can imagine Isabel's bursting into a thousand questions in her mind, and in her mind only. For it was Louisa, not Isabel, who hung on to Dick's arm, and it was only when Richard observed a copy of

Disraeli's romantic novel *Tancred* beneath Isabel's arm that they exchanged any remark. The book had become her Bible.

'You are reading that?' Richard inquired.

'Yes,' she replied stoutly, 'it is the book of my heart.'

Just before this little group broke up, Richard inquired if she came often to these gardens.

'Oh yes. We always come and read and study here from eleven to one, because it is so much nicer than staying in the hot rooms at this season.'

According to Isabel, Richard turned to his beautiful companion as they left, saying – 'Do you know that your cousin has grown charming? I would not have believed that the little schoolgirl of Boulogne would have become such a sweet girl.' And lo, in her fantastic world, she heard her newly-married cousin retort, 'Ugh!'

The next day Isabel was there waiting, between the hours of eleven and one. She waited for him, and he did indeed arrive. She was there the following day, and the day after that, and each time Richard promised to be there, too. He kept his word.

There were no others present. Only the instantly recognisable strangers in the parkland on those balmy days between August and September. Isabel, at twenty-seven, was not in need of a chaperone. Isabel's enemies have rightly pointed out that she is always doubly loquacious when there were no witnesses. But in this matter the lady must have her say. We do know that Richard strolled for a fortnight at Kew with his lady.

Courtship among the military demi-class, clinging to the revenue of unearned substance, was a matter of decorum. The old Byronic days of fornicating Royalty had passed away into the pages of romantic novels. A sense of propriety had grasped the maiden's arm, and according to *Household Words* and *The Englishwoman's Domestic Magazine*, courtship and the art of blushing and the territorial heel and toeing that went on was all part and parcel of a game entitled 'the smile which lurks in the half-dropped eye.'

Richard told Isabel of his plans to try for the Nile source from the east. He had all the money now, and it was merely a matter of finalising port arrivals with the East India Company. He would be away for three years at least. His furlough was good for the first twenty-four months. If the expedition was only partly successful money would be forthcoming readily for yet another trip. He was the right man to lead this exploration. In truth, he could tell this young woman anything, and he received the same open-mouthed adoration. This time there were no tutting aunts to frown back, no cynical failed father to shut his ears to the drivel, no distant and nervously charming mother to push him away at arm's length. After a couple of weeks of these soul searching perambulations around Kew, Isabel records that he leaned towards her and caught her eyes in that black-vice gaze of his, and asked —

'If you could dream of doing anything so sickly as to give up Civilisation, and if I could obtain, say, the Consulate at Damascus, could you go and live there, too?'

It is more than likely he meant that, if nothing came of the Nile Expedition, he could no longer continue with the East India Company Regiments after these endless furloughs, and there was only one outlet left for him: to take up a minor post in a Consulate where he might make use of his languages.

She did not reply immediately. Suddenly, all her dreaming, all her childhood infatuations over this man, had come to a head. The fable had to be faced. She looked back at him, at his bony face with a grotesquely dramatic moustache and thick eyebrows, and her mind, as she admitted later in her diary, was full of wonder and presentiment. He helped her along, his words soothed —

'Don't give me an answer now, because it will mean a very serious step for you — no less than giving up your people, and all that you are used to, and living the sort of life that Lady Hestor Stanhope led. I see the capabilities in you . . . but you must think it over.' [Hestor Stanhope, who had died seventeen years before, the lady who had braved a pilgrimage to Jerusalem, was the very heroine of all Isabel's dreams.]

'Forgive me,' Richard murmured, '. . . I . . . ought not to have asked so much.'

'I don't want to think it over [Isabel suddenly sprang to life] . . . I have been thinking it over for six years. Ever since I first saw you at Boulogne on the ramparts. I have prayed for you every day, morning and night. I have followed all your career minutely. I have read every word you ever wrote. And I would rather have a crust and a tent with you than be Queen of all the world! [Her breath literally sprang from her lungs. She could not stop herself. Her uncoiled heart released a torrent of emotion.] . . . And so I say now . . . Yes! Yes! Yes!'

To his horror, he now had to sit down and listen to her six-year long trial of patience and endurance. It must have come as something of a shock to him. He certainly did intimate to her, in a round the houses fashion, and with no great sense of guilt, that she was the kind of gel he might like to share Damascus with. But that was all he intended.

That night, Isabel returned to her parents' house, and wrote in her diary —

would have suffered six years more for such a day. Such a moment as this. All past sorrow was forgotten in it. Men might as well undertake to describe Eternity. I then told him all about my six years since I first met him. And all that I suffered. When I got home, I knelt down and prayed, and my whole soul flooded with joy and thanksgiving. I feel that I have at last met the master who can subdue me.

It looks as though Richard had overplayed his hand, and she had called his bluff. In view of subsequent events, all he probably intended was a sally, tentative and devious in the direction of her sexuality. A clumsy pleasant little trick which might bring a blush to any normal laughing and witty girl like Louisa. In no time at all he was invited to the Arundell household for a grim cup of tea with Isabel's disapproving mother. It was not possible for Isabel to announce an engagement but the hints were flying all around the house.

Poor Richard was not aware of an 'engagement' as such. He informed no other of his verbal intimacy with Miss Arundell. But the avalanche of affection her whole being poured out towards him took him off balance. He had never truly loved anybody in all his thirty-five years. Not with a love which forsakes all else. Not with a love he was prepared to die for.

A torpor overtook him now. He allowed the days to control him. The plans for the Nile trip were so well under way, he and John Speke already had their berths booked on the *Elphinstone* for Bombay. He had time to glance at an engraved Virgin Mary Isabel wanted him to keep. He said he dared not wear it. Natives would cut his throat to get at the gold in the chain.

Richard and Isabel arranged to meet at the opera, but Isabel sat alone. That night she dreamed he had taken his leave; he appeared to her in this dream and spoke in tones any reader of Isabel is by now familiar with — 'I am going now my poor girl. My time is up and I have gone. But I will come again — I shall be back in less than three years. I am your destiny . . .'

He had indeed gone without speaking to her. It was a sudden, illusive and quite taciturn decision, cruel in its emotional abruptness. He imagined it might cut the devotional cord this particular Penelope gripped so tightly. On the following morning, Isabel's sister received a note posted from the dockside. Richard asked her to reveal his departure to Isabel with as much tact as she might muster. In the envelope he enclosed a poem

I wear thine image, Fame
Within a heart will fit to be thy shrine!
Others a thousand boons may gain,
    One wish was mine —

The hope to gain one smile,
To dwell one moment cradled on thy breast,
Then close my eyes, bid life farewell
    And take my rest!

And now I see a glorious hand
Beckon me out of dark despair,
Hear a glorious voice command,
    'Up bravely dare!

'And if to leave a deeper trace
On earth to thee Time, Fate, deny,
Drown vain regrets, and have the grace
    Silent to die.'

She pointed to a grisly land,
Where all breathes dead — earth, sea, and air;
Her glorious accents sound once more,
    'Go meet me there.'

Mine ear will hear no other sound,
No other thought my heart will know.
Is this a sin? 'O, pardon, Lord!
    Thou mad'st me so!'

The previous morning, he had posted from the dockside an identical copy of this poem to Louisa Segrave.

XI

Lucetta damsel pondered beside shores
of unknown lakes and began to tell lies
which one day would assume the
proportions of truth.

RICHARD AND JOHN SPEKE ARRIVED AT THE ISLAND OF
Zanzibar after an eighteen-day voyage. They were met by a sickly
British Consul, Colonel Atkins Hamerton. He was of Irish descent, and
from the looks of him both Richard and John soon understood what
almost twenty years of colonial administration like this could do to a
man. Hamerton was a wreck. At the age of fifty he had fallen into a
torpor based on boredom and increasing isolation from his home
country. In due course, British Colonial Administration would
remember him, recall him, and provide Zanzibar with a much younger
man.

Richard and John stayed there for six months. In part, Richard still
hoped his friend Steinhaeuser might yet join the expedition, and he
held out grimly for this. But in vain. The dry season made any travel
into the interior that much more difficult. The Wadis would be low in
water. The intensity of the heat, with so little moisture in the air, would
have been conducive to no more than five miles a day across the sandy
plains of a heartland south of the great Central Plateau.

So they stayed and frittered their days. Speke allowed that Richard
spent most of his time compiling a thousand pages of notes based
around local custom and the general condition of Zanzibar itself—a
filthy place with bodies floating in shallows and open sewage feeding

THE
SOURCES OF THE NILE
adapted
from Capt. Speke's Map
by
RICHARD F. BURTON

Scale – Statute Miles

these shallows. The explorers were not shy in making known their plans, despite the tale of a French missionary who had gone before them from Bagamoyo on the East African shore and headed west-north-west across the Masai plains in the belief that the Mountains of the Moon lay north of Tabora. Unfortunately, certain natives had tortured the hopeless evangelist, savagely mutilated his body and eventually sawed the man's head off. The route across the Masai plains was indeed the most obvious choice. There were known to be smaller lakes in that direction. The going would have been easier. In addition, had they gone further than the tragic missionary, they would have reached the lower eastern shores of what was to be called Lake Victoria; this fabled inner sea which in fact provided seventy per cent of the flow of the great Nile. After a fact-finding mission up to Mombasa, however, with the idea of an attempt across the Masai plains very much in mind, Richard decided against this route. The Masai warriors had suffered massive loss of cattle in the recent drought and Colonel Hamerton again reminded him of the fate of the French-man. Richard looked at Jack Speke, remembering their humiliating quarrel in Somalia, and decided it was a wiser bet to avoid another situation like that. Jack was angry. In the notes which he later put together as *What Led to the Discovery of the Source of the Nile*, he stated his conviction: 'I thought we could easily have walked around the Masai.' Jack knew it was good hunting territory. There was water ahead in the known smaller lakes such as the Olduvai Gorge, and enough hippopotami to keep his trigger-finger pumping. Richard was procrastinating. He still had not heard if Steinhaeuser could join them on the big march west. He took Jack with him from Mombasa on a pointless survey of Fuga inland, and no sooner had they arrived there than Richard confessed to his companion that he really wanted to visit Kilimanjaro. Speke did not lose his temper over the petty ruse, and as both men came down with a violent fever the plan had to be abandoned. They returned to Zanzibar, Richard on a stretcher.

The abortive journey to Fuga did produce for Jack Speke an element of good fortune. Of the porters provided, one, a freed slave, Seedy Mubarak Bombay, became a long-lasting friend and servant to Speke. Bombay was patient and understanding. He allowed Jack to take his time and stumble over his Hindustani until he at last made sense. He made Speke feel like a leader again. He wasn't totally at Dick's mercy when it came to skill with languages. Bombay was a hard worker; he had an open frame of mind and a degree of honesty which was a surprise to Jack. One ought not to imagine for a moment that any of these famous white explorers, in the 19th century, ever overpaid their bearers. So who can blame the *Kaffir* or the 'nigger' for taking what he could?

On June 16, 1857, Richard and Jack gathered all their equipment and men at a point a few miles south of Bagamoyo, on the African mainland. They were going to approach what they believed to be the area of the source of the Nile on a long overland trek which would take them 750 miles into the heart of East Africa. One hundred and thirty-two porters and thirty donkeys assembled. The two Britons had nine thousand pounds in weight of equipment. Guns, food, cotton, ammunition, sabres, beads, various crates of instruments carefully boxed in London and wrapped with rolls of cotton, prismatic compasses, rain gauges, sextants, barometers, even a domestic bath thermometer. The general agreement was that any man who returned with them to Bagamoyo would collect the best part of ten English pounds. If the entire trip took two years, a porter would be on three pennies a day, and what he could eat, and what he could take on the side. What most porters, perhaps with the exception of Bombay, did not realise was that their white masters had anticipated enough deaths and desertions to bring the final company at the end of this mammoth voyage to a handful. Richard knew the rules best. If they ever got back themselves, there'd be few men left to pay off.

The caravan stretched a mile in length, and it required a posse of Baluchi soldiers sent up by Colonel Hamerton to urge the whole train into action. By the 27th, the expedition was moving at four miles a day. Richard was not satisfied with this. They had bog and jungle and thick undergrowth ahead of them before they reached the first of the Usagara Hills. But command of the caravan was not totally in his control. For many of the Africans had agreed to come only as far as Kazeh, now Tabora, on the understanding they could indulge in a certain amount of slave-dealing on the side.

Basically, they were following known caravan trails, old paths carved out by ancient slavers, but following their compass they frequently deviated from what might have been a much simpler passage less than a mile to their north. Both white men contracted fever. They were delirious, and had to be carried by the donkeys. After a month of this they reached Morogoro, a township rife with smallpox. Their porters were now convinced the white men would die on their hands. And the Baluchi tribal soldiers had had enough. Richard faced them down with a revolver in his hand. But he was faint with weakness; sores and delirium took their toll.

The journey grew ever worse. Jack was unable to shoot at anything, and began to suffer painfully from ophthalmia. Richard could not cope with the numbers of donkeys who died from the tsetse fly, and each morning it was apparent yet another porter had absconded. The more weight each man had to carry the greater his complaint. And if large wooden crates weren't stolen, they were simply dumped at convenient places along the route, for later collection.

On November 7, 1857, they came in sight of the slave-dealing and ivory-trading citadel—Kazeh. It was ruled by an old and patrician Arab warrior Snay bin Amir. Dick Burton spoke Swahili well enough to keep up with all his porters, and now he could use his knowledge of Arabic to great advantage over Jack. Snay, a wise and cunning nightjar of these hot lands, appreciated Burton, and Jack had to rely solely on Bombay's erratic interpretation. A humiliating experience. Richard was at pains to tell the Amir of the poor state of his caravan. He'd lost two-thirds of the donkeys, some forty men, and almost half the food-stuffs, cloth and ammunition he had set out with. In addition, every other day on the caravan trail they had been blackmailed by the euphemistic *Hongo*, or local 'taxation' culled from them by numerous warriors promising 'safe conduct' in return. And the Baluchi tribal soldiers were no defence against this extortion. Snay was very sympathetic to Richard's case. Goats and bullocks were slaughtered in his honour. Snay, undoubtedly, was well aware of the necessity of 'taxes', if a traveller wished to survive. But there is no doubt that in Burton he saw great kinship. In later notes, Dick did not spare Speke, doggo and sullen, racked with ophthalmia:

Here were the times when Jack was at such a disadvantage from want of language; he could join in none of these things, and this made him, I think, a little sour, and partly why he wished to have an expedition of his own. Snay bin Amir was familiar with the language, the religion, the manners, and the ethnology of all the tribes. He was of a quixotic appearance, high featured, tall, gaunt, and large limbed. He was well read, and had a wonderful memory, fine perceptions, and passing power of language. He was the stuff of which I could make a friend, brave as all his race, prudent, ready to perish for honour, and as honest as he was honourable.

Jack, however, wrote a wholly different interpretation of these linguistic proceedings:

To save repetition, I may as well mention the fact that neither Captain Burton nor myself were able to converse in *any* African language until we were close to the coast, on the return journey.

All Richard gleaned from the Amir was that an inland 'sea of Ujiji' lay to the west immediately ahead of his planned route, and a 'sea of Ukewere' lay to the north. The Ujiji was to become the great Lake Tanganyika, and the Ukewere would be known in future years as Lake Victoria. It is apparent that Dick's enthusiasm for putting Speke in his place was greater than his use for the scraps of information the Amir fed him. Dick it was who made up his mind to continue westward, come what may, and he could not allow himself to be drawn by Jack's insubordination. He had to emphasise what he assumed to be his natural authority. Speke, half blind and in agony, could yet summon the strength to beg Burton to take the route north of Kazeh. The route to Ukewere. Richard would not. He reiterated how dangerous such a trek was, according to the Amir's gospel. Neither Jack's command of Arabic nor Bombay's was in any condition to question Burton's interpretation of Snay bin Amir's words. Jack could not forgive easily, but Burton could not forget Berbera; the partnership beckoned deep ruins of distrust.

Half their porters stayed behind at Kazeh. Some agreed to wait for the explorers on the return march. Meanwhile the wise Amir sent his outriders back across the Central Plateau to fetch adequate provisions for the Britons when they returned via Kazeh. The caravan, now reduced to some eighty men, set off from Kazeh on December 14. They had made fifty miles across hard hot terrain when they halted at the Swahili village of Msene. Dick announced it was Christmas. Seedy Bombay told the porters a white man's holiday was upon them. And for two energetic weeks the men drank *pombe* and chased the girls in Msene. Seedy fell in love with one young charmer. Jack Speke's eyes improved, but he held back from the sinful goings-on outside his tent. He only dreamed of trekking north towards the fabled inland stretch of water called Ukewere. Burton was not above relishing certain pleasures of the body here, and described this holiday at Msene —

> I remarked three beauties who would be deemed beautiful in any part of the world. Their faces were purely Grecian, they had laughing eyes, their figures were models for an artist, like the bending statue that delights the world, cast in bronze. These beautiful domestic animals smiled graciously when, in my best Kinyamwezi, I did my *devoir* to the sex, and a little tobacco always secured for me a seat in the undress circle.

In fact, the *pombe* alcohol and the girls' services were all paid for out of Dick and Jack's combined pocket. No wonder Speke grumbled.

There is no suggestion that he was homosexual. He just thought the entire caravan was wasting time and money — his money. After Msene they eventually set out on the last leg of their great journey. In the following two months they had no contact with anyone to the east; it was a slow and painful march across a country of burning remorseless heat sheen.

Malaria apparently racked Burton. Speke's eyes worsened, and no matter how he shielded them the horizon was nothing but a blur of silver heat, and the agony etched itself into his mind. Both men held grimly on to their donkeys, and endured the joint discomfiture of too many ills, as Burton describes:

> Burning and painful eyes, hot palms and soles, a recurrence of shivering and flushing fits, extremities alternately icy cold, then painfully hot and swollen, indigestion, sleeplessness, cutaneous eruptions, fever sores, languor, dejection, all resulting from torpidity of liver, from inordinate secretion of bile, . . .

The explorers allowed their servants to haul their donkey mounts up a final slope which surveyed a broad valley basin. Richard's eyes were good enough to face the sun sinking ahead of him. Jack Speke could see little but 'a misty veil'. At last, they breasted this hill, clad with sparse thorn tree, and Jack's donkey buckled beneath him and died in the hot dirt.

Seedy Bombay helped Speke to his feet. Dick was already ahead on the ridge.

'What is that streak of light which lies below?' Jack asked Seedy.

'I am of opinion,' Seedy replied, 'that that *is* the water you are in search of.'

It was truly a great moment, filled with pain and wonder. Jack could not actually see the water, he had to have it described to him. He could see nothing but this silver haze of pain. Dick's legs had failed him. He could not descend from the donkey. Porters lifted him bodily and carried him upright to the edge of the hill. He could just make out villages dotted along the great lake, which must have been thirty miles from shore to shore. Jack's face was wildly distorted. The fever created a nervous spasm in his jaw. He seemed to be perpetually chewing cud. His teeth ground together. He was haggard and bent into the horizon, screwing up his eyes, the blindness at this crucial moment a bleak laughing irony.

The caravan was treated with implacable unconcern at the village of

Ujiji. The white men had no slaves to buy or sell. The villagers were frankly astonished at the condition of the two explorers. In due course the caravan camped alongside the inland sea, which would be known as Lake Tanganyika. Burton was now eager to explore the northern end of the lake, and he ordered Jack to travel north a few miles in search of a dhow which Dick had been assured of. The dhow was large enough to take a crew and provisions as far as he needed. Days later Jack returned with his four porters in an even worse physical condition. Burton was angry when his colleague confessed he could not hire the dhow for less than an absurdly inflated sum of money, and even then it would be three months before the natives were ready to put the boat out to hire. Jack with his poor command of the language, and inability to deal on any level, had bungled the plan. The natives treated him with contempt. They found him bumptious and ignorant. This white man was not getting their dhow for less than £200.

Richard ordered two canoes from the village instead. In his opinion, Jack was an idiot. He was 'wet to the bone' he later wrote. Indeed, considering the care Jack usually took over his guns and ammunition, scarcely any wonder is it that Burton came to this decision when he saw his countryman limp back to Ujiji, his hunting rifles engrained with rust and all his powder-magazines soaked through. Speke did not waste his breath to explain. A grim silence fell between them. Burton had no idea of the private torment the younger man endured. For Speke had fallen asleep one night and a small beetle contrived to crawl deep into the tympanum of his ear. Jack had gone wild. He attacked the determined insect with oil and salt. Nothing could slow down its curious scraping of the poor man's most sensitive membrane. In his words —

> . . . I therefor tried melted butter; that failing, I applied the point of a penknife to his back, which did more harm than good: for though a few thrusts quieted him, the point also wounded my ear so badly, that inflammation set in, severe suppuration took place, and all the facial glands extending from that point down to the point of the shoulder became contorted and drawn aside, and a string of boils decorated the whole length of that region. It was the most painful thing I ever remember to have endured; but, more annoying still, I could not masticate for several days, and I had to feed on broth alone. For many months the tumour made me almost deaf, and ate a hole between the ear and the nose, so that when I blew it, my ear whistled so audibly that those who heard it laughed. Six or seven months after this accident happened, bits of the beetle — a leg, a wing, or parts of its body — came away in the wax.

Both men wanted a detailed hydrograph of the lake. For thirty-three days, eight men rowed the explorers towards the supposed outlet river which, according to all their dreams, fed northwards into the Nile. Whenever they paused they were told again and again that, yes, there was a river further up, it was this same Rusizi they had heard about, but it was not flowing out of the lake, it flowed *into* it. Dick was weak with exhaustion. The native rowers would not continue further north. A lake storm almost drowned the canoes. Dick had totally lost heart in any further progress. In his opinion they had both done enough: 'We deserved the Victoria Cross, we were heroes, braves of braves; we wanted to be looked at by the fair, to be howled at by the valiant.' Both men compiled scanty notes. They guessed the lake was 250 miles long, but in fact it was over 400. Jack used his bath thermometer to hazard the altitude at 1,800 feet. It was actually 2,500. As for the hydrographic purpose of the great lake, Dick with an inspired guess believed it to be a reservoir which received a network of streams in a natural depression of land. It would take eight years before proper readings were taken, and Lake Tanganyika's curious western swamp outlet discovered. For this stretch of water did not feed to the north, but through marshy soak-aways, on a massive scale its weight of water delivered itself west into the magnificent Congo River.

Jack was blind. Dick's fever made simple walking an arduous feat. They had lost most of their scientific equipment, and now lake monsoons threatened their last chances of exploring Lake Tanganyika to the full. From Burton's point of view, they had done enough. The seal of approval, that famous Gold Medal from the Royal Geographical Society, was theirs to claim. The expedition could ask no more of its leaders nor of its porters and servants. With hindsight one feels that a more carefully recruited expedition could have achieved more in less time, with nothing like the injurious cost to health and sanity. There is a certain casualness in Burton's approach to the trek. He led with no formal discipline; every arrangement he had with Jack was based on a gentleman's word — the separation of money, duty, risk, responsibility, sheer basic logistics, who spoke what language, who led when, who held the donkeys, and who held the job of muniments recorder. But there would have been no expedition at all without Jack's cash contribution. He paid up in advance almost a third of the total costs. Burton used Speke for the money and he abused the younger officer for his lack of knowledge. Could he not have shown, if not magnanimity, a shred of partnership?

By the time they stumbled east towards Kazeh, Speke was at the end of his tether with his companion. He halted a few days on a hot sandy plain outside Kazeh when the Amir forwarded to the caravan the first batch of mail either man had received for twelve months. With the mail arrived enough food and the extra equipment from Zanzibar which Burton had requested.

Dick opened an enormous file of magazine clippings, and letters regularly posted out to Zanzibar once a week since he left London. There is no counting the words young Isabel wrote to her champion. She included every item of news she could find. It looked like a patchwork quilt of cut-out information, interpretations of political and social events, and whatever reviews she could cull which mentioned his name, no matter how brief the reference. It was an avalanche of words. Dick was engulfed with gratitude. It was not a great love he recognised. It was something more paltry, a washing of sentiment, enough to heal wounds and keep back fever. He heard the cry of a stubborn lonely woman in the dark terraces of a suburban life, an act of slavish hope, a torrent of notes which amounted to a form of sacrament.

A letter from an aunt in Bath informed him of the sudden death of his father. The news was nine months late. Joseph Burton had left an estate, inherited from his wife, of more than twenty thousand pounds. After sundry legal matters, Richard, Edward and Maria had automatic division of these spoils. Being the eldest of the two brothers, he would collect the greater share. It was normal practice in those times to provide the senior son with nine tenths of the inheritance even if, as often occurred, there were girls in the family who were several years older. It did not take Richard many moments to assess his new wealth.

Before they packed camp to go on to Kazeh, Jack penned a letter to a friend, Dr Norton Shaw and handed it to the Amir's outrider for safe journey to Zanzibar and the HMG blue postbag bound for London. Jack's spleen atrophied—

Burton has always been ill: he won't sit out in the dew, and has a decided objection to the sun . . . there is literally nothing to write about in this uninteresting country. Nothing could surpass these tracts, jungles, plains for dull sameness, the people are the same everywhere in fact the country is one vast senseless map of sameness . . .

As soon as they had reached the relative comfort of Kazeh, Jack made up his mind to strike north with Seedy Bombay to the rumoured great lake, the so-called sea of Ukewere. At this point Burton did not care to argue. Jack was half blind, and Dick showed a certain lack of compassion. In fact, Dick wrote a formal letter, to be posted in the near future, to the Royal Geographical Society explaining Captain Speke's 'voluntary' offer to trek north. Years later, when this was published in an account of the march by Speke, Burton scribbled beside the printed letter, 'to get rid of him!'

It was a twenty-five-day expedition, to what Speke had already made up his mind to call the 'Nyanza Victoria'; at the onset, Seedy Bombay notwithstanding, Speke had difficulty communicating with his porters and they decided to while away an afternoon chatting and drinking. On the rest of the trek he insisted on not rousing everyone until six in the morning. He was just below the equator and he must have known daylight filled the cool first air as early as four in the morning. He did not seem to realise that every hour in the cool early light was worth two in the slow burn of the latter part of the day. On the 30th of July he led his donkey to the creek which flowed on past a couple of hamlets. In the distance lay that misting light which indicated a great floor of inland water. He named this creek 'Jordans Nullah' after his family house in Somerset. Three marches on and he stood on a hill above the vast sheet of water. There could be no doubt in his mind. This was the mother feed of the great White Nile. He named the hill he stood on 'Somerset' as a matter of course, after his home county. The porters were curious at this exotic habit of handing out names. What was this white man's ritual in aid of? As he descended to the shore of the lake he informed Seedy he would name the Nyanza Lake Victoria after, and in honour of, his great Queen. Seedy dutifully translated this piece of information to the porters.

Once Jack Speke had taken hasty readings of the water table, and found it to be considerably higher than Lake Tanganyika, it took him but seconds to convince himself that those northernmost peaks he had seen in the distance at Tanganyika must be the fabled Mountains of the Moon. Then, on a hill near 'Somerset Hill', he asked a number of natives and village chiefs for details about the great Nyanza lake. One said it could not be circumnavigated because it 'went on until the end of the world'. Another suggested no boat could reach the far side, if such a shore existed. Speke was exhilarated. He had achieved the impossible. Dick Burton looked an ass. He stood two thousand feet above the Nile in Egypt. The gradient of the water (at seventy feet every mile) plus the difficulties of the trailing Sudd (floating densities of green matter) made any attempt on the Nile source from the north an impossibility. He was right. He would stay right in exploration history. And yet he grabbed at the evidence with the rapacity of a deprived child. He dubbed this neighbouring grassy pinnacle 'Observatory Hill'.

There was no gallop back to Kazeh to confront Burton until the last night of the return trek. Jack then could not control his impatience. He slept barely an hour, then climbed out of his tent and harassed the porters to wake up and march with him. It was lucky for Burton that an early rising porter stirred him in time to explain that the other white man was within gunshot of Kazeh. Burton hurriedly dressed and ate a hastily prepared breakfast. He barely found a tea-pot to empty when Speke strode into the tent compound with a look of *eureka* across his scorched and angrily scarred face. In Dick's words —

> We had scarcely, however, breakfasted before he announced to me the startling fact that he had discovered the sources of the White Nile. It was an inspiration perhaps. The moment he sighted the Nyanza, he felt at once no doubt but that the lake at his feet gave birth to that interesting river, which has been the subject of so much speculation and the object of so many explorers. The fortunate discoverer's conviction was strong. His reasons were weak, were of the category alluded to by the damsel Lucetta, when justifying her penchant in favour of the *lovely gentleman*, Sir Proteus —
>
> > I have no other but a woman's reason —
> > I think him so because I think him so.

It wasn't a dramatic event. It was a flat and dull exchange of confidences. Jack blurted out his beliefs. Dick Burton munched his water biscuits and greatly condescended. Speke can be forgiven his enthusiasm, and later history would virtually prove him right. As far as Burton was concerned the puppy had turned into a rabid competitor. Jack's own account of this meeting has always had a certain bitterness about it, what little friendship the two possessed now curdling into silence and the knives of common niceties —

> Captain Burton greeted me on arrival . . . I expressed my regret that he did not accompany me as I felt quite certain in my mind that I had discovered the source of the Nile. This he naturally objected to, even after hearing all my reasons for saying so, and therefore the subject was dropped.

Burton considered Speke's venture a lucky ride to the shores of a huge lake, a '*trouvaille*'. As far as he was concerned, Speke's measurements made no sense. Neither, for that matter, did his own at Lake Tanganyika. But Burton had commonsense in this matter. Both lakes, Victoria and Tanganyika, had flood levels in January. But the Nile in Egypt was fast sinking in January. It did not make sense. Either there remained a further vast lake to the north, where perhaps finally lay these mysterious Mountains of the Moon, or the true feed to the White Nile had a different source from either lake. Dick's argument was crystal clear. Lake Victoria could not be the ultimate and superior source for the Nile. It took months for Burton to write down his contempt for Speke. When he did, the rancour poured—

Jack changed his manners to me from this date. His difference of opinion was allowed to alter companionship. After a few days it became evident to me that not a word could be uttered upon the subject of the lake, the Nile, and his *trouvaille* generally without offence. By a tacit agreement it was, therefore, avoided, and I should never have resumed it, had Jack not stultified the results of my expedition by putting forth a claim which no geographer can admit, and which is at the same time so weak and flimsy, that no geographer has yet taken the trouble to contradict it.

Now, for the first time, although I had pursued my journey under great provocations from time to time, I never realised what an injury I had done the Expedition publicly, as well as myself, by not travelling alone, or with Arab companions, or at least with a less crooked-minded, cantankerous Englishman. He is energetic, he is courageous and persevering. He distinguished himself in the Punjab Campaign. I first found him in Aden with a three years' furlough. His heart was set on spending two years of his leave in collecting animals north of the Line in Africa. He never *thought* in any way of the Nile, and he was astonished at *my* views, which he deemed impracticable. He had no qualifications for the excursion that he proposed to himself, except that of being a good sportsman. He was ignorant of the native races in Africa, he had brought with him about £400 worth of cheap and useless guns and revolvers, swords and cutlery, beads and cloth, which the Africans would have rejected with disdain. He did not know any of the manners and customs of the East; he did not know any language except a little Anglo-Hindustani; he did not *even* know the names of the Coast Towns. I saw him engage as protectors, or *abbans*, any Somali donkey-boys who could speak a little English. I saw that he was going to lose his money, and his *leave*, and his life. Why should I have cared? I do not know; but as virtue is really its own reward, I did so, and have got a slap in the face, which I suppose I deserve. I first took him to Somaliland; then I applied officially for him, and thus saved his furlough and his money by putting him on full service. You would now think, to see his conduct, that the case was reversed—that he had taken me, not I him; whereas I can confidently say that, except his shooting and his rags of Anglo-Hindustani, I have taught him everything he knows. He had suffered in purse and person at Berberah, and though he does not know French or Arabic, though he is not a man of science, nor an acute astronomical observer, I thought it only just to offer him the opportunity of accompanying me as second in command into Africa. He quite understood that it *was* in a subordinate capacity, as we should have to travel amongst Arabs, Belochs, and Africans, whose language he did not know.

One can disregard all the righteousness about who knew what language. (Did James Bruce, in the 18th century, speak Swahili?) What we do know, is that for all these disabilities in Jack Speke, Burton did find it 'only just to offer him the opportunity' because without Speke's money there would have been no 1858 expedition to the presumed source of the great White Nile.

For four months the two white men, with their surviving porters, trekked back to the coast. For weeks, both explorers suffered the returning blights of fever and ophthalmia. At one time Dick nursed Speke through the night, while the man howled with an incoherent cry from his subconscious. His humiliation at Berbera came up like vomit. At the end of this breakdown Speke gasped from his hammock, 'Dick the knives are sheathed!' It was not to prove much of a prophecy.

At Konduchi, in February 1859, they boarded a boat for Zanzibar. All the time, Dick tried to persuade his companion to stay on at Zanzibar, renew their furloughs, and make a further and final attempt on the mysterious Nile source. Jack would have none of this. As soon as they reached Zanzibar they learned that bills for the expedition still stood at more than £2,000. Dick contributed over half this amount to settle porters and East India Company suppliers. Jack was more than reluctant to contribute a further £600. Burton made a blunder here. He would not pay those he believed had cheated him on the expedition. He had vouched for all services and goods in his own name as leader, he had recently inherited his father's money, but on the dockside at Zanzibar he quibbled over each penny with the parsimony of a pawnbroker. Speke was embarrassed.

They stayed five weeks at Zanzibar. Jack was eager to get back to England. Burton and he took a clipper to Aden where ships were bound weekly for England. Burton stayed with John Steinhaeuser, who himself observed Speke's erratic, almost schizophrenic responses towards Burton. When Jack was pleasant his eyes shone with a kind of fear. When he ever questioned Dick over the smallest matter, a look of stray mongrel affection entered into his face. Dick decided to take a later boat, a week away, for England. Jack sailed from Aden on HMS *Furious*. Dick obligingly informed Speke he'd rather spend extra days in Aden with Steinhaeuser. The British in Aden had already heard of the possible 'discovery and solution' of the Nile problem. Gossip and covert fame surrounded the two men. It was an unnerving time for both. They were by no means cured. They had various forms of fever and skin diseases to cope with, and after thirty months of each other's constant company, they shared a closeted formal insanity. Months of casual intimacy and pain and suffering had brought them to the shores of indifference and fear. Dick allowed his natural arrogance to lead him. Jack nurtured a subtler emotion — vengeance.

On the dockside, Burton spoke the last words he would ever again address to his younger companion. They would see each other briefly, in a hall, and in a private salon, but they would never ever have the opportunity to express their fundamental differences face to face.

'I shall hurry up, Jack, as soon as I can,' Dick called out.

'Goodbye old fellow,' Jack rejoindered, 'you may be quite sure I shall not go up to the Royal Geographical Society until you come to the fore and we appear together. Make your mind quite easy about that.'

We only have Burton's word for this telling remark. There were no other witnesses. On plain merit, it damns Speke for a bounder and a cad. These were words he had no intention of sticking by yet there is irony here. If Jack *had not* uttered those strangely disconnected words, he would never have assumed the caddish immortality which overtook him. There is room for doubt. Dick recorded only what he chose to record. Jack had been the achiever, albeit accidental. He had yearned *to see, to grasp* that fame, give hillocks absurd sobriquets, above all — try. It was Dick who had hesitated, held back, waited.

What delayed him, what held him back, what held the secret to all his starts and many stops? Withdrawing at the crucial moment. An uneconomic use of his being. It was as if he found fame a kind of gaudily illuminated alleyway. He was afraid to enter.

It was inevitable that Jack Speke, being the first to reach London, would receive all the hurrahs of the newspapers. He docked on the 8th of May, and he was in London the next morning. Some revilers have barely given him credit for finding a room at Hatchett's Hotel, Piccadilly, before sprinting down Kensington Gore for the portals of the Royal Geographical Society. In fact it was not until the evening that he met with the RGS President, Sir Roderick Murchison, and outlined the discoveries, '*trouvaille*' and otherwise, he and Burton had made in the East African Expedition. The great misunderstanding over Speke derives from his having gorged the praise. He was the social lion of London. He could not help but be fêted, and he could not resist it. And who could have done for that matter, after stumbling through East Africa with malaria and ophthalmia for over thirty months? Doors were hurled open. Suppers were laid. Whippersnapper journalists asked impertinent questions. Ladies giggled and millinered aspidistras swooned. Society craved any morsel which might allay the shameful Crimean past. Society was hungry for a hero in civvies. Jack Speke, tall and fair, in misty blue and grey evening clothes with tinted new spectacles for his weak eyes, struck a fine figure. But there was a misunderstanding. He had not rushed to Murchison to steal Dick's limelight. He explained his own belief in the Lake Victoria source, though he admitted it lacked hard evidence. Sir Roderick Murchison, quite rightly, informed Speke that the RGS had the sum of £2,500 to spend on a further trip to the source of the Nile and he and Burton, either together or individually, could apply for this money at the next Grant Committee Meeting, which would be in a month's time. Jack had every right to put his claim first for the grant. There were four weeks left in which to claim it, and he knew at least six others would put in an application for that same money. To pull back was not Jack's nature.

When Burton arrived in London thirteen days later he was angry at the publicity which now surrounded his companion. There was Jack blabbering night and day about a vast inland lake he had called Victoria, and everyone had forgotten that it was his, Dick's expedition, and he had led Speke to Lake Tanganyika. Dick declared, 'My companion now stood forth in his true colours, an angry rival.' Jack Speke had agreed with the RGS on an award-presenting dinner immediately Dick arrived in London. Murchison toasted both men, but he undoubtedly declared his own interest in Speke's mysterious lake. It was a recognised achievement to have reached Lake Tanganyika, but, generally speaking, its existence was anticipated enough for Burton's discovery to be considered a received discovery. But Jack had indeed stepped into the unknown. That vast water he had found was a geographical pearl; and this was the crude reason why the public and the press and the less knowledgeable experts who should have known better were so entranced. At the RGS supper Dick was awarded the highest prize the Society could offer – the Gold Medal. But Jack received the lesser but still prestigious Founder's Medal. And still Dick privately fumed.

Blackwood's Magazine invited Speke to show them his journals of the expedition. In due course he took up their offer to publish them, and agreed to spend the summer working on them at Jordan's, his family's estate in Somerset. Dick spluttered and squirmed. He had made up his mind Jack had stolen the glory. He insinuated that a young journalist, Laurence Oliphant, whom Jack had met on the boat home, had put him up to this publication through Oliphant's association with the Scottish magazine. Jack was modest enough to inform *Blackwood's* he did not want to assume the mantle of leader of the expedition by publishing this journal. And if Dick wanted to contribute to *Blackwood's* then he must be free to. This seems hardly the attitude of one who had tried to pull the carpet out from beneath Dick's feet.

Dick and Jack maintained their separate courts for a month. On the 20th of June, when the Grant Committee for African Exploration presided at the RGS, Dick submitted a half-crazed scheme to cross the Juba desert disguised as an Arab merchant and approach the lakes with as small and inconspicuous a camp as was possible. He suggested that local chieftains were becoming increasingly nervous of white men with large caravans, and as he was conversant with the various languages this was the only way to allay the suspicions of the inland tribes. The Committee could not persuade Dick to give them a definite date for departure. There were good enough reasons for this: in the first place he had already embarked on an 800-page commentary to be titled *The Lake Regions of Central Africa*; secondly, he was in daily fear of the East India Company's decision on his perpetual furlough; and thirdly, any day he could be summoned for an account of the bills at Zanzibar.

It took the Committee a week to make up its mind. Naturally Jack presented to them his plans for a return trip to Lake Victoria via Kazeh. This time he would follow the lake north as far as it would go. This time he would not fail. This time he would not spend a mere three days on its shore, designating hills. The Committee held fire with Jack's plan. They threw out Dick's familiar cloak-and-dagger ploy. Privately, although it was the Summer Recess, the RGS commenced an agreed course of plans with the Foreign Office. It was a scheme to allow Speke the money and the full backing of the government agencies concerned. But the decision was not made public for months.

During these succeeding months Jack continued to reiterate his beliefs from salons to public halls. He made it known, without any real evidence to this effect, that his Lake Victoria reached all the way north to Gondokoro. He took advantage of Burton's tentative description of the hills north of Lake Tanganyika; Dick was astonished when he heard Jack call them the true Mountains of the Moon.

In November, Burton received the two bitterest blows of his life so far. The RGS announced a £2,500 Grant for Speke's second expedition to the Nile Source. And then Dick received an official reprimand from East India House, Bombay, over his treatment of native porters in Zanzibar. His two careers, explorer and officer, were in dire jeopardy.

As regards romance, the months which followed Dick's return to an England awash with Jack Speke's fame are a curious series of hide and seek events. Before his return Isabel received a letter from him in Zanzibar stamped May 1859. At this time he was arguing with Speke over completion payments for the expedition, and a new Consul had arrived named Christopher Rigby (the same Rigby the linguist Burton had defeated in East India Company examinations years earlier). Rigby all along took sides with Speke. Dick must have felt an outcast. Isabel's letter contained a single sweet page:

TO ISABEL

That brow which rose before my sight,
As on the palmers' holy shrine;
Those eyes — my life was in their light,
Those lips my sacramental wine;
That voice whose flow was wont to seem
The music of an exile's dream.

Alas, we do not learn if a copy was also penned for Isabel's pretty cousin Louisa! Clearly the sly fox dandy wanted to be sure of at least one lass waiting at the dockside. And following Isabel's flood of letters and cuttings he could well afford a gushing sextain from the heat of Zanzibar.

According to W. H. Wilkins, Isabel's friend and biographer, she called 'at a friend's house' the day after Dick landed. The friend was not at home. She asked the maid if she could wait. A moment later a loud knock came to the door, and she heard Dick's unmistakable voice demand, 'I want Miss Arundell's address!' Whereupon she raced downstairs and threw herself into Ruffian Dick's arms. To her shock the man was a shadow of what she had known. He was emaciated and his hair and skin had the appearance of someone exposed to the most gruelling dehydration. In-no time at all, they were arm in arm out in the street searching for a taxi. They sat together in a hired barouche and circled aimlessly around the town. Their conversation according to

Isabel was a riot of loving intimacies newly restored. She drew his portrait in the cab. He drew hers. They exchanged lockets and hugs and God knows what else.

Her ardour is astonishing and disarming, Nothing would shake her thoughts. 'My earthly god and king,' she designated the poor sick fellow, 'and I could have knelt at his feet and worshipped him. I used to feel so proud of him; I used to sit and look at him, and to think — *you are mine and there is no man on earth the least like you.*' She was like a walking blanket. She poured out an onslaught of suffocating affection. But she also stood by him. She was implacable. If ever a man needed solace like this it was Dick Burton. Here he was, under the impression *he* had discovered *one* of the main sources of the great Nile, while there lay the rest of literate London convinced that Jack Speke had discovered the *only* source of the Nile. He certainly needed her.

According to Isabel, they met daily in secret, she informed her parents of their intention to marry, he even visited her parents with this in view. What actually happened? Within a week Dick was off to Dover to stay with his sister. Maria Stisted kept him under convalescence for six weeks. He was so ill he could not attend the Grant Committee meeting at the Royal Geographical Society. He followed Maria to Paris to see his sick brother Edward. He went on to Vichy to take the waters for a touch of gout. He returned to Dover to work on the long manuscript of *The Lake Regions of Central Africa,* but for some reason he was unable to complete the work there. He had no rooms in London to go to, so he took himself off to Boulogne to finish the book. There he found many of his old friends and neighbours. The dates speak for themselves; he did everything in his power to stay out of London.

By the summer of 1860, the proofs of his book were with the publishers. Jack Speke had finally selected a young officer from his own Indian Regiment, James Grant, to take on the second Nile mission. James Augustus Grant, born 1827 and educated at Aberdeen, was a mild fellow, well spoken, and, most importantly as far as Jack was concerned, this new companion would do what he was told. Although Grant was not averse to hunting and shooting, he was at all times a quiet and scholarly figure, and in his own right he would reach the pinnacle of his career as a colonel of the Intelligence Department in the Abyssinian Expedition. Jack could not have chosen a greater contrast to Burton.

Speke and Grant departed for darkest Africa two weeks before *The Lake Regions of Central Africa* was published. Speke had seen nothing of the proof copies of the book before he departed. It would have been a simple matter of courtesy for Burton to have asked for copies from his publisher. He did not. And on publication day it became evident of his anger towards his companion. The anger rolled off the pages, and not once did he mention that companion by name:

> During the expedition he acted in a subordinate capacity, and, as may be imagined, among a party of Arabs, Baloch, and Africans, whose language he ignored, he was unfit for any other but a subordinate capacity . . .

And on and on. He could not get the pent-up ire out of his system. He remonstrated with the RGS for allowing this puppy explorer to 'secure for himself the right of working the field which I had opened'. It seemed that nothing would satisfy his loss of face.

The book was well received, but was unlikely to be a best-seller like David Livingstone's *Travels and Researches in South Africa*, a publication which had immediately caught the fancy of the public. Essentially, Dick's book was a sturdy and careful attempt to plot the Nile source. He did not claim everything for his Lake Tanganyika. He made light of the claim for the unknown Lake Victoria. It was not enough to half-find Tanganyika. It was not enough to half-dismiss Victoria. The public wanted a brave and valiant mystery, and a positive belief in a single source for the Nile. Unwittingly Jack had created the required mythology. For thus lay the mood of the times.

XII

Dick Burton magicked away ten
thousand pounds, and brandy and
cigars could not amend his imprudent
marriage to a vertiginous maiden.

DESPITE THE ONLY MODEST SUCCESS OF HIS BOOK, DICK WAS
now taken up by Society in a big way. A generous Duke of Somerset
invited him to Bulstrode, a fascinated Lord Palmerston got him down
to Broadlands, a horsy Lord Derby called Dick to Knowsley, and
Monckton Milnes, an old friend, taster of the esoteric and patron of
poets, invited Dick to his London home. Isabel did not accompany
him on these country-house weekends which, in the manner of the
period, could last as long as a month.

As soon as the book was out in the shops, Dick settled all his
financial affairs in London. His bank account safely nestled more than
£14,000. Maria had a small inheritance from her dead father. And there
was enough money left over to support Edward Burton in a home for
the disabled. Dick never lost his affection for the young brother
with whom he had shared so many scrapes in his youth. Sadly, Edward
never recovered from his accident in Ceylon. [Edward Burton (1825–
1895), an army surgeon, suffered brain damage, as a result of a fight
with a Ceylonese tribesman in 1859. He died in an institution.]

Having wangled yet another furlough, Dick packed his bags,
acquired a new revolver, and boarded the liner SS *Canada* bound for
the United States. Via Washington he journeyed to Salt Lake City to
investigate the polygamous Mormon society which was ruled by

Brigham Young. In predictable tones, Isabel Arundell tried to cover up the dismay she felt when she discovered her idol had departed again without a word in her direction. She larded the shock with premonition. She was, it seems, struck by a vision of his going, when out on a walk with chums. Later, she announced to her sister she would not be meeting Richard on the following day as they had arranged. Within hours, a messenger arrived at her door with a note from the idol. According to her he had left like this because he could not bear the pain of parting from her, and she insisted her mother had forbidden their plans of marriage. She blamed this sudden lack of contact on his sensitivity to farewells. At twenty-eight she was old enough to marry whom she wished. But Dick's diary declares his intention 'to drink myself to the level of the aborigines', and for the next six months he would fortify himself with a daily drown of 'mint-juleps, brandy-smashes, whisky-skies, gin-sling, cock-tail sherry, cobblers, rum-salads, streaks of lightning, morning-glory', in the pleasant company of John Steinhaeuser, whose presence on this voyage Isabel never later admitted.

Neither did she take all that kindly to the news of his departure. To begin with she collapsed on the hall carpet, as most young ladies of a similar breeding were in the habit of. To follow that, she contrived a general state of total physical breakdown, so all-pervasive that it would leave her family in no doubt as to the true nature of her affections for this man —

> I was for a long time in bed, and delirious. For six weeks I was doctored for influenza, mumps, sore throat, fever, delirium, and everything that I had not got, when in reality, I was only heartsick . . .

In a London suburb, Charles Dickens was writing *Great Expectations*. Darwin had just published the second hurriedly rushed out printing of *The Origin of the Species by Means of Natural Selection*. As a junior army officer, at war with his contemporaries and with no war to indulge in, Leo Tolstoy settled into an orgy of drink and women at a cold and cavernous town house in Moscow. Meanwhile in a gaudy uniform, on board the SS *Canada*, travelling first class across the watery Divide Captain Dick Burton preferred whisky to cribbage, preferred laughter to nervous bodices. As he leaned into the westerly wind on the upper bridge an irony struck him: fast approaching his fortieth birthday, he had all the talents and potential abilities of any member of his own generation, a virtual Paladin, swordsman and crackshot, explorer and poet, and a firstborn British anthropologist. And as he considered these many talents they retreated before his gaze. He liked to coin a self-description – 'a blaze of light without a focus' – and neither gods nor continents, neither money nor toil, neither applause nor titles, would persuade his soul to break cover and show itself naked. And he would always reserve his secrets, that schoolboy who performed practical jokes on gullible tutors; he would for ever contain his self in an armour of stylised inscrutability – whatever he would write, say, do, in the years to come, the summary of these endeavours would be a palimpsest devised by the child in him for the deception of adults.

At the end of the year he returned to England via the Panama Canal. He carried 500 pages of manuscript describing his journey to Salt Lake City and the Mormon Brethren, *The City of the Saints and Across the Rocky Mountains to California*. In his own words, 'my eyes were full of sight-seeing, my pockets empty, and my brain stuffed with all manner of useful knowledge . . .' But he was tired after these months in the States. Before he left for home, the American public had voted Abraham Lincoln their new President.

Isabel spent Christmas with a large and wealthy Catholic family in Yorkshire, the Cliffords. On the 25th she read in *The Times* a brief announcement, 'Captain R. F. Burton has arrived from America'. Isabel was incarcerated in a great country house, surrounded by a snowstorm, and some ten miles from the nearest station. Nobody will ever know exactly how she achieved it, but according to her legend she contrived a telegram addressed to herself ordering her to London immediately.

Within three days, she and Richard came to a joint decision. In her telling, Dick blurted, 'Our lives are being spoiled by the unjust pre-judices of your mother, and it is for you to consider whether you have not already done your duty in sacrificing two of the best years of your life out of respect to her. If once, you really let me go, mind, I shall never come back, because I shall know that you have not got the strength of character which my wife must have. Now you must make up your mind to choose between your mother and me. If you choose me, we marry, and I stay; if not, I go back to India, and on other explorations, and I return no more. Is your answer ready?' To which, in her own legend, she replied, 'Quite. I marry you this day three weeks, let who will say nay.'

Dick couldn't have given a fart in a bustle factory whether her mother's feelings were becalmed. And as for really letting him go anywhere at any time—from Aden to Gondokoro, from Berbera to Zanzibar, and from Boulogne to Salt Lake City—Dirty Dick had been going and would continue to go as far as he could devise, Isabel notwithstanding. Memory and logic were a confused mosaic in her mind, forming an agreeable version of the facts. One can't harden the heart to her, though. She had plundered a fine depth in her being. She wanted to bleed for the man.

Burton's niece took a very grim view of this marriage. 'Marriage!' she declared. 'This step, upon which much misplaced sentiment has been lavished, surprised both friends and relatives; those who knew him best were perfectly aware that it surprised him most of all.' The couple were wed in a Bavarian Catholic Church, in Warwick Street, Central London, on January 22. She did not tell her family of the great day. He met her outside the church puffing a large cigar. The service was performed by a priest and a registrar. As far as her family was concerned she was going away for three weeks to stay with friends. Dick had rented a two-roomed furnished flat in a type of building more commonly called 'bachelor lodgings'. After the service and a wedding breakfast with the registrar and eight friends, the newly married couple retired to his chambers. Surprisingly, his sister Maria was present at the ceremony. The following day, Dick penned a letter to Isabel's father,—

My dear Father,
   I have committed a highway robbery by marrying your daughter Isabel at Warwick Street Chapel and before the registrar—the details she is writing to her mother.
   It only remains for me to say that I have no ties nor liaisons of any kind, that the marriage was perfectly legal and 'respectable'. I want no money with Isabel; I can work, and it will be my care that Time shall bring you nothing to regret.
                                        Yours sincerely,
                                        Richard F. Burton

Aunts espied her entering these same bachelor's lodgings, and they told her mother. His letter just in time dampened the scandal down. But the honeymoon was very short. He packed her off home after a week to explain fully about the wedding. Meanwhile he went to stay with an aunt who possessed a large house.

Dick was not averse to encouraging outrageous rumours in club smoking rooms and torpor-filled barracks. He found those rumours a form of anodyne. They appeased his dreams. These tales were fed back to him with an ever-expanding licence for conjecture. 'He had been caught in a Turkish harem and buggered most foully for his curiosity'; 'He had been fornicating with young boys in homosexual Karachi brothels, and received dreadful extremes of syphilis'; 'He had boasted of killing savages with the ease of a fly swatter'. It is not too difficult to imagine the natural anxieties of Isabel's respectable family. They were but thirty years after the Catholic Emancipation Bill and the Catholic Relief Bill. Unlike the Jews, they now possessed the right to sit in the House of Lords, but rank and status were sensitive areas for high-minded Catholic families. The job of Sovereign to the British people, or Regent, or Lord Chancellor, or Lord Keeper, or even Lord High Commissioner to the Church of Scotland was forbidden to the papist brethren. These high Catholic families did not relish a Burton in their midst.

The tryst in that Bavarian Church was a perverse and peremptory arrangement; it looked for all the world less like a service to God and registrar, and more like an arraignment of his earlier achievements. One can see what was in their minds—the priest to declare the Holy Roman Rights in order to placate her family, and the registrar appointed for Dick's non-conformist oath. Purists on her side have claimed Burton a Catholic convert from this ceremony, and rumours were spread that he had joined the Roman Church in India ten years earlier. This was not the truth. The man could not be confined to such a secular oath.

And there was a sense of bewilderment amongst his friends. For Burton was in love neither with Isabel, nor with the depth of her purse. Burton was not a member of her Church. And why hadn't he discussed these nuptials with the friend who always had urged him on to translate eastern erotica—John Steinhaeuser? Or the jovially rich companion and collector of literate pornography—Monckton Milnes? Even that scurrilous chum of Burton's from Paris, purveyor of erotic novellas—Fred Hankey?

Isabel had wed a man without a career. Perhaps she had an inkling that she was not exactly Dick's Louisa Segrave, the pretty thing. And yet, with heart-breaking guilelessness she described her newly married life in their tiny lodging as 'seven months of uninterrupted bliss'. It is difficult to understand her pleasure. Richard appears to have spent most of his days in pubs in Fleet Street, drinking with a variety of articulate or down-at-heel literati—William Black, Tom Hood, James Hain Friswell, George Augustus Sala, Wilfrid Blunt the poet, Edmund Yates, Bernal Osborne, Carlo Pellegrini a caricaturist; and it was

Dick's pleasure to join the Garrick Club, and the Arundel Club, and the Beefsteak Club.

Isabel had the guts to keep her family at arm's length. She dutifully followed her husband to Monckton Milnes' country mansion Fryston, but she was not in the least reduced by the sight of Thomas Carlyle or William Thackeray at supper; Milnes, by no means a major author, had compiled an incredible library of poetry and *belles lettres*, of so broad a spectrum that he insisted on having French and German and Portuguese literary journals delivered to his hall table. There Dick was in his element, and Carlyle jovially called him 'Perpetual President of the Heaven and Hell Amalgamation Society'. In due course, Milnes persuaded Lord Palmerston to give an evening party for Isabel to enable her to acquaint herself with the variety of friends and admirers Dick possessed. The social year for Isabel was capped when Lady Russell arranged a 'casual' introduction to Queen Victoria. It was held at an afternoon sitting in the Russells' house, casual but very contrived. The Queen attended this drawing-room assembly, and it was not exactly the Court. Victoria had a stern ruling at these drawing-room tea parties, hen houses for aspiring crinolines; she would not touch hands with a girl who had eloped. Isabel must have bloomed. *Ipso facto* her own marriage was no jilt job, out through the hansom cab exit with a licence and two midnight train tickets to Le Havre. She had conquered.

Meanwhile Dick relied on his absenteeism from the marriage, but Isabel was happy and determined. She kept by her bed in the small apartment her own list of dos and don'ts in marriage. It has a tragic undertone:

1. Let your husband find in you a companion, friend, and adviser, and *confidante*, that he may miss nothing at home; and let him find in the wife what he and many other men fancy is only to be found in a mistress, that he may seek nothing out of his home.

2. Be a careful nurse when he is ailing, that he may never be in low spirits about his health without a serious cause.

3. Make his home snug. If it be ever so small and poor, there can always be a certain *chic* about it. Men are always ashamed of a poverty stricken home, and therefor prefer the Club. Attend much to his creature comforts; allow smoking or anything else; for if you do not *somebody else will*. Make it yourself cheerful and attractive, and draw relations and intimates about him, and the style of society (*literati*) that suits him, marking who are real friends to him and who are not.

4. Improve and educate yourself in every way, that you may enter into

his pursuits and keep pace with the times, that he may not weary of you.

5. Be prepared at any moment to follow him at an hour's notice and rough it like a man.

6. Do not try to hide your affection for him, but let him see and feel it in every action. Never refuse anything he asks. Observe a certain amount of reserve and delicacy before him. Keep up the honeymoon romance, whether at home or in the desert. At the same time do not make prudish bothers, which only disgust, and are not true modesty. Do not make the mistake of neglecting your personal appearance, but try to look well and dress well to please his eye.

7. Perpetually work up his interests with the world, whether for publishing or for appointments. Let him feel, when he has to go away that he leaves a second self in charge of his affairs at home; so that if sometimes he is obliged to leave you behind, he may have nothing of anxiety on his mind. Take an interest in everything that interests him. To be companionable, a woman must learn what interests her husband; and if it is only planting turnips, she must try to understand turnips.

8. Never confide your domestic affairs to your female friends.

9. Hide his faults *from everyone*, and back him up through every difficulty and trouble; but with his peculiar temperament advocate peace whenever it is consistent with his honour before the world.

10. Never permit any one to speak disrespectfully of him before you and if any one does, no matter how difficult, leave the room. Never permit any one to tell you any thing about him, especially of his conduct with regard to other women. Never hurt his feelings by a rude remark or jest. Never answer when he finds fault; and never reproach him when he is in the wrong, *especially when he tells you of it*, nor take advantage of it when you are angry; always keep his heart up when he has made a failure.

11. Keep all disagreements for your own room, and never let others find them out.

12. Never ask him *not* to do anything—for instance, with regard to visiting other women, or anyone you particularly dislike; trust him, and tell him everything except another person's secret.

13. Do not bother him with religious talk, be religious yourself and give good example, take life seriously and earnestly, pray for and procure prayers for him, and do all you can for him without his knowing it, and let all your life be something that will win mercy from God for him. You might *try* to say a little prayer *with* him every night before laying down to sleep, and gently draw him to be good to the poor and more gentle and forbearing to others.

14. Cultivate your own good health, spirits, and nerves, to counteract

his naturally melancholy turn, and to enable you to carry out your mission.

15. Never open his letters, nor appear inquisitive about anything he does not volunteer to tell you.

16. Never interfere between him and his family; encourage their being with him, and forward everything he wishes to do for them, and treat them in every respect (as far as they will let you) as if they were your own.

17. Keep everything going, and let nothing be at a standstill; nothing would weary him like stagnation.

Clearly this charter for a slaver of carpet slipper oligarchy was written before her marriage by a virgin of twenty-nine at a desk beside her bedroom door in a house crammed with brothers and sisters on the outskirts of Worthing. A certain sadness pervades these commandments when one observes what has been left out. There is not one mention of children. Not a whisper about old age. And not a murmur of sharing the Dark Angel's door where the timely Reaper hails the last sod turned. Isabel had merely made a desperate cry from unwedded bondage. She was chained to this totem in her mind. If Dirty Dick only took pity on her, when he strode up that Bavarian Catholic aisle stubbing out his angry cigar, at the very least it was humane and compassionate.

She hugged his knees beside a little comfy fire glow beneath a mantel-valance decorated with Persian arabesque, silver weave fabric Dick swore he stole from a Turkish *caravanseraglio*, and she called him Jemmy. In the little room he was pleased to see she had laid out stoned dates on a side-table next his brandy. The room had a stuffed dark prune drabbet crepuscular about it, and Dick called her his Zookins.

During this time, with the aid of the well-known scientist, James Hunt, he announced a new group, The Anthropological Society, and it was the intention of this new body to publish a magazine and maintain London offices for the more learned members of the fraternity. It was meant to be a formal off-shoot for his own publishing schemes. He had had his fill of publishers squeezing his marginalia into obscurity. Later the august group became the Royal Anthropological Institute of Great Britain and Ireland. But in early 1861, it did not possess funds for such grandiose designations, and amazingly enough Dick managed to sneak into the same London offices a further society dubbed the Cannibal Club, which met regularly above an Italian restaurant and claimed Swinburne and Monckton Milnes as members. One can see why Burton's schoolboyish humour attracted few serious anthropologists. It wasn't pomposity which kept them away from him. It was his flair for confusing the laughs with his own paranoia. It didn't make sense to munch olives and pasta and cheese macaroni and make wild jokes about black pudendas downstairs, and then hasten to the more formal meeting hall of his Anthropological Society upstairs and lecture there on the eremitic sequestration of the vulgar nest-building equatorial ape from the Gabon. Upon being invited to join the upstairs society, the eminent Thomas Huxley demurred. Burton was asking for trouble.

He was now forty years old. He had achieved two great feats of exploration, and spoke two dozen languages. The East India Company's administration of India had now ceased, its charter was to be dissolved in 1858, and though it took time for government tape to wind up its vast affairs, it was inevitable that the Company's troops would be merged wtith the regular British Army. The Bombay Army, Dick's force, had to come to a final decision over its motley officer class. Half were killing themselves with expatriate boredom in barracks flung on far shores; the other half were donning civvies and enjoying the fat life of home on full-pay. It was an extravagant situation. And some of the men had to be made examples of.

As soon as his commission was placed under the umbrella of the regular army, its pecuniary worth was almost nil. What was the advantage of 'buying' Dick's Indian Commission when it was cheaper and more rewarding to acquire an equivalent post in Greys, Guards or Dragoons of the Queen's Own? Furthermore, it was too complicated to volunteer for India now. Britain had seceded her dependent states. Vast lands like Rajputana and Hyderabad were virtually kingships. Times changed rapidly. And the Foreign Office had its eyes on East Africa, on Zanzibar, and on a colonial military penetration of this coastline; it could be done by devious means, using naive missionaries and vain explorers as outriders. It could be done by sheer hypocrisy — by creating huge public support against slavery in these parts. Occupation by force had to be ruled out so long as the German or the Portuguese nations kept their distance. It was the silent and cunning war which the British Foreign Office excelled in. As for India, in future, this great territory would remain under Crown Protection, but each governor-general to be appointed would receive the additional title of Viceroy.

The order of calamities for Burton in 1861 went accordingly; he knew by the time he was back from the States that his Indian Commission was worthless, and being grafted into the main army would mean a return to uniform and barracks, and furloughs as long and as distant as the African horizon would from now on be out of the question. Secondly, during the eight months abroad his personal fortune had mysteriously dwindled. Thirdly, various trunkfuls of Persian and Arabic manuscripts, a collection of costumes (mainly genuine gemmed and beaded Arab gowns) and a personal library of rare dictionaries and reference books, were all destroyed in a fire at a warehouse. It is quite possible that here he lost his first attempts at a translation of the *Arabian Nights*, which he had discussed with Steinhaeuser ten years earlier. Unfortunately nothing was recovered. Finally, he was vain enough to believe the British Army could continue with him on his present record. But there were many senior officers who would jump at an excuse to be rid of him. Without as much as a word in the direction of the East India Company, who were, after all, still supplying him with £300 a year, he applied to the Foreign Office for the post of Consul in Damascus. The reply from the office of Lord John Russell, then Foreign Secretary, said that a position might be open to him on the tiny island of Fernando Po, a Spanish colony twenty miles from the west coast of French Equatorial Africa.

It took the Foreign Office a while to inform the regular army authorities that Captain R. F. Burton had applied for a consulship, and it was apparent what he was up to. He assumed he could keep his half-pay and at the same time find himself a sinecure sufficient for wife and self. Of course it didn't wash. The Foreign Office confirmed the Fernando Po consulship, at £700 a year, and Dick professed amazement when he read in the Bombay Infantry rolls that he had been struck off the register! He spluttered to Isabel that plenty of other 'Indian fellahs' were on half-pay plus a government stipend, and he above all comers deserved it too. But why? He had virtually missed the Afghan War. He had seen four months of the Crimea War. And now he wanted a salary to support himself and his Gold Medal from the Royal Geographical Society. It simply wasn't on.

Dick's finances were in a most peculiar state. One year he had inherited over £15,000, the next year he had less than £4,000. His niece hardly bothers to explain just what happened to this sizable inheritance

> When his wife's debts and his own were paid, Burton had only four thousand pounds remaining from his little patrimony, a sum which, prudently invested in a joint annuity, brought in about £200 per annum. Besides this majestic income there was his half-pay.

He had no more than £1,200 to pay out in Zanzibar, after he inherited from his father. As for the trip to the States, that Mormon Tribe and his whisky-skies, the basic expenses did not exceed £1,000. And as for Isabel's so-called debts — there was a hat from the milliners, a cab ride or two home, and a dozen opera tickets. She hardly needed new clothes. Most of the last eight years of her adult life had been spent in stitching elbow shadows in front of the morning-room grate. Apart from a trousseau of all her dreams and ambitions, she had a wardrobe of dolmans, pelisses, paletots, and muffs, Algerine and Sultane demi-shot chine, and the frou-frou for decorous sobriety the equal of any Winterhalter painting. It didn't make her spendthrift by any means. The art of the sober middle classes was an industrious business of home domestics and hearth-side make do and mend.

Where had £10,000 gone? Since there are blanks and missing months in his American tour from the Rockies to the Panama Canal, it does seem most likely that he actually spent it, blew it, drank it, fornicated it away in cow-poke clapboard shanty towns. Dick needed secrets.

After seven months of marriage, he sailed for Fernando Po on August 24, 1861. He did not return to London until December 1862. Isabel Burton closed up the fusty rooms in London and returned to Worthing to live with her mother and father.

Dick sailed down the west African coast stopping at every port from Sierra Leone to Gambia and on to Lagos. On board the boat, for quirky motives, he grew to detest west African natives. This culminated in his refusal to sup first class with a handful of black Monrovians. He stopped at Fernando Po for a week. Just enough time to take in the mountainous little island, be warned of the fierce wind *harmattan*, and disappear back to the mainland with the excuse that he had to hire a cook, a carpenter and a 'nigger-boy', if the lad was quick-witted enough.

Fernando Po was known as 'the Foreign Office grave'. Out of 250 white inhabitants, seventy-eight had died from a sudden influx of yellow fever. Burton was quick to liken himself to 'Prometheus with the Demon Despair gnawing at my heart', and he considered suicide at Fernando Po. He found he could barely tolerate more than a month at a stretch in the place. He had taken to a flask of brandy a day, and for every forty-eight hours he spent in his island house at *Buena Vista*, he made sure of at least forty days on the African mainland, great sandy bar witness to the South Atlantic rollers.

He canoed up the Congo River. He studied black justice in Sierra

Leone. He reviled white missionaries in Dahomey. He looked for gorillas in Gabon, and he completed fourteen journals of his travels which made up some three thousand pages of print when he later consigned *Wanderings in West Africa, Two Trips to Gorilla Land, A Mission to Gelele, King of Dahome,* to the British publishers. None of this assuaged the agony in his own mind. It wasn't the ghastly conditions of Fernando Po. He once declared 'man found it hard to live but uncommonly easy to die'; and in effect he had now been stranded; cast alone on this island he was Prospero forced to double up as Caliban. By now he had spent thirteen months on this coast and only the frequency of British ships to the island enabled him to gad about so much. Now all enthusiasm for the slave-trading coast had melted. He tended his garden, and the number of servants rapidly increased. One biographer has suggested he was enjoying a 'black bed' and the privileges of a slaver without the hindrance of social condemnation. Perhaps here in his first consulship scruples slipped a little. The very fact a fellow was married, but on his own in an outlandish place, made it appropriate to take up what urges the sensual gods decreed. For the single man, consul or not, it was not so easy to act in public without discretion, for the bachelor was a marriageable target in colonial life. In addition to his daily flask of brandy, a subtler and more inevitable way of life overtook Dick, and, in that steamy mosquito air through the transparent shield of netting, tender nights crept up on him with curious balm at once disinterested and subjugated; and on that Gulf of Guinea, sea-girt continental bay enclosing the Biafra Bight, a vast living port of black flesh dragged to exile with no promise of a future beyond that new horizon, there was not one black girl who'd hesitate her arms. The black pretty giver on that shore had nothing left to receive but the wide sea void of an unknowable oblivion. Even if Dick lacked pity, especially for the West African, a touch of sentiment was not beyond his reach. He drank as he wished in his Foreign Office grave, and brandy was not his only intoxication.

In London Isabel marched into the appropriate room within the Foreign Office, promptly burst into tears and unashamedly beseeched the nearest official at hand, who happened to be the famous Ninevah archaeologist Henry Layard, at the time an Under-Secretary for Foreign Affairs, to send Dick home. She had heard dastardly rumours that her Dick was running a seraglio of black girls on the run from their Arab slaving masters. She had been a grass widow for fourteen months, and the startled Layard of Ninevah wrote out an official recommendation for a four-month furlough. It was processed that afternoon.

Dick was on trial, and he knew it. That Fernando Po posting was the bottom of the official consular gazette, and he could slip no further. The episode didn't make or break his marriage either, but it was the start of a long and terrible slide. To get off this slippery slope he was not too sure Isabel wielded the best remedies. But bless her, she did the screaming. And it proved quite efficient.

If the Foreign Office was under the impression a four-month furlough would make Dick a good boy, it was to be disabused. The four months lasted twelve months, and a good deal of that holiday, on full pay this time, with all expenses paid, was spent carrying the diminutive and paralytically drunk Algernon Charles Swinburne up staircases in Monckton Milnes' country estate of Fryston. Richard Monckton Milnes, first Baron Houghton, was born in 1809, educated at Cambridge and he entered politics to become a Liberal on Peel's conversion to Free Trade. Monckton Milnes maintained all his life a fast friendship with Dick.

What was preying on his mind? The vulture shadows of Speke and Grant once more heading west from Bagamoya and on up to the far shore of this unexplored great Lake Victoria which only Jack had seen? This did not help the sale of Dick's *The Lake Regions of Central Africa*. The great reading and buying public was not willing to buy a book which could not possibly be the terminal essay on the mysterious source of the White Nile. The public was absorbed with central and dark Africa. The white mythology of unknown Africa had three-legged black giants, men with eyes in their chests, native women with the sex gorge capacity of were-man-cravers, unknown animals of startling proportions and lake-monsters who required sacrificial canoes of blood—in fact, it is a rewarding study of Victorian behaviour to catalogue white middle-class fears and fantasies about the 'dark heart' of the famous continent.

Dick Burton also got precious little return from his book *Wanderings in West Africa*, published in 1863. It was more of an anthology of his pet topics and digressions, pages crammed with his very own by-the-wayness, these curious and compelling references to anything from narcotics, the use of toothpick, colonial government wages (he was very keen on that subject), with a few foul words tossed in to make a very ugly anthropological salad about the general human baseness of Jews, Irish and Americans, dressed with the efficacy of the Kola nut as an aphrodisiac when dunked in lime cordial with a garnish of ice cubes.

It wasn't that he was noticeably cracking up, it was that something within him had begun to run down. He himself could not see it. In loneliness, lost abilities steal away from the spirit with the silence of shadows, and Richard Burton was losing his grip on the outside world which he so constantly mocked. He had an idea that the 'pygmies', those petty civil servants, were taking over, that all his novelties had ceased to fascinate the public, and all he could do was strike out with the arrogance of a being who could stride the stones of a Giant's Causeway.

On his way back to Fernando Po in January 1863, Isabel persuaded him to let her sail with him as far as Tenerife. There they stayed for what she called a glorious holiday. He had kicked a drunken sailor out of their cabin on the voyage out. He had marched her up to the highest peak he could find in Tenerife, smoked a cigar whilst she prayed ('It was Passion Sunday,' she recalled), and marched her down again. Husband and wife had a pretty heated quarrel round about here. She insisted on accompanying him back to Fernando Po and his consular house (equipped with a retinue of black servants), and with perfunctory ease he slammed her. She had to return to England. She cried and begged him, but he would have none of it. The last place on earth he wanted her snooping about was his little haven on that island, and besides, he had recently discovered the natives were in the habit of fermenting a fine palm-toddy.

The Foreign Office gave him a job as Queen's Commissioner to be received at the Court of King Gelele, a rather murderous chieftain in Dahomey whose wont it was to decapitate in one afternoon dozens of prisoners as offerings to the gods. It was a dangerous task. The new Commissioner was given a seventeen-gun salute from HMS *Antelope*, and a retinue of a hundred servants washed Dick ashore to this uninviting kingdom. Burton was obliged to stay three months here, much against his better judgment. For half that time the wily Gelele simply kept him waiting. To be received at Court was not easy. Dick considered it humiliating to have to observe multiple atrocities in the capacity of Commissioner. But in a land like this he was powerless.

Eventually, the purple and white silken clothed figure of Gelele invited Burton, accompanied by a naval surgeon and a Wesleyan minister, into his Court. It was a place filled with female warriors and courtiers who could accommodate as many as sixty wives each. Slaves and servants prostrated themselves on the ground, and the Commissioner was invited to drink from the skull of a former prisoner. There was an acrid smell of slaughter over the whole place. Gelele's father had originated this army of native women. On the father's death, Gelele murdered five hundred as a divine offering.

The King was not over-enthusiastic about Burton's gifts, the most princely being an unfortunate forty-foot-round tent designed with so many confusing ropes and pegs it was extremely difficult to erect. Upon inspection, Gelele announced it was too small for him. Richard resorted to reading out the Queen of England's message to the black despot. The message was, in effect, that Victoria would greatly appreciate it if King Gelele abolished his practice of wholesale slaughter, and put aside his evil traffic in slavery, because these activities ran counter to her religious beliefs. Not surprisingly, the despot pointed out that, apart from palm oil, slavery was his country's principal export trade, and if Her Majesty would like to pay him £50,000 a year in lieu of his losses he might take into consideration the White Queen's pleas.

Dick packed his bags within four hours of this retort, and returned to Fernando Po. He had had time to observe many aspects of circumcision and cicatrization amongst the hordes of slaves, but the sight of so many heads impaled on wood railings and the stench which pervaded this landscape of arbitrary execution, had quickly tired him of Dahomey. As for Gelele's notorious army of two thousand women armed with flintlocks and broad shaped cutlasses, he was of the opinion that an equal number of British charwomen, armed only with broomsticks, could have cleared them off in a few hours.

Although Dahomey was to become sandwiched between a British and a German colony in years to come, not until 1892 was it conquered by the French. And Britain's designs on this hostile African shoreline came to little fruition. The last British slaver had been prosecuted forty years before Burton arrived at Gelele's gates. There was a simplistic assumption behind Dick's mission. For three hundred years Europeans had indulged in an inhuman diaspora of Black Ivory. It has been estimated that eleven million slaves were shipped from the west coast since the 16th century. And Gelele's faith in his principal industry was but a drop in the ocean compared with the monopolistic slaving devices of Charles II's 17th-century Company of Royal Adventurers. It was a thankless task for Burton to persuade this black despot to adapt to changing codes of white behaviour.

It was now August 1864. Richard had come home again and Isabel raced down to the docks to meet him. It was his last government mission to the dark continent. In London, Speke and Grant had returned amidst extraordinary scenes of public acclaim. Britain had, at last, found true heroes for the hour. And now the illustrious David Livingstone had joined the other explorers in England after his arduous Zambesi River march. Richard was not altogether excluded from this limelight. Within a few days, he was to witness one of the most tragic moments of his life.

XIII

Jealous and mortal, white soulling ant bleeding from an African heart, there was no going back.

ONE WOULD IMAGINE FROM BURTON'S BITTERNESS THAT JACK really had been given his second attempt at the Nile source on a silver platter. It came as something of a shock to Speke and Grant, once they had embarked on their monumental expedition, to learn that the Foreign Office had reneged on its contribution to the voyage and furthermore the RGS themselves had reduced their offer *pari passu*. Jack had to dip into his pocket for a further £1,000.

Speke will always be spoken of in the shadow of a Burton book, yet it was Jack who first strode west of Lake Victoria to the Kingdom of Karagwe, where King Rumanika offered him considerable hospitality, and it was Jack who first entered the Kingdom of Buganda where the fearsome Mutesa ruled. At Karagwe, while Grant fell ill with fever, Jack amused and amazed himself by measuring one of Rumanika's outsize wives. He recorded the startling girths of 23-inch arms, 48-inch chest, a thigh of 31 inches and a calf of 20 inches. Quite unintentionally, this proto-anthropologist made rather a fool of himself in choosing such details, for when they were published from his *Journal*, it was apparent that rather than a brilliant and curious anthropologist-explorer, he was a man who remained all his life quite mystified by the proximity of women —

. . . After getting her to sidle and wriggle into the middle of the hut, I did as promised and then took her dimensions . . . and I believe I could have obtained this more accurately if I could have laid her on the floor. Not knowing what difficulties I should have to contend with in such a piece of engineering, I tried to get her height by raising her up. This, after infinite exertions on the part of both, was accomplished, when she sank down again fainting, for her blood had rushed to her head. Meanwhile, the daughter, a lass of sixteen, sat stark-naked before us, sucking at a milk-pot, on which her father kept her at work by holding a rod in his hand; for, as fattening as is the first duty of female life, it must be duly enforced by the rod if necessary. I got up a bit of a flirtation with missy, and induced her to rise and shake hands with me. Her features were lovely . . .

As for King Mutesa, and his three hundred strong harem, his habit of executing the girls daily and of burning servants alive, and his insistence on Jack taking three girls in their early teens as brides—well, Speke trod carefully. He distracted Mutesa with his ability to shoot birds out of the sky with one of his many muzzle-loaders.

Jack was now close to the northernmost tip of the lake, and he made up his mind to trek alone the remainder of the journey. He wanted to find the mysterious outlet of water which would prove him right. Pretty much on a trumped-up scheme, he sent James Grant north by north-west of his own passage along the lake shoreline, up to the further Kingdom of King Kamrasi's Bunyoro. Poor Grant, in addition to fever, had a very painful leg, but he accepted his commander's proposal. Jack had a ten-day journey to find the waterfall of his imaginings. On July 28, 1862, he reached a broad stretch of stones which dipped below the lips of the great lake and seemed to evacuate a mass of water across many hundreds of yards. It was an awesome sight, and yet it wasn't the gigantic falls of spume white exultance he had hoped for. In his mind he had pictured something much more ostentatious for the source of the White Nile—

. . . The scene was not exactly what I expected; for the broad surface of the lake was shut out from view by the spur of a hill, and the falls, about twelve feet deep, and four hundred to five hundred feet broad, were broken by rocks. Still it was a sight that attracted one to it for hours—the roar of the waters, the thousands of passenger-fish, leaping at the falls with all their might, the Wasoga and Waganda fishermen coming out in boats and taking post on all the rocks with rod and hook, hippopotami and crocodiles lying sleepily on the water, the ferry at work above the falls, and cattle driven down to drink at the margin of the lake, made, in all, with the pretty nature of the country — small hills, grassy-topped, with trees in the folds, and gardens on the lower slopes — as interesting a picture as one could wish to see . . .

He stood splash centre of the pearl of Africa. It was he, Jack Hanning Speke, who had reached the goal of all European dreamers, and nobody could take that away from him. In the future, his geographical alignments could be taken to the cleaners with derision, even his working methods were to be chastised, but he had discovered the main water source. He tried to persuade his porters to shave their heads and kneel to pray with him for deliverance. Not unnaturally, Seedy Bombay demurred. And continuing with his former practice he named the vast and shallow cataract the Ripon Falls, after the new President of the RGS. If that wasn't a hint for the Society's Gold Medal, what was? To the average porter lugging an eighth of a ton of Speke's hunting bags it must have meant little. For untold centuries men had fished and ferried themselves around these falls, and one wonders what they had in their minds when presented with these first white adventurers. Did they believe in the determination to see water-falls and climb hills and designate the hills with strange titles? Or did they entertain the most colossal suspicion of these motives? After these explorers, and later missionaries, who might follow?

Speke and Grant were believed dead by London after the first eighteen months of their expedition. Consul John Petherick was sent up to Gondokoro with money and provisions. He, too, suddenly disappeared. Immediately, the wealthy sportsman Sam Baker and his lovely wife set off in pursuit of Speke, Grant, Petherick, and indeed the Fountains of the Niles if they were lucky enough.

Speke and Grant reunited in Bunyoro, and they made their historic final march up to Gondokoro by February 1863. The Bakers first greeted them, and then Petherick turned up from nowhere, much to Speke's anger. Speke assumed the man had been ivory trading and slave dealing, and complained that Petherick was responsible for delivering goods and equipment over a year too late. With Jack's new fame came a quick and easy arrogance. When Jack Speke and James Grant returned to London they were the men of the hour. They bathed in the applause.

Dick's *The Lake Regions* had infuriated Speke even before he had read the book. Two years before he reached his Ripon Falls, he wrote —

. . . Burton has published some bitter things concerning myself in allusion to the lake expedition, and I must now say that if he has been impinging my honor [*sic*] I shall be very sorry that I have glossed over many of his translations . . . it is a lamentable affair going into contest with one with whom I was associated for such a length of time, but it must be done if he has published *such* matter as he wrote to the Govt. unless he has also published my response which I am sure he would not do . . . If the spirits of Burton's victims could only raise their voices to England now and tell their tale without a fault what strange rebukes would appear against the would be injured man who injures without scruple yet feels more sensitively than most other men . . . I promise . . . not only a large book, but one that justifies my every action no matter from what side attacked. If for no other object I desire to return as speedily as possible to set men's opinions on a proper train for judging fairly between us.

Before Dick got back to London from Fernando Po, Speke had declared publicly, 'Had I been alone on the first expedition, I should have settled the Nile in 1859', and later, to another audience, 'I don't wish to say anything about Captain Burton. I taught him at his own request, the geography of the countries we traversed.' Jack incorporated the new phrase 'Honour est a Nilo' in his Somerset coat of arms, and in a haze of sneer and wrath, as one contemporary put it, Burton crept back to England and this emotional gunfight which compelled him on to a platform of retribution.

Sir Roderick Murchison, and the RGS, were quick to arrange a confrontation between Speke and Burton, with the eminent Living-stone taking the chair, at a meeting for the British Association for the Advancement of Science in the East Wing of the Mineral Water Hospital at Bath. It was an annual event, to enable travellers to meet a select audience. What promised to be a black Barnum of a do, was not ennobled by Jack's hasty, 'If Burton appears on the platform at Bath I will kick him', and in order not to be upstaged by 'Honour' Jack, Burton replied with a suitable rebuttal, '*That* settles it. By God, he *shall* kick me!'

Many observers were far from convinced by the 1864 publication of Speke's *Journal of the Discovery of the Sources of the Nile*, and his *What Led to the Discovery of the Sources of the Nile*. There really is no account-ing for Speke's extraordinary willingness to appear on a platform with Burton. Even with two books out that year, a hero's welcome, the applause of the nation, he was acutely aware of the shortcomings of his own argument. Because, (a) the Lake Tanganyika still stood seven or eight hundred feet above *his own* measurements, and he was in grave doubt about these measurements; (b) the lake of his Victoria still didn't match the fall of the Nile further north in the dry season; (c) his assessment of these 'Mountains of the Moon' was demonstrably weak. Jack guessed Dick would have half a dozen arguments to bring forward at the Bath conference. Burton intended to explain to the audience that Lake Victoria actually swelled in the lower Nile's dry season, therefore how could it feed the Nile? In his opinion, the southern borders of the lake flooded for up to thirteen miles, whereas the northern shore shallows were not inundated, this meant there was not enough pressure to pour forth a single Nile source at the so-called Ripon Falls. And in his opinion, there was no lake anywhere that could be taken so freely as the head of a river. Was Lake Baikal the head of the Yenessie River? Was Lake Geneva the head of the Rhône, simply because the river issued from it? Or Lake Winnipeg the head of the Saskatchewan?

On the day before the grand debate there was a crucial and silent confrontation between Speke and Burton on the platform at Bath. Isabel Burton recorded the event with her own peculiar asides. For some reason she felt slighted. Dick hadn't been invited to join the most superior people in a more advantageous seating arrangement. Nevertheless there came a crude moment when Speke was about to take up a chair within spitting distance of Burton. 'He looked at Richard,' wrote Isabel, 'and at me, and we at him. I shall never forget his face. It was full of sorrow, of yearning, and perplexity. Then he seemed to turn to stone. After a while he began to fidget a great deal . . .'

It was an excruciating moment. There were dozens of celebrated scientists staring poor Jack out. Was he or was he not going to kick Dick Burton off the platform? Those closest at hand held their breath; the pause was deafening. Suddenly Jack threw up his hands and lurched from his chair. Was this to be the moment of the proffered foot? No. Speke blurted out,

'Oh, I cannot stand this any longer!' and he attempted to leave the platform. Whereupon a courteous and seemingly hypnotised neighbour on the file of chairs beside him asked,

'Shall you want your chair again, sir?' But Speke was already in motion. 'May I have it?' the neighbourly gent continued. Speke was well across the platform heading towards the stairs, to the tune of the neighbour's plaintive, 'Shall you come back?'

'I hope not!' Speke answered in his retreat.

That was at 1.30 in the early afternoon of Thursday, September 15; by 4.30 that same afternoon Jack Speke lay dead in a field beside a low stone wall six miles away to the east of Bath. He had arranged to stay at Neston Park, by the village of Box, a long straggling hamlet. The Park belonged to an uncle, John Fuller.

On this particular afternoon Jack hurried back to Neston without a word to anyone else in that hushed conference hall. The six-mile journey took him the half-hour of a crisp cab trot. At two in the afternoon he had plenty of time to catch up with his cousin George Fuller, a surgeon Thomas F. Snow, and a game-keeper Daniel Davis, who were partridge shooting.

Jack carried a Lancaster muzzle-loading shotgun. It was a heavy instrument but it possessed feather-light hammers. He was walking 600 yards behind the others in the direction the beaters indicated As he reached the low wall the keeper, according to George Fuller, turned to see Speke atop the wall gripping the gun by the muzzle. Fuller states that when he heard the gun fire he looked round to observe Speke falling off the low wall. The keeper was marking birds for the two guns, Fuller and Snow, and the two men stood sixty yards apart. Neither witnessed the firing of Speke's gun. The wall consisted of loosely knitted dry-stone segments, and it is not at all unlikely that Jack's foot slipped, and the subsequent jerk on the Lancaster loader released a cartridge. Fuller and Davis sprinted back to the injured man. His gun lay beside him. The left barrel was empty. The right barrel was at half-cock. The gun had no safety-clasp. The only safety measure was to carry the gun unloaded and broken. The cartridge had passed upwards through his left lung penetrating the auricle of the heart. Speke lay on the ground bleeding profusely. He warned Fuller away from him.

'Don't move me,' he murmured.

The surgeon came running up to the group. There was nothing he could do. Jack Speke bled to death at their feet. The blood, flesh and gut havoc of that spewing cartridge at such close range left him little life. He died fifteen minutes later. Jack appeared to have stumbled and touched the gun hammer against the stonework. The slightest rub could have slipped the hammer. It seemed to be an act of thoughtlessness. So accustomed to guns was he that he didn't bother to unload the gun and break it before stepping on to and over the broken part of the wall.

Fifty years later, Fuller in his dotage wrote a rambling and highly inaccurate description of the events leading up to the fatality. Nevertheless, no matter how many dates and details his memory failed him on, his words on Speke's gunmanship that day are important:

My gamekeeper, who was with us, and I, both noticed this carelessness in the use of the gun by Hanning. We therefor avoided being very close to him when walking the fields, and in crossing the wall where the accident happened both the gamekeeper and I were at some distance from Hanning.

On the Friday morning an urgent meeting was called in a private room of the Bath assembly hall. The RGS Council huddled together. Meanwhile, the Burtons took the platform to await the arrival of Jack Speke. Shortly after, David Livingstone and Roderick Murchison took the platform, and in front of a hushed, expectant and crowded hall, Murchison announced that Captain Speke had been killed in a shooting accident the previous afternoon.

Dick slumped into his chair like a man thumped in the heart. 'I saw by the workings of his face,' Isabel declared, 'the terrible emotion he was controlling, and the shock he had received.' There is no evidence to the effect that he reeled back from the platform crying, 'By God he's killed himself!', but this legend persisted in the weeks which followed this extraordinarily dramatic death. Dick Burton retired quickly from the platform, after a few garbled words about life in Dahomey, and left the hall. The assembled audience was in hushed uproar. They had been robbed of the argument of the year, and were now confronted with a baffling death nobody could explain. Dick returned to his hotel rooms in Bath and as Isabel records, he burst into tears.

Five days after the tragedy, Burton wrote to a friend in Fernando Po: 'Nothing is known of Speke's death. I saw him at 1.30 pm and at 4 pm he was dead. The charitable say that he shot himself, the uncharitable say that I shot him.' Either portion of that remark can be taken for a cheap parting shot at poor Jack. Burton was thrown into temporary confusion; he was offended by *The Times* obituary which came down heavily on Speke's side as the discoverer of the source of the Nile, and smiled with self-satisfaction now that word was coming through from Samuel and Florence Baker's expedition to the Luta Nzige (renamed Lake Albert) and the third of the mysterious water plains south of Gondokoro. The Bakers had been sighted, and their news was that this Lake Albert was as large as Lake Tanganyika! It was a gross exaggeration, but it suited Dick's basic theory that there was more to the true source than Speke's broad and shallow falls. Dick promptly ordered the printing of a nasty little essay under the title of *The Nile Basin*, some 15,000 words which amounted to what would have been the principal refutation of Speke at Bath. The text was augmented by a malicious piece of rubbish by James Macqueen, the journalist, more an addendum to Dick's essay, titled *Captain Speke's Discovery of the Source of the Nile*. The battle, in Dick's mind, was still very much on.

But to be fair to Burton, no matter how he felt obliged to pursue the battle, he could not restrain a kindly impulse the following year:

> I do not stand forth as an enemy of the departed; that no man can better appreciate the noble qualities of energy, courage, and perseverance which he so eminently possessed than I do, who knew him for so many years, and who travelled with him as a brother, until the unfortunate rivalry respecting the Nile Sources arose like the ghost of discord between us, and was fanned to a flame by the enmity and the ambition of *friends*.

Dick saw light at the end of the tunnel. Perhaps Baker's lake would add fuel to his belief that the River Rusizi flowed out of Tanganyika north into Luta Nzige. Indeed, the RGS had to take very seriously Baker's claims for another true source of the Nile. For Baker had no axe to grind; he wasn't in deadly geographic combat with anyone else, a fact, when he published his fascinating account of a grand expedition with Florence his wife, *The Albert N'Yanza, Great Basin of the Nile*, heartily endorsed by an eager public who rushed out to the shops to buy the book. The reader of the day wanted the warming, almost domestic picture of a young wife like Florence risking death, starvation and fevers to travel alongside her good man into the densest *unknown* of the black heartland.

It was to take the further explorations of Livingstone, V. L. Cameron and Henry Stanley (twice), over the next eighteen years, to persuade Dick Burton he was wrong about his Lake Tanganyika. Burton need not be too harshly blamed for his intransigence. Livingstone believed, for example, that it was *his* Lualaba which flowed into the Nile. It wasn't. Stanley in a famous and monumental trek found this river swerving west to merge with the flow of the great Congo River. It was V. L. Cameron who proved conclusively that the western side of Lake Tanganyika flowed and flooded through marsh and shallow inundation out on to a minor river, and ultimately into the Lualaba.

Speke's end brought about another death. For much of the discussion about Jack's suicide originated with Burton's 'the charitable say that he shot himself, the uncharitable say that I shot him'. It wasn't a phrase of wishful thinking. It was an abdication from reason. Within himself Dick was talking about an assassination of his own spirit. No longer now, with Jack gone, was there a chance of storing up bile.

Dick had had his weapons taken away from him. Furthermore, the popularity of Baker's book proved just how fickle was the reading public. They now looked further afield for their African Lords of Conquest.

As far as the Royal Geographical Society was concerned he was not their man for future explorations. The Society, let it be said, had already given him enough encouragement. No university wanted his Arabic and linguistic abilities. No publisher was keen to take up any more of his peculiar sorcery of footnotes the size of novellas. Dick Burton had become his own worst enemy. His narrative texts were inflated personal malice, thereby reducing his anthropological brilliance in the notes to a form of *grangerism*. And he had managed to achieve a literary style as obscure as his professional standing in the Foreign Office.

The years to come were going to dash every expectation he had of his own geographical prophecies in Africa. To borrow from Kenneth Ingham of Makerere University, Uganda, both Speke and Burton were 'still on trial'. Speke was now dead. But Dick burned, he lay wounded and hungry for the truth about those great lakes he might never return to.

By the close of 1864, he had one booklet underway, a strange and personally humorous poem, published anonymously. For four more years he would publish nothing else. The silence was deafening. He had published seventeen works, ranging from the Sind travels to *Falconry* and *Bayonet Exercise*, and from the Mecca and Harar marches to West Africa. And of them all, *A Personal Narrative of a Pilgrimage to El-Medinah and Meccah* (1855) is a masterpiece of hazardous orientalism. It ought to have made him the most famous explorer of Europe. The youthful mixture of cocksureness and diverting addenda did not prepare the public for the serious and dazzling anthropology it contained. *The Lake Regions of Central Africa* (1860) was not perhaps as fine a book, for contained within lay the seed of incomplete exploration and the chapters were in themselves only stepping stones to the Nile solution.

If Burton had died at the age of forty-four, his memory might have happily collected that peculiar posthumous quality only the English can supply: he would have passed away at the peak of his abilities. It could have been recorded that his promise was infinite. And a puritanical English phlegm could bracket him in that virgin's closet — a cult figure quite unsullied by the decay of the years.

His achievements would have been just enough to distinguish his name with the perpetuity of *firsts* — Mecca and Harar; for there is very little in the British imagination which allows for the maturity of years. How often has one heard the words *promise* and *potential* bandied about in English Letters? Poor old Dick looked jolly promising at forty-four. Death would have forgiven him his excesses. If any Briton was a victim of the national pastime of not playing the game, not sticking to the rules of genial understatement, it was Burton. Dirty Dick, bad hat, he would look out across the years for more time than he cared for.

He was, in fact, the very opposite of Conrad's Mr Kurtz, in *Heart of Darkness*. Kurtz had spent time writing a report on the necessity of the white man entering Africa as if he were a God; in order that the natives might learn the Fall, and in order that this White God might more accurately observe the black recognition of baseness. Mr Kurtz lay sick as the narrator hove in view, dying of the most complete expression of self-knowledge — a deep awareness of his mortality. Kurtz witnessed the Fall, and lay siege to the baseness in his character at one and the same time. The horror was too great a vision of reality for him to absolve. And Kurtz was made mad. An eyewitness to too much light.

Dick, the fox, was run to ground. None of this blinding light for him. Dick skulked. Beside a man like Kurtz, Burton was a model of sanity. It was an intellectual strait-jacket he had himself designed. Now, the years would not matter. Isabel might bathe the wounds, and the threadbare carpet might beckon his slippers, and the fire glow a draught redeemer from the cold of the hostile 'pygmies' outside. Sip the brandy. Cut the cigar.

As for *his* Africa, others would take it from him. His Afrophobia would return to him again and again. The passions he had once entertained in the continent so newly penetrated were to echo back at him whenever a new discovery was made or a question uttered like chieftain Comoro's to Samuel and Florence Baker in 1864: 'Suppose you get to the great lake, what will you do with it? What will be the good of it? If you find that the large river does flow from it, what then?'

But it was years before he was able to accept the utter estrangement between Africa and himself. Seventeen years on he declared, 'There is a time to leave the Dark Continent, and that is when the *idée fixe* begins to develop itself. Madness comes from Africa . . .'

As Karen Blixen bade farewell to her African Farm in the Ngong Hills, Kenya, never to return there, she wrote, 'The noble wave of the mountain rose above the surrounding flat land, all air-blue. But it was so far away that the four peaks looked trifling, hardly distinguishable, and different from the way they looked from the farm. The outline of the mountain was slowly smoothed and levelled out by the hand of distance.' Her leavetaking held none of the torment of Burton's faintly melodramatic words. Unlike Karen, his 'hand of distance' wounded him. His white soul lay in exile.

And melodramatic has been too often the only means of describing Burton. He is elusive and he hides from us. It is not easy to espy him with a form of inductive phenomonology. And to make use of Husserl's 'normal standpoint' and say yes, there he is, this is Dirty Dick plain. The nature of the man glints at us slyly. Then there comes a sudden change of focus, and the image refracts.

The Foreign Office travels to come would never reimpose the strength of the African voyages on his mind's retina. The older he was the closer the horizons walled in, until in due course, they would assume the nearness of a window where he leaned watching the winter migration of birds which tapped on the glass pane. Cunningly, and with heart's wound disguised—his longing, his first encounter, thrilled foundling eye of discovery, knowledge sought in a hundred religions and forty languages, the blunt realism of confrontation with the outside—how they would all shrink into a desuetude.

XIV

Almost savage, he strove with none,
for none was worth his strife: he chose
to not see the beast in the hour-glass.

TOO MUCH STRESS HAS BEEN LAID ON THE MINOR ROLE OF A
consul, in particular in the case of Burton. The British consul, in fact,
did quite well for himself on an average income of not less than £500
a year, plus all travel found, clothes and family supplementary grants.
Poets and political adventurers from Wilfrid Scawen Blunt to Sir
Roger Casement were usually much younger than Burton when they
took up posts far from United Kingdom shores. Lord Russell, at the
Foreign Office, with a certain patronising cant not unduly concealed,
offered Dick the post of consul at Santos, in Brazil. The small port
town had its own value as a trading station, but beside Rio de Janeiro,
Pará (now Belém) and Bahia (now Salvador), it was a relatively small
outpost. It was within reasonable distance of 'social Brasil', the royal
court at Petropolis, the richer estates around Rio, and it was two days'
hard ride to São Paulo. Dick accepted.

The Anthropological Society now claimed 500 members, including
the young and celebrated scientist William Crookes, and Charles
Bradlaugh, politician and Free Thinker. At a farewell supper for the
Burtons, Dick toasted everybody's health including the late Speke's.
He virtually apologised for the scurrility in his slim volume *The Nile
Basin*, and he asked the members present to make a contribution to
Jack's memorial bust.

He took his wife to Portugal for a two-month holiday, and in his usual way departed alone for Rio, leaving her to go back to London and pack and pay sundry bills. She would follow him out. Isabel spent a week at a convent in Kensington, and the rest of her month was filled with goodbyes and packing. He had entrusted her with the normal Foreign Office grant of £150 for 'sundries' and it happily covered all unpaid accounts for brandy and cigars. She followed him out in August 1865, in her role as the consul's wife.

Almost as soon as she stepped foot on Rio harbour she became delirious with a fever. Dick took this as a fine opportunity to practise hypnosis, and he discovered to his delight his powers of concentration definitely calmed her. The fever remained, but her mental panic had subsided. It was definitely not the last attempt at such a strange, even unique form of control over his wife. For he had, like many others of his day ever since Queen Victoria's unwisely publicised efforts to reincarnate her late Consort's voice, become fascinated with the rapping tables and foaming mouths of ether which had made spiritualism so popular. In England this came to a glorious head when William Crookes could not persuade the august body of the Royal Society of the amazing feats of Daniel Dunglas Home.

Dick and Isabel loathed their new house in Santos. Isabel called the steaming hot shoreline a place 'knee-deep in mangrove swamps'; and they hastily moved inland to São Paulo, where she discovered a derelict and cavernous convent. It had a large garden, but much more important for a stranger new to Brazil's climate the house stood more than 2,000 feet above sea level. Dick chose a forty-foot-long former communal dining room as a study. It was there he began an untiring vigil which would later produce his two-volume *The Highlands of Brazil*, a translation of the great Portuguese poet Camoens' *The Lusiads*, and a collection of Hindu tales, *Vikram and the Vampire*.

Almost as soon as the Burtons moved into the convent, with the aid of a thirty-five-year-old black dwarf named Chico, Dick left for a twenty-day expedition to inspect a lead mine. The purpose of this trip had nothing to do with his consulship. He had acquired a share in the mine's equity, and believed a fortune lay at his feet. Consuls are expressly forbidden by HMG to indulge in commercial exercises, and Dick knew this. Meanwhile, Isabel rode horses, studied the language, decorated the large rooms, and practised fencing with her husband's sabre. We discover Dick at this time panning for rubies in rivers and his wife writing letters of self-introduction into the diplomatic circles of Petropolis. Dick gave two lectures to invited audiences in Rio. They were both presented to the Emperor, Don Pedro, who kept officers of much senior rank in queue while he appeared fascinated by Burton's remarks.

Dick carried out as few of his consular duties as possible. Unfortunately he could not avoid the acute embarrassment of a quite charming event. A young couple urgently requested the consul to marry them. Dick could hardly refuse, as he had no excuse at the ready. He grimly pronounced the happy couple man and wife in a British Civil Ceremony, and shot off immediately for a nine-month expedition down the mighty river São Francisco in an effort to hunt a rumoured El Dorado of the forest. The century before, a Portuguese rascal called Raposo wrote a sketchy description of a lost city in the jungle. He and his comrades were trying to get back to the coast, when to their surprise they stumbled upon high walls, tall temples, and statuary encrusted with what looked like gold. Raposo and his men were exhausted, alas, and the snakes and the hunger drove them back to the coast. Future generations, including the vainglorious Percy Fawcett, have been fascinated by Raposo's tale. Dick travelled the 1,500 miles of the river searching for strange stones marked with drawings perhaps a thousand years old. He made detailed notes on villages and river-life, and when he emerged from the Rio São Francisco with not a trace of any city in the forest, he was peeved indeed to discover Isabel was unable to meet him off the river-boat in Rio. Poor woman, she had waited beside every commercial launch for the past ten days and by accident she had missed the crucial conveyer of her earthly bliss.

She took one look at his yellow features and high fever, and rushed him home to the convent in São Paulo. Doctors were promptly called, and she daily administered 36 glasses of calomel, a purgative, and castor oil. The local doctor added his knowledge to hers, and covered Dick's legs and arms with leeches. Isabel believed he nearly died from a combination of 'liver congestion' and 'inflammation of the lung'. If, as does seem likely, he had suffered a dose of hepatitis, from the São Francisco river water, he could have died from their ministrations. One can only presume he kept a sizable crate of brandy beneath his hammock and sweated it out. Dick was still a strong man. In her diary Isabel wrote that he screamed out in pain. Sufferers from hepatitis may rarely do that, but a man purged with half a gallon of mercurous chloride and forty leeches every day might be forgiven his screams.

It was at this stage in his life that something definitely cracked.

In July 1868, he suffered what resembles a breakdown. Dick informed his wife that 'he could not stand it any longer'. Isolation and obscurity were too painful. Isabel wrote of São Paulo:

It had given him that illness, it was far away from the world, it was no advancement, it led to nothing. He was quite right. I felt very sorry, because up to the present it was the only home I had ever really had quietly with him, and we had had it for three years; but I soon sold up everything, and we came down to Santos, and embarked on the 24th of July, 1868. Here he applied for leave, as the doctors advised him not to go to England at once, but to go down south to Buenos Ayres for a trip, and he asked me to go to England and see if I could not induce them to give him another post. I saw Richard off down south, and taking an affectionate leave of all kind friends, embarked for England.

In her luggage she took a number of manuscripts. They were all in various degrees of completion. They were her own hand-copied versions of his unfinished translations, the Camoens' poetry, the epic poem *Uruguay* by Basilio da Gama, and parts of Dick's descriptive narrative *The Highlands of Brazil*. On the voyage home she would continue with her copper-plate writing, and in some passages even supply the necessary editing. He had begun to allow her access to his work. She could copy out with her clearer hand his scrawled impatient slant. Isabel had gratefully accepted this new role. She had become, in the absence of any greater emotional demand made on her, a carrier, a secretary, and a nurse. It made up just a little for his refusal to share his wanderings, those forays down rivers and into forests, quests and truant runs into the unknown, in which he specialised. And this was just about all he considered her good for. In due course his cruelty would rebound on him. For Isabel was developing a deft hand at warding away these blows, a thickness of skin was hers now, and as for the editing, he hardly cared for the books he was churning out; if she could add a line here or a line there, so much the better. And she did.

As soon as Isabel was safely out of sight, Dick climbed out of his sickbed and dispatched himself to Montevideo in Uruguay, and then on to the eastern shore of the Paraná River, on the Paraguay border. Between 1865 and 1870, Paraguay suffered a humiliating war against the combined armies of Brazil, Uruguay, and Argentina. In the most simplistic terms, it appears to have been Brazil's fault. First they attacked little Paraguay. Then the extremely incautious Paraguayan dictator Francisco Lopez led an army into Argentine with the intention of surprising Brazil from the south-east. In no time, Uruguay sensed it might also be overrun by Lopez' army, and all three countries declared war against the landlocked territory of Paraguay. Lopez' country was reduced by 1870 from an estimated population of 1,400,000 to 221,000.

Dick spent over two months 'convalescing' on the Rio Paraná border with Paraguay. He made enough notes to compile a manuscript entitled *Letters from the Battlefields of Paraguay*, but he had a fairly luxurious view of Paraguay, from the winning team's heights. If he had trekked west above the Chaco desert on the Rio Paraguai, he would have seen death and malnutrition and slaughter on the scale of a diaspora no Arab slaver or West African black emperor ever conceived. Dick hugged the border lines, and sympathised with Brazil, and then returned to Montevideo to hunt out an English Club on the Plaza Independencia. Much to his dismay this centre of an Englishman's world was nowhere to be found. He went on to Argentina, where Wilfrid Blunt, the poet, met up with him in the teeming English society of Buenos Aires. Twenty years Dick's junior, wealthy and equipped with charm and good looks, from early days he had been impressed by Burton. Dick had become a legend to younger men, this socially unacceptable and embattled scholar of Arabic with a Byronic streak about him, now tossed on the farthest shore of the Foreign Office's imagination, this 'desperately learned man' still associating with those 'pygmies' whose 'dress and appearance were those suggesting a released convict'.

Blunt had been influenced by the D'Orsays and Dickenses of his day, he was a dandy in his white suiting ribbed with silver and feather *voile*, and his sensibilities were shocked by Burton's brandy stains:

> Burton was at that time at the lowest point I fancy of his whole career, and in point of respectability at his very worst. His consular life at Santos, without any interesting work to his hand or proper vent for his energies, had thrown him into a habit of drink . . . and he seldom went to bed sober.

It quickly became apparent to Dick he was in the presence of a new generation, younger and bolder, yet rather too well laundered for his liking. It is as if Dick literally started to bellow across the elegant *bodega* floor —

> In his talk he affected an extreme brutality, and if one could have believed the whole of what he said, he had indulged in every vice and committed every crime. I soon found, however, that most of these recitals were indulged in *pour épater le bourgeois* and that his humanity was more pretended than real. Even the ferocity of his countenance gave place at

times to more agreeable expressions, and I can just understand the infatuated fancy of his wife that in spite of his ugliness he was the most beautiful man alive. He had, however, the power of assuming the abominable which cannot be exaggerated.

Dick talked about crossing the Andes with pack-horses, of riding to Chile, of exploring Patagonia, in particular (it struck Blunt) taking up any route which might offer secret gold or unplundered mysteries: the brandy was getting out of hand. In private he was worried stiff about whether any publisher would take the books he had sent on ahead with Isabel. He hoped she might drip her charm and tears under the nose of the Foreign Office with some effect. And he was on the verge of chucking his Santos consulship in a final letter of bitterness to London. He was not going to impart these lowly worries to Blunt, but Richard was too drunk to notice the mask slip. The young poet was no dullard like Jack Speke; Wilfrid Blunt was of a new breed, sharp and clever, with his sonnets neatly tucked up his perfumed sleeve. Blunt was a convinced Home Rule man, he passionately believed in the cause of a United Ireland, and it struck him dourly, this sight of Burton, his hat and head askew, this errant son of yet another minor English family who had benefited from landed wealth based on clearances and the impoverishment of the Irish.

I came at last to look upon him as less dangerous than he seemed, and even to be in certain aspects of his mind, a *sheep in wolf's clothing*. The clothing, however, was a very complete disguise, and as I have said he was not a man to play with, sitting alone with him far into the night, especially in such an atmosphere of violence as Buenos Aires then could boast, when men were shot almost nightly in the streets. Burton was a grim being to be with at the end of his second bottle with a gaucho's navaja handy to his hand.

From September 1868, Dick virtually disappeared until March the following year. He did indeed cross the Andes, and he is rumoured to have travelled with the notorious 'Tichborne Claimant', a fat figure of a man who had laid claim to a vast fortune and estate in England following the death of a baronet, and who later was exposed as an extraordinarily convincing impostor, as much a character of intense fascination to the British then as perhaps the life of Grand Duchess Anastasia, daughter of Czar Nicholas II, is for us now; and more tittle-tattle reported Dick in hand-to-hand fighting on a Peruvian mountainside when he suffered a fearsome wound and dispatched four villains, we are led to believe.

Treating himself to yet another bottle of the best stuff, Dick is to be discovered in a café in Lima, Peru, after this gap of six months. Perhaps, at long last, he had emerged from his self-imposed exile.

Malcolm Lowry's consul, from *Under The Volcano*, had sat too long at the bar table for the waiter to clear up the artillery of glasses. For him, his exile was of a similar nature:

The consul dropped his eyes at last. How many bottles since then? In how many glasses, how many bottles had he hidden himself, since then alone? Suddenly he saw them, the bottles of aguardiente, of anis, of jerez, the glasses, a babel of glasses – towering, like the smoke from the train that day – built to the sky, then falling, the glasses toppling and crashing, falling downhill from the Generalife Gardens, the bottles breaking . . . the consul sat very still . . . How indeed could he hope to find himself, to begin again when, somewhere, perhaps, in one of those lost or broken bottles, in one of those glasses, lay, forever, the solitary clue to his identity? How could he go back and look now, scrabble among the broken glass, under the eternal bars, under the oceans?

An acquaintance approached Richard Burton from across the street in Lima and congratulated him. 'What for?' Dick muttered. Word had reached Lima that Burton had been offered the consulate at Damascus. It was the extraordinary decision of Gladstone's new broom in government office. It was a highly controversial posting. Burton had leaped over many heads. But it was a glorious stroke of luck. Dick lurched forward blearily, half afraid it was the shadow in the eternal bar of his mind which had spoken.

Damascus was the job he had always yearned after. It meant back to Arabia. Back to the city he was later to call 'the beauty-spot of Allah upon Earth'. Burton hastened to post off two acceptances. He boarded a boat and sailed for Buenos Aires, voyaging around Cape Horn in the Drake Strait. It was just as well he set off. The posting reached him over four months after the decision was taken. And three months after Isabel's last victorious letter to him aburst with the good news.

While he was in South America Burton displayed a total lack of curiosity for the indigenous population of Brazilian forests. The ethnologist in him disappeared. There were over two million Indians in the South American lowland forests. These lowland tribes were principally made up of Carib, Tupi, Arawak and Jê groups. If he'd possessed the inclination to explore, his natural abilities would have overtaken such groundwork laid by the brothers Richard and Robert Schomburgk in British Guiana. The entire basin was a virgin paradise for the anthropologist and fieldworker in comparative sociology between the indigenous groupings. Burton dismissed these forest-dwellers in a few words found in his later *Unexplored Syria* (1872): 'The aborigines of the New World were savages that can interest only in Fenimore Cooper.'

XV

Damascus aborted, and their lives
filled with flight and chaos, indebted to
darkness.

DICK RETURNED TO ENGLAND, COLLECTED HIS PAPERS FROM THE
Foreign Office and signed his agreement. The job at Damascus offered
him £1,000 a year, a genuine increase of £400. Nevertheless, he could
not help but feel slighted when Lord Clarendon confronted him with
the points raised by those many who objected to this new posting.
First of all, Damascus was a city of 200,000 souls, of which more than
two thirds were Muslim. The remainder were Jews, Greeks, Armenians, even a Muslim renegade sect called *Shazlieh* who had adopted the
Syrian Christianity. Ten years earlier, 3,000 Christians were butchered
inside the walled city by Muslims, and, to put it bluntly, Clarendon was
disturbed at the prospect of sending this unbeliever Burton to such a
city, after his notorious ride into Mecca a quarter of a century ago. It
did not help matters to find on his return that the publishers were
galloping into a third edition of Dick's *Pilgrimage to Meccah*. Clarendon
indicated that if Dick could not vouch for a most proper and rigorous
performance of his official duties as consul he would have to recall him.
Dick was obliged to get down on his knees to assure the Foreign Office
'to undertake to act with unusual prudence, and under all circumstances, to hold myself only answerable for all the consequences'. It was
a rash oath. But, at the time he had no choice. He desperately wanted
the job. Clarendon told him there were other, largely unnamed,

protesters from the Christian fence. Dick was rumoured to be a black-guard heathen; how much more strife might he kick up in Damascus?

There is some indication that the Foreign Office had not the nerve to renege on this posting; and so to cover all their tracks Lord Clarendon asked for Dick's undertaking he would closely inform his superior Consul-General in Beirut, S. Jackson Eldridge, of all his actions. Clarendon had been warned of the danger of employing Burton for Damascus by Sir Henry Elliot, British Ambassador at Constantinople. Elliot never ceased attacking Dick in private. The two men had never met, only corresponded, and yet for an unknown reason Elliot definitely had it in for Burton. He had already written to the Foreign Office, from Constantinople—

Damascus is probably the most fanatical town in the Empire, and the presence there, in the character of British Consul, of a person who had penetrated to the Prophet's shrine, is regarded as certain to cause exhibitions against him that may be productive of very undesirable consequences.

By the Musselman population Captain Burton is regarded either as having insulted their religion by taking part as an unbeliever in their most sacred rites, or else as having, at that time, been a Mohammedan and having become a renegade.

Under either supposition he would be regarded with aversion by most, and with hatred by very many of the population, and it is my duty to draw your Lordship's attention to a consideration which was probably lost sight of when Captain Burton was selected for the post.

Elliot was a career diplomat. Son of a famous father, he had followed a diplomatic life from Russia to Australia and was a Privy Councillor. Elliot's work possessed that infallible doggedness of a dutiful Crown employee, neither one to grab honours nor one seen to do the imprudent thing. Elliot was the son of Lord Minto, and it is indeed probable Minto, like the Blackwood family (near neighbours on the east side of Scotland), was a regular host to Jack Speke at the pinnacle of the explorer's fame. Being a Privy Councillor made Elliot a frequent judge of Indian and colonial appeals, and many a time Burton's name must have come up in his wrangles with the East India Company.

There were other natural enemies, in particular the then Amir of Syria, Mohammed Rashid, a rotund speck of ghastliness, the last living word in corruption, a filthy and besmirched jewel in the rotting Ottoman Empire, who ended his life at the vigorous hand of an assassin. Or so the British textbook will have us believe. Nowadays there is something very suspect about these classic schoolboy images we inherit of wicked Turks and the like; one only has to glance at the terms the Great Powers dunned from the Ottoman Empire at the signing of the 1878 Berlin Treaty—Cyprus was carved out to Britain, Bosnia and Herzegovina were gobbled up by Austria, Montenegro was ceded to Roumania, Italy had its eyes on Tripoli and Greece was claiming Crete. It suited Britain down to the ground to topple the Turks either by treaties or insults. This Syrian Amir did not like the idea of a consul turning up in Damascus who could speak Arabic and could easily be seen as yet another cursed English spy. And what was Dick's response to the furore raging about his head? He took six weeks off to tour France in the heady company of Algie Swinburne, Sir Frederick Leighton the painter, and a well-known opera singer Adelaide Kemble Sartoris. They were having such a good time that Dick in his inimitable fashion ordered his wife home to London to continue with the Damascus packing. Meanwhile, our man still supposedly ill with hepatitis, led his merry party on towards Vichy for the *waters*. Three weeks later, Isabel rebelled and rejoined Dick in the company of a mutual friend, J. J. Aubertin. Aubertin had lived in Brazil for many years, poet and scholar, he was once Superintendent of the British-built railway between Santos and São Paulo. He became a prosperous cotton merchant.

One can never quite get to the bottom of Burton's hepatitis. The sensation seeker will always murmur how he seemed to show classic symptoms of syphilis in a recumbent stage. Isabel was always quick to point out a fever which attacked his breathing, as if this was the most respectable way to describe the malady. On the other hand, any drinker as heavy as he could easily display all the debilities—yellowing of features, chronic thinness, wasting etc—of a man with cirrhosis. This was an illness Isabel would not record.

Dick gave Isabel the slip again in Turin. He would take the boat on to Beirut. She would go back and pack once more. Their relationship was distant enough to stretch to these insulting separations. Certainly she had the spirit to argue, sometimes she would turn back and join him in his fun; but she remained dutiful. She was his skivvy, a serf biding her time; yes it was a kind of love, she held on relentlessly, and he needed her for this. He was sure she would never leave him, neither would nor could. She was not going to give up and return in defeat to her parents. She was never going to desert her own Faith. And she had made an oath to herself, that week trembling before her wedding ceremony; she must train herself to take every kick, every blow that fate in the shape of her Richard presented. It took Isabel two months to clear up the sundries in London before she could depart for Syria.

Isabel quickly acquired a highly inflated picture of Burton's consular duties: she was under the misapprehension that her husband was representative for her Britannic Majesty from Baghdad in the Iraqui east, to Nablus deeper south in the Palestine Territory, to Aleppo in the north, almost 500 km above Beirut. She had created an imaginary principality. It would have struck Burton's immediate superior Eldridge, stationed in Beirut as Consul-General that he himself sat *half as close* to Aleppo as did Damascus. Isabel's mind ran a riot of grandiosity. Earlier, in Brazil, Wilfrid Blunt detected similarly awkward traits: 'She was indeed a very foolish woman, and did him at least as much harm in his career as good . . . it is a fine trait in his character that he should have borne with her absurdities for the sake of her love so long.'

Dick was under a tight rein. Neither Eldridge in Beirut nor Elliot in Constantinople was prepared to risk trouble with our man in Damascus. The Foreign Office had at last devised a scheme whereby they could get rid of Dick. It was apparent that some of his superiors were handing Burton enough rope with which to hang himself. How could he resist the opportunity to explore Syria, and Jordan, and the inexplicable giantism of the Baalbek stones in the Lebanon? Who could stop him comparing new languages with the tribes in the unexplored deserts of the Mogharibeh or with the fifteen holy sects within Damascus? As soon as he arrived within the walls he was well served with British company. There were fifty English men and women, a mixture of missionaries, soldiers and a remarkable woman, the adventurer Jane Digby, who had formerly married Lord Ellenborough, and now was heavily ensconced in Arabic wedlock with Sheikh Medjuel el Mezrab. (Burton's niece described this sheikh with customary snobbery: 'Jane Digby had capped her career by marrying her Arab camel-driver'.) Jane's eastern life was every bit as romantic and courageous as those other wonder-women of a period gone before—Hestor Stanhope and Lady Mary Wortley Montagu. Half her months were spent in comfort at Damascus, the rest of the year she travelled through the desert with her Bedouin man and his tribe. Jane had command of a dozen dialects in the desert, and though she was over sixty she had strength and beauty and vitality which Burton was obliged to praise in 'the cleverest woman I had ever met'. Out of the first year of his consulship, Dick spent 183 days riding camel and mule, through all kinds of distant horizons, with not a word in Eldridge's ear, and a couple of summer months with Isabel at a watering-hole called Bludan, a green and charming cool place on a hillside, writing and putting the finishing touches to *Vikram and the Vampire* and *The Battlefields of Paraguay*.

Isabel, with her new-found glory and a decent salary to back up her husband, arrived in December 1869 in Damascus with five dogs, a maid and enough luggage to last them a lifetime. Quickly she took stock of the consulate. It was a tall, grubby building in a street which seemed to be in a perpetual state of market-day. She made immediate acquaintance with Jane Digby, a Jesuit priest, and a family of Protestant missionaries. In no time at all she was out in a carriage on the edges of Damascus searching for a more fitting house for her consul. She found an ample terraced and balconied property in a Kurdish hamlet (now a suburb to the town) less than four miles from the walls of Damascus. The house at Salahiyyeh stood next to a Mosque, and ironically her study window on the upper floor lay an arm's length from the minaret where the daily Muezzin made his call to the faithful. The house was suitably stationed above a running brook, and all the rooms were therefore cooler. Opposite, across a lane, the Burtons cultivated a garden hidden behind a high wall with roses and jessamine and an orchard of apricot trees. Isabel acquired a dozen horses, two boys for grooms, and an extraordinary zoo of exotic pets from cats to guinea pigs, from goats to panther cubs, all of whom were allowed to roam freely through the garden and the courtyard at the back of the house. One report has Isabel keeping 'fifty pariah dogs' to the bargain; she does seem to have taken the romance of a new life too far, and done her level best to spend whatever her husband earned.

In that first year, Isabel and Richard, with two young visiting admirers, Edward H. Palmer, an orientalist, and Charles Tyrwhitt-Drake, an archaeologist and landscape artist, travelled with untold enthusiasm: suddenly life was much easier. They could write down to consulate expenses seventeen camels, oats for twelve horses and a bodyguard squadron of Bedouin tribesmen. Meanwhile the Amir of Syria, the all powerful Rashid Pasha, listened to tales of the Burtons adrift and sailing across the sea of desert with ever gloomier prognostications. They must be spies. They must be pursuing British Governmental machinations to the cost of the Ottoman Empire. It did not occur to Rashid that these Britishers were indulging their passion for travel with the tenacity of children suddenly provided with untold funds. Isabel and Richard were intoxicated with the new freedom. She had never travelled like this with him before. Others have suggested he worked five hours a day in his terrace home, and that Isabel kept Sundays clear for feeding the poor in her hamlet, and Wednesdays clear for entertaining the many sects. It cannot have been so. If he had been doing his duty, and had been seen to be doing it by Rashid Pasha's spies, nobody would have turned a hair.

Rashid wanted a clue to Burton's spying. Then he could report back to London with due outrage. When Dick returned from another expedition with his young friends, he found Damascus in a troubled state. Two Jewish lads had scrawled crosses on the walls of a Muslim lavatory. A Catholic had been whipped by a Muslim when he returned to collect money owed. It was believed there would come a riot on August 27. Would there be a repeat of the massacre of three thousand Christians? Dick, seeking no permission from any other authority, harangued the town council to lock all Christians and Jews in their homes and post armed guards at street corners. He announced another massacre was imminent. The advice was taken (Burton at that time toted two pistols in his belt, to the incredulity of the town legislature) and a Union Jack was raised above his consulate building. As it happened there was no massacre. Isabel, and every Jew and Christian, felt grateful to the consul. The Muslims seethed with anger. The consul had begun to divide and rule. It looked very clumsy.

Rashid had enough of an argument against Dick to put to London. This was added ammunition. But there was more to come. The consul had a distaste for Jews. And, more often than not, it befell the Damascus consul to settle disputes over money matters. A money-lender would complain to the consul that a certain Bedouin had failed to keep to his agreement. Usually Richard complied with the usurer's request for aid. But not any more.

It was rumoured that Burton had called in the Jewish lads who had desecrated a Muslim lavatory with their crosses. Burton had tortured these children. Burton had stripped them and flogged them. Within days of this, he put up a notice on his consulate door—he would no longer give the normal Britannic Majesty assistance to money-lenders who could not collect their dues. In private, Dick believed that British-protected Jews had milked villages of everything the Bedouin possessed, and he did not see himself as a bailiff for blood-suckers. The Jewish community in Damascus was outraged. Why was Jewry thus pilloried for a perfectly legal form of commercial enterprise five thousand years of civilisation had by no means confined to members of the Promised Land? When Charles Doughty visited Damascus ten years after Burton, he too noticed how greedy the Arabs were for loans of any kind, for borrowed money is still 'sweet' to the Bedouin, it is like the booty of other men's goods, and the day of reckoning is not yet:

The lending at usury, disallowed in the Koran doctrine, is practised even in these puritan countries. The villagers are undone thereby; and the most Bedouins fall every year behindhand, thus losing a third in the use of their little money. In Syria, the Muslims lend not, for conscience sake: but the people are greedily eaten up by other caterpillars, to the confusion of the name of Christ! by the iniquitous Nasara [Christians]; twenty-five yearly in the hundred is a merciful price among them for the use of their money.

(*Travels in Arabia Deserts*, 1888)

In England, the Chief Rabbi of London put a personal protest to the Foreign Office. Other leading Jews accused Isabel Burton of being a bigoted Catholic. And the Foreign Office had to pay attention. To Rashid Pasha, it appeared that Burton was cutting his own throat. First he had enraged the Muslim population with the populist fear of a second massacre, now he had the Jews in the walled city up in usufructuary arms. Rashid bided his time.

It would have been more justifiable in Burton's case if he had posted a notice outside the consulate forbidding *all* moneylenders to come to him for British protection, but he confined his remarks to Jews, in a walled city which included Greeks, Armenians, Abyssinians and a smattering of British bankers and commercial entrepreneurs, the 'Nasara' of Doughty's description.

First it was the Muslim community feeling slighted. Dick had raised the temperature and taunted the elders of the city with the shadow of another Christian massacre. Now, the Jews turned against Burton. They did not spare their zeal. For months now, Isabel had had a Jesuit confessor of her own, Fray E. Forner, a Franciscan priest. Forner had lately come into contact with the renegade tribe Shazlieh. Originally these were Muslim, but the priest had converted them to a half-form of Christianity which involved a considerable amount of evangelical mysticism. A couple of hundred Shazlieh had been baptised by the priest, to Isabel's naive satisfaction, and yet these new converts in private maintained an admitted devotion to their own Mohammad. It looked, on the surface, like another hasty western blunder with Christian fools rushing in with holy waters. The poor creatures were of neither one faith nor the other—merely a curious hybrid of Jesus and Mary and Mohammad. All over the Turkish Empire this sect had begun to emerge. It is believed to have originated in the military barracks of Constantinople. The groups were invariably small. But they created consternation within the Muslim framework of the Ottoman Empire.

Isabel appealed to her husband to offer this sect in Damascus the protection of Her Britannic Majesty's Government. Dick hesitated, until came a moment when he was convinced of the risks this sect ran when twelve of its members were sentenced to death by the Damascus authorities. Dick strenuously appealed on the Shazlieh behalf, and these sentences were reduced to formal banishment from Damascus. But Isabel was not satisfied. She wanted to witness a baptism of this sect. And she persuaded Dick to entertain the idea of buying the Shazlieh a plot of land. Isabel imagined a village home, free of local taxation, and possessing the unhindered right of worship at its hybrid font.

To the astonishment of the Foreign Office, Burton actually wrote to ask for official protection from the sect and, furthermore, he formally invited the Patriarch of Jerusalem to perform a mass baptism in Damascus. The London office could not have had their misgivings more positively confirmed. The thought of mass baptismal waters in the teeth of Turkish opposition and Muslim cries of treachery in the broiling sun of Damascus took the Foreign Office by storm. 'The Shazlieh,' Doughty wrote, 'are abhorred by the Muslims.'

An old friend of Dick Burton, Algie Freeman-Mitford, who was in the employ of the Foreign Office, called on the elegant terrace house outside Damascus. Freeman-Mitford was astonished by Isabel's behaviour. Far from being the rumoured lady of bounty who gave parties twice a week for all sects, he found a woman whose —

> manner with the Mohammedans among whom she lived, and whom it was her business to conciliate as far as in her lay, was detestable . . . It is only fair to Burton's memory to show how heavily he was handicapped.

Algie Freeman-Mitford was the first scout the London Foreign Office ordered out to Damascus to make a check on Burton. He wasn't the last. Freeman-Mitford was a long-standing friend. Eight years earlier Dick had wanted to take Algie on his West African expedition into the Cameroons. He was on Burton's side. Others were definitely not.

Sir Henry Elliot, from his eyrie in Constantinople, had already posted to London a number of Amir Rashid's woeful tales of discontent over Burton. Rashid's complaints were music to Elliot's vindictive ears. The situation had become so malevolent that, on the least excuse, such as hearing of Burton travelling to a Bedouin waterhole in the desert, the Amir would cannon off another diatribe. Rashid was in the habit of penning his remarks in French, in the form of *notes-verbales*: 'Les relations le plus intimes avec les gens des plus malfamé dans le pays.' He believed Burton indulged every opportunity to roam abroad in his beloved desert, seeking out unknown tribes and ancient Syrian ruins. He further complained: 'M. Burton a, on ne sait pour quel motif, une aversion toute spéciale pour la nation Musulmane'. If anything, Rashid was telling the truth. At least, it was a verifiable truth from the Amir's point of view. Dick Burton had already promised to buy a tract of land for Muslim converts to Christianity.

In the early months of 1871, Jane Digby, or, as she preferred to be known, 'the Englays woman of el Mezrab', took full advantage of Isabel's hearty admiration for her. She dictated to Isabel her autobiography. Isabel maintained that she transcribed Jane's long history of adventure, numerous husbands and considerable travel achievements. Many months later *The Times* prematurely announced Jane's death in Damascus. It was an embarrassing error due in the main to the distance between London and Syria, and the result of a garbled account of the adventuress's disappearance. Isabel wrote to correct the obituary the instant Jane surfaced alive and well. Isabel also made great play of the fact that she alone was entrusted with Jane's autobiography, and much to the annoyance of the Digby family, intimated that only she had access and right to this manuscript. Jane's family complained to their famous adventuress/traveller and under great pressure Jane Digby denied publicly she had ever handed such a manuscript into Isabel's 'safekeeping'. But in the next post Isabel received a demand from Jane for the return of the manuscript! It was Isabel's turn to consider that she had been humiliated. The adventuress had told a lie to shut her family up, and now Isabel decided she wouldn't even hand the manuscript over to its rightful owner. Isabel seemed determined to muscle into any and every conceivable matter. She did not believe herself important enough in her man's eyes. She had to grab at straws – anything which might enlarge her position. She meddled, fiddled, burst into tears, and told whoppers because she craved some attention. She was being reduced from a wife to the role of bank clerk, teller, packer and secretary.

The Burtons had been in Damascus fifteen months. In April 1871, Isabel and Dick and Charles Tyrwhitt-Drake, with a dozen servants, two horses each, and various camels and mules, set off for a genteel pilgrimage to Jerusalem. Isabel, quite naturally, was keen to attend two masses and receive Holy Communion in the Sepulchre on Easter Sunday. Ten days after this the splendid caravan of *Englaysie* and their retinue reached Nazareth, and that night they camped outside a Greek Orthodox Church, which seemed a safe enough place. Equally securely were placed a number of other caravans – an American tourist group, a similar German group, and two British camps. Dick and Isabel and Charley hid themselves from the rest, for they did not like to be identified with the common tourist parties in the other sand-dunes. All evening on May 5, the Feast of St George, Arabs, vagabonds, sellers and water-carriers drifted from one tent to another. Late into the night, a Coptic Christian took it upon himself to steal into Isabel's black tent. Isabel sat up and shrieked as any respectable young married woman might in such circumstances. The young Coptic character fled from the tent. Six of Burton's servants caught him as he ran, and they searched him, to no avail, then they roughed the fellow up and warned him with the flat of many fists not to enter an *Englaysie* woman's tent unless invited. The culprit withdrew, licked his wounds, bided a half an hour, and returned with a sack full of stones the size of sweet Israeli melons. He began to hurl them on Isabel's tent. Once more the servants climbed to their feet. They chased the Copt, who was by now hurling, if not stones the size of melons, dreadful execrations in the direction of the fair lady's tent. Once more the servants grappled with the persistent Copt, and within full view of the door to the Greek Orthodox temple they set about the chap with no end of curses and kicks. Within moments, other Greeks, late night faithful worshippers, emerged from the Church to witness this one-sided punch-up. Dick and Charley, by then fully dressed, made the classic mistake of hurrying across the sand with their belts crammed with pistols. More Greeks ran out of the church, and became incensed at the sight of one of their Faithful being attacked by a mob of *Englaysie* tourists. More servants joined in the scrap. The Greeks soon numbered one hundred and fifty and, ever mindful of the holstered pistols, hurled stones from a distance. To Dick's credit he did not draw his pistols. He stood his ground. A servant, sensing the odds so much against them now, shouted to the Greeks:

'Shame! Shame! This is the English Consul of Damascus!' followed immediately by the rejoinder, by no means evincing much confidence in Her Britannic Consular Servant:

'So much the worse for him!'

Isabel panicked. She grabbed a pair of her husband's breech-loading pistols and raced up a sand dune to raise help from a group of American campers. More white tourists swarmed across the dark sands, and the rioters disbanded. Dick suffered a lacerated arm. Two of his servants

180

had been indecorously held to the ground and had earned cracked ribs and bruised skulls.

In London, the Foreign Office was examining a report on Burton by C. M. Kennedy who had visited Damascus in the hope of studying the Consul at his desk. The London Office wanted an on the spot recommendation that a small post such as Burton's could be reduced to the level of Vice-Consul, and thereby certain savings made in the diplomatic wage packet. Of course this was all so much hooey, none other than the treacherous Sir Henry Elliot at Constantinople lay behind the scheme. He knew that if Dick was offered such a demotion, the humiliation of it would drive him out of Damascus. At the time of Kennedy's visit, however, the peripatetic consul had temporarily disappeared; in fact, Kennedy was reduced to riding up and down desert tracks in the company of Isabel inquiring at any encampment for news of Burton's passage. Kennedy eventually gave up the ghost. He returned to England and presented the Foreign Office with a description of a consular office which for the most part was locked and empty.

Within a fortnight of the Nazareth disturbance the town's Greek Orthodox Bishop had written to London to complain of Burton's behaviour. The Amir Rashid was positively gleeful when his spies brought back their fanciful reports. Dick had fired into a crowd of innocent Coptic children, Dick had torn down paintings inside the church and shot a priest at the altar, and his wife had marched down the aisle wearing only a nightshirt; cables were raining down upon London with these interpretations.

Dick did not bother with an account of the *fracas* to his Consul-General superior in Beirut. Lord Russell repeatedly urged him to report back to London, in stronger and stronger terms, from 'serious complaints have arisen' to a 'demand for immediate explanation'; but Dick sat firm. He did make a legal effort to have a dozen Greeks in Nazareth arrested for inciting the attack of stones, but basically a diplomatic torpor had hold of the man. When at last he understood the weight of the accusations piling up, he sent a cable thirty-five days after the event:

MY SERVANTS UNPROVOKEDLY ATTACKED BY GREEK ORTHODOX AT NAZARETH ON ACCOUNT OF A SLIGHT QUARREL WITH AN INSOLENT NEGRO. THREE OF MINE SERIOUSLY HURT. HAVE APPLIED TO LOCAL AUTHORITIES FOR REDRESS. GREAT OPPOSITION AT FIRST FROM GREEK CLERGY WHO NOW OWN THEMSELVES MISTAKEN AND WISH FOR AN AMICABLE SETTLEMENT. DETAILS BY POST
                                    RICHARD F. BURTON: CONSUL

The Foreign Office waited a week for the details they were promised in the post. None were forthcoming. Finally Lord Granville informed Sir Henry Elliot in Constantinople that he was free to announce to the Turkish Government the immediate recall of the Damascus consul. Rumours were rife that Burton had already been dismissed. Even Jane Digby could not resist the opportunity to send Isabel a note:

My Dear Isabel,
    I was calling at a native house yesterday, where I found assembled some leading people of Damascus. The conversation turned upon Captain Burton and the present British Consulate. One word led to another; and I heard to my surprise and consternation, that men famed for their *various pecuniary* transactions are boasting about everywhere that, upon their representations the consul is to be recalled . . .

In this case she was referring to the Jews; but now it was a more serious matter. Burton did not seem aware of this at all. The very week the Vice-Consul to Eldridge in Beirut, Thomas Jago, was preparing to ride for Damascus to take charge of the consulate, Dick and Charley Drake were to be found in the cooler mountain retreat of Bludan on an exploration. Burton had had the nerve to inform Eldridge in Beirut he needed urgent sick-leave, and had promptly vanished from Damascus.

On August 16, a messenger reached their mountainside house in Bludan from Thomas Jago. It said that Jago had taken command of the Damascus consulate as of the past forty-eight hours, and that he, Jago, had the full authority of the Consul-General in Beirut. At that precise moment, Isabel and Charley and Dick were in the courtyard saddling up their half-breed mounts for another trek into the high hinterland. Their servants were ready beside their mules. The picnic hampers were strapped to the animals.

Isabel liked to recall that Dick and Charley galloped all the way to Damascus, and on to the terraced house in the village of Salahiyyeh. And there, on the hall table was the ultimate insult, Lord Granville's letter from the Foreign Office, in London. As he tore the official envelope away, the grim paragraph he hastily scanned confirmed the worst: 'I regret to have now to inform you that the complaints which I have received from the Turkish Government in regard to your recent conduct and proceedings render it impossible that I should allow you to continue to perform any Consular functions in Syria.' The harshness of the address, the hard uncompromising patronage of a master to a student cad Flashman burned into Dick's confidence. Granville completed his letter: 'You will, therefore, make your preparations for returning to this country with as little delay as possible.' Dick was in his fiftieth year. He had received a scolding as he had never envisaged before. Dick leaned inside the doorway of the house. Opposite, just across the narrow path, lay his apricot orchard, and in the courtyard beyond the inner curtains there were those ghastly chickens and strays and chained leopards Isabel tried to make pets out of. Now the creatures were absurdities. For eighteen months, he and his wife had careened up and down these desert hills playing at nabobs on £1,000 a year; it was a rash performance. After a swig of brandy, and a change of horses, Dick led Charley Drake down the narrow lanes into the centre of Damascus. Whoever this 'puppy' Jago was—he'd give him a bite of his sharp teeth, by God!

Charley Drake followed Burton into the consulate office. Burton was spluttering with indignation but there was little else he could do; and Jago possessed official confirmation of his new post as Vice-Consul in Damascus. Best face forward for Dick was to collect his brass inkwell and his dromedary's heel ash-tray, not forgetting an ivory handled swordstick with a spring release he cherished, and walk out with a swagger. Dick scribbled a message for his wife and a servant from the Salahiyyeh house rode away on his mule with it. He didn't ask Charley to accompany him across the desert to Beirut. He took half a dozen water bags, packed whatever journals he had left on his desk in the village house, and rode off into the night with a square lantern swaying on the pommel. In the morning, Isabel opened his note: 'Don't be frightened. I am recalled. Pay, pack and follow at convenience.'

In the early hours he was making good progress towards the coast when he reached a view of the Syrian hills. His recollection was a rare phrase of recrimination: 'The sight of Bludan mountains in the distance at sunrise, where I have left my wife. *Ever again*? Felt soft. Dismissal ignominious, at the age of fifty, without a month's notice, or wages, or character.' One has to feel a pang of compassion for him, indeed there is a case for considering him ill-used by the scheming Elliot in Constantinople, and the nosey Amir Rashid. But account ought to be taken of Burton's bizarre stupidity. His failure to communicate.

In a state of panic, Isabel set off for Beirut twenty hours after Dick had saddled up. She had no clue where to find him. In the end, after a brave ride through the desert, she came across her petulant husband pounding up and down the harbourside. They collapsed into each other's arms. They withdrew to a hotel in Beirut for a further day, to await his boat home. Brave and silly she may have been, but she showed extraordinary strength of mind and body. This frantic and possessive woman was racked by love for a selfish caddish odd sod who had not the grace to pause and ride back from Damascus to explain what had happened. He did not care. And in their bedroom on Beirut harbour front when he cried, she held her breath and didn't, she would save her tears for later.

Dick wasted no time seeing his superior, Eldridge, in Beirut. Leaving Isabel to wind up their affairs he boarded the first ship out. He intended to skulk about London quietly. Rent a couple of tiny bachelor rooms and smoke his cigars and perhaps look up Algie Swinburne for the brandy, and Monckton Milnes for the gossip. As for the Foreign Office, well, he'd wait for Isabel to get back; she'd do her familiar trick of bursting into Russell's room, leaning against one of those black leather library chairs and letting the tear ducts flow. Dick would lie doggo in his rooms. Better that way. Swagger around at dusk with half a flask of brandy mayhap. Call on the doctor and get him to remove the abscess on his neck. And tell the doctor a rousing yarn about some scoundrel Copt's dirty teethmarks. The doctor might not have heard that one before.

Isabel closed up the house on the outskirts of Damascus. She asked Charley Drake to take on the remainder of the three-year lease. She appreciated the thirteen friends who came to deplore Dick's treatment. She held a small auction in the morning—clothes, trinkets, goats and her lovely half-bred horses; but she still did not have enough money to get back with. She was forced to send a cable to an uncle in England for funds to get her safely aboard a ship. It took her two months to pay and pack all her bags and manuscript parcels, all her crates and upright-this-way portmanteaux. She made her final call on the one person she needed to hear her—the confessor Jesuit priest, Fray Emmanuel Forner.

Now that her man was safely away, she could conceal the truth with her little white lies. It wasn't *really* true he had been recalled, was it now, Isabel? 'It is monstrous for any missionary of the British Syrian schools or otherwise, to pretend that my husband was recalled, because I defended myself against the man who attacked me!' And what was the real reason for Foreign Office malevolence? The real reason why he went back was entirely different to what has been presumed. 'The real cause was very different; it was his one endeavour to do what England professes to admire, what Richard did in practice, namely, to sacrifice himself for Christianity's sake!' And what was the reaction to those rumours in the desert? '. . . Dick always sacrificed himself to the poor, the ignorant, and the oppressed.'

Dick arrived in London with a cloth valise, a trunkful of special and private books and manuscript diaries, and an empty pocket. The Foreign Office had cut off his pay. He took a cab straight to his sister's house in Norwood. The Stisted family had removed themselves to a square detached villa in a backwater of south London. Like Dulwich, Brixton Hill, and Ruskin's lair at Herne Hill, these newly paved crescents were a modish retreat from the richer side of the Thames below Piccadilly.

According to his niece Georgiana, when he arrived on the doorstep the man was at his wits' end:

> Never had we known him so wretched, so unnerved; his hands shook, his temper was strangely irritable, all that appreciation of fun and humour which rendered him such a cheery companion to old and young alike had vanished. He could settle to nothing; he was restless, but he could not leave the house; ailing, but would take no advice—it was indeed a melancholy spectacle!

To calm himself down he stayed at Norwood for two months, counting his meagre coins, *not once* attempting to come to any sort of reconciliation with the Foreign Office, and rewriting a pile of manuscript pages based on his early days in East Africa, which had been inexcusably buried for five years in the Bombay office of the Royal Asiatic Society. The manuscript had been forwarded to Burton at the close of 1871, and with an additional chapter of rage and vilification (once more) at Jack Speke, Dick was determined to wrestle the pages into a two-volume study, *Zanzibar: City, Island and Coast*, making some 1,022 pages plus various prefaces, which an unwilling and grumbling publisher in the shape of Tinsley Brothers, of the Strand, took to the printers for him.

Isabel returned to London equally short of money. She had with her a dozen crates of his books which she immediately dumped in rooms beside Montague Place where her parents were renting accommodation. So low, in fact, was their joint purse, that she advised Richard it was best they closed themselves in under the in-law umbrella of rooms in central London, from where, at least, they could replenish their coffers with a certain decorum. An address in Norwood, and one where she was not particularly welcome anyway, was an hour's cab ride back and forth, and would prove in the end too costly. Isabel approached two elder members of her Arundell clan and raised £40. The rooms in

Montague Place were paid for, but Dick had to support his wife and his wife's maid, the Syrian girl Khamoor (from all accounts a decorative but work-shy addition to the party whom Isabel treated more as a daughter and confidante), and Dick needed about £12 a week to sustain them.

Between October and January, he compiled a further two volume 760-page book, *Unexplored Syria*. The manuscript was a hotch-potch of essays by more than one hand; Isabel makes an anonymous contribution to the text, so does their friend and fellow adventurer Charley Drake. There are nearly three hundred pages clustered with notes of the famous Burton variety, the usual discursive marginalia. The entire book from exploration to ancient Syrian archaeology bears all his weaknesses and few of his earlier energies. The undaunted curiosity and sense of searching in the man had become drained. The Tinsley brothers published the volumes in bright red cloth wrappers, and the author even suggested he might follow this up with an account of his personal travels across the Syrian deserts of the Drusic tribes and through the valley of the Euphrates. Like many another promise this was never followed up. It was more the sad echo of a voice seeking its old audience. The public wasn't going to ask Dick to guide it through almost a thousand pages now that the great David Livingstone was rumoured to be returning from his Lake Tanganyika quest, and the remorselessly confident Welsh-American journalist Henry Stanley had come upon the much loved doctor on a lake shore after one of the most extraordinary marches across Africa ever recorded.

Dick was relieved to join his own family, the Stisteds, in Edinburgh, for the January month. He also put in a sterling visit to his brother Edward who lay incarcerated in the Surrey County Lunatic Asylum. In a year when psychotherapy was hardly advanced in this country beyond the primitive Christian morality of equating insanity with sinfulness, when Hippolyte Bernham or Henry Maudsley were still considered dangerous humanists toiling on the outside edge of experimentation, it must have been a shock to his system to come upon Edward Burton in a *home* which, like many another institute, had not given up the use of a 'rush chair' to quiet the insane, a 'whirling bed' to ease a simpleton's fiery mind, and a device known as the 'hunger cure' for the patients who required more punishment to return them to reason. Where, one wonders, are Dick's notes on that visit?

Crammed as they were into three small rooms with their maid, their crates of books, and their piles of costumes and exotic ephemera which gave proof to Dick's wide travels, neither Dick nor Isabel could resist a high social invitation. A certain hostess, Marian Alford, seemed at a loss to know how to entertain the Prince of Wales and the Duke of Edinburgh his brother (a ghastly dank naval second son of Victoria's with an unquenchable thirst for Gaiety Girls). The hostess, with the approval of her illustrious Teuton guests, approached the Burtons with a proposition. Would they be willing to attend the party dressed to their eyebrows in a mad oriental disguise along the lines of a Bedouin Sheikh or whatever these greasy characters wander about in in the middle of the desert. It would be most awful jolly fun if that maid of yours can skip in after brandies with a silver tray of toffees and wiggle and wriggle her bottom around. Amazingly enough the Burtons took the engagement on. Dick trumpeted and bellowed from guest to guest speaking all kinds of languages, and the attractive maid Khamoor with bump and grind eastern promise undulated to tickle snicker-gadfly approval from the guests of honour. It had got so low. Dick Burton was reduced to a charade.

He sent Isabel to the familiar Foreign Office portals. He knew the consulate at Teheran was vacant. He dreamed of other, better posts, but it was no consolation to him when she returned with the news that on the contrary, Teheran was already bespoken to an old friend of his at the FO, Ronald Thompson, and all there remained on offer was the Amazon sea-port of Pará (now Belém). Dick sniffed and remarked it was not a berth to his liking or to his expectations, after the glamour of Damascus. It was really a case of how long he could hold out in the name of pride. The Foreign Office was only too aware of this, for he had spent the previous month compiling a fat sheaf of papers protesting his sudden recall to England. These notes, in the form of 141 pages privately printed by Clayton Brothers for the Foreign Office, and stamped 'office use only – not to be circulated', took the shape of Amir Rashid's letter of complaint and Burton's formal reply and an introduction written in clearly grieved tones. It was a summary of an unjust dismissal. Although privately printed for internal use, it had been forced upon the authorities by the sudden death of Rashid and his subsequent disgrace in public life, and by the not unreasonable complaint of Dick's about so many enemies sniping away at him (Elliot etc). Nevertheless, the Foreign Office offered him no recompense and no apology; they accepted the findings of their internal investigation without further comment. It was like being released from a dog kennel only to be kept on strict rations of biscuit and bone meal.

A mining speculator offered him the princely sum of £2,000 to spend three months making a detailed report on sulphur potential in Iceland. Dick set off for Edinburgh to stay with the Stisted family again, *en route* for the cold north; it was May 1872 and he would not return to Isabel until September 15. She was angry at the anonymous backer's decision to pay for only his round trip. Dick arrived in Reykjavik on June 8, and set about surveying what he hoped would become a profitable enterprise. It would seem the world's major supply of sulphur came from Sicily, and speculators wanted mines which rested in less politically volatile earth. Dick slogged away at his job like a man possessed. He risked frostbite and extraordinary changes in climate to explore every possible mine shaft he could reach by Icelandic donkey. The early mornings were taken up with interminable rides across stony bleak tracts. In the late afternoons, with the sudden announcement of freezing hurricanes, his party would have to take cover in village huts built nest-like against any slope which might offer protection in this desolate and open interior. With light from the oil-glow, and an ever-present cold wax smell of fish from a hearth stove, night after night he described every detail of the working day, from the economics of the fishing industry to the units of pressure required to set off the hot springs and geysers.

More than three years would pass before he could persuade any publisher to touch this exhausting double volume of data and windy exploration, *Ultima Thule; or, a Summer in Iceland.* All the stale mannerisms remain, the ceaseless questing after digressions and the like marginalia, the astonishing variety of subjects he broaches; every page is marked with a soul's tiredness. This sturdy work provides an invaluable anthology of Dick's limitations. One can observe between the lines the confession of a man whose entire system has run down, identify a physiological basis for Burton's neurotic doggedness. His notations are often closed premises, his reasoned arguments slide into self-congratulatory gratification, and he cannot escape analogies to his own past horizons. When Dick found the famous geysers in the lowland plains he recorded how they *reminded him* of Central African frog-pools. Dawdling about waiting for the day to take shape *was similar* to Peruvian donkey boys uncertain of the steep Andean climb ahead. The mosquito in the fish smelling log cabin was *on a par* with the midge of Maine. The writing often slips into the irreconcilable — for want of a better description he calls the Icelandic southern wind *a relative* of Sind breezes, and any odd mound he might push his donkey over *could be mistaken* for a nest of African termites.

The spirit of exploration in him had become immobilised. Nothing he could see, nothing which presented the face of novelty in Iceland, could be seized upon, as of old, with the energy of first touch, that dice-throw gratification. The gambler of firstnesses had ceased here. The body of his writing was hide-bound; there was a hardboiled insistence on the mirrors from his past. 'Nothing can change as long as man is armoured', was Reich's assumption for a career filled with *fear* of living, *fear* of mobile comprehension. The midge of Maine, and, for that matter, a breeze in Sind, had become decoys, lights in the closed fist of his mind.

It was July 1872. Strangely enough, Lord Granville from the Foreign Office wrote to Isabel, and not Richard. He had reasonably good news: would Dick accept the consulate in Trieste? He urged her to ask her husband quickly, and to take into account what few other berths there were about. Isabel, even if she did fire off a letter to Reykjavik, certainly wasted no time waiting for Richard's reply from Iceland. She informed Granville ten days later that the answer was a grateful yes. They faced the reality of a reduction in salary (£600 p.a.) compared with Damascus, but it left hope for a better post in the future, perhaps Morocco.

Although Dick did not return to London until the September, he had heard of Isabel's not inconsiderable woes. Her mother died in June, and in August her youngest brother died at sea on a naval commission. Yet more bad news was to follow: when Dick returned from Iceland they learned that the anonymous speculator had absolutely no intention of coughing up the promised sum of £2,000 for the Icelandic survey expedition.

He returned to England to spend six weeks packing his books back into those dozen trunks. They jointly cheerioed the Duke of Somerset, the Earl of Derby, Edward Bulwer-Lytton, Monckton Milnes, and the painter Sir Frederic Leighton; broke as they were, Dick was not bereft of friends. Finally he left ahead of Isabel for Trieste. She stayed behind to settle sundries and pay for freight. The Foreign Office accountant wouldn't pay for all the sundries a consul would pile up while settling in a far port like Trieste. And with Dick's finances perched on such a precarious wire, it is possible that his wife was forced to take each item of freight and account for it by receipt to the Foreign Office. Clearly, the Burtons did not want to spend their own money, sail away into the blue, and then wait six months for the Foreign Office to reimburse them.

Trieste was a dismal port in the Austrian Empire, seventy miles east-north-east of Venice. Its principal articles of export were wool, woollen goods, paper, sugar, and light machinery. It boasted the see of a Bishop, and the entire harbour suffered from a British controlling interest based on quasi shipping rights under the aegis of the Austrian Lloyd Steamship Company. It is hard to imagine what strategic powers such a firm grasp on this port, set in a sea of obscure principalities from Gradisca and Istria to Goritz, the Foreign Office believed it was exercising. But the British authorities had found the perfect place to deposit their greatest living orientalist, in this hole-in-a-wall Illyrian province so recently promoted to the rank of an 'imperial city' under Austrian suzerainty.

Dick took four weeks to reach Venice, yet Isabel made it by an overland route in eight days. A fellow consul escorted Isabel to a boat by the Piazza in Venice, and to their mutual shock she and Dick collided in the lower saloon. The fellow consul never forgot the fascinating spectacle.

'What the devil are you doing here?' demanded the upright figure of the husband, with his broad shoulders and his puffy black Luciferian moustache, half a mandarin's, half a Serbo-Croat infantryman's upper-lip decoration sartorial.

The wife, so taken aback was she at the sudden appearance of her husband, who, she was firmly convinced, had already arrived in Trieste to take stock, find rooms, and light a stove ready in wait for her, that this round and bonny wife snapped at him —

'Ditto!'

Each Burton held a bizarre creature under the appropriate elbow. Dick clasped a war-scarred black and red fighting gamecock equipped with whittled talons (had he spent the past month gambling in discreet cockfighting arenas putting up his fancied Old English gamecock against those scruffy foreign froggie Millefleur Barbu d'Uccles, Belgian Bearded Sebrights and the like?). And Isabel, on her hip, balanced a fat-faced bull-terrier. They took stock of one another for a long moment. And then they both sat down on a bench and shared the reamed letters each had begun to the other.

Others have called this a perfect example of their unity, as if they were a couple of brothers. Would it not be more realistic to suggest that now all they were concerned with was a form of survival with dignity? He had his brandy flask. She, poor lady of eagernesses and doggy devotion, had in all probability passed through her menopause, and, customary as it was to those of her class, this spelled doom for the marital bed. Ladies then were of the opinion the menopause heralded the end to physical contact with the male. It was the start of a second life, shorn of the nauseating demands of the opposite sex, a time to observe the more serious aspects of one's life—devotion and service to others and spiritual comfort, into the bargain.

Richard had no intention of living out his future years in a state of matrimonial war. If anybody capitulated now, it was our hero. He was aware of the cruel fading of the hours. There had come to him that harsh blow of realisation—he had failed to match his ambition. In the future it would be Isabel who gained ground. Richard was tired and careless now; the dark was not welcome, and 'who must die must die in darkness', according to a Columbian legend, 'even if he is a seller of candles'. Feuding had dogged Burton too long. He wanted to acquiesce. The calm shore was an inviting thing. He was to write:

> Blood-feuds are most troublesome to the traveller, who may be delayed by them for months: and, until a peace be patched up, he will never be allowed to pass from one tribe to their enemies. A quarrel of the kind prevented my crossing Arabia from Al-Medinah to Maskat, and another in Africa from visiting the head of the Tanganyika Lake. In all such journeys the traveller who has to fight against Time is almost sure to lose.

She grew strong in the absence of his will. He, being quite unable to forgive the past, had no confidence left with which to face the future. He had a secret worry that perhaps Isabel's way of social greed and holy mores was what he should have clothed himself in, years earlier. And yet oh clearly how he despised such an image. They were not enemies. More a version of 'Tom and Jerry' of mid-Victorian times, lives filled with flight and chaos and never an apology in sight; only in the case of the Burtons the blows were real and hard, and neither of them could forget the true provenance of their social slights. Curiously alone with each other, and within this context of isolation—cigars and carpet slippers, brandy and Holy Rome bespoken—there were yet such gulfs and chasms of misunderstanding, such vagaries in their insipid domestic intimacy, he could not be expected wholly to give up the crafty art of the fox.

XVI

PRINCE When? . . . Where? . . . and how much?
ACTRESS Tonight . . . Your place . . . Free!
RICHARD Pay, pack . . . and follow.
ISABEL No, won't . . . shan't!

FOR TWO YEARS AND FIVE MONTHS RICHARD MADE HIS HOME IN Trieste, and did not return to England until May 1875. Both Burtons travelled extensively during this period, and of perhaps greater importance – they travelled together. Austrian, Spanish and Mexican royalty gave Richard and Isabel invitations to all sorts of functions. Trieste, which was well connected by rail (Paris, Rome or Madrid could all be reached by express service) proved a fortunate location for the socially observant traveller.

Dick prepared for publication two and a half million words within a short canter of twenty-nine months. All his energies flowed through a deluge of indifferent pages. The passionate scribbler was determined to annotate every single issue he could fall upon, on the condition that nothing penetrated the veil of his marriage and the sealed container of his inner being. And a deluge it was.*

---

* Richard prepared for publication a translation of Lacerda's journey through Cazembe in 1797, *The Lands of Cazembe*; published for the RGS, and the only edition, by John Murray; a 94-page introduction to a translation by Albert Tootal of *The Captivity of Hans Stade of Hesse*; published in 1874 as no. 51 of the first series of pamphlets by the Hakluyt Society: two articles on Rome for Macmillan's Magazine; a pamphlet which might have been intended for a speech to the Royal Society of Edinburgh called *Volcanic Eruptions of Iceland*; another pamphlet, *The Castellieri of Istria* which he posted on to his own Anthropological Society in London; a 60-page prima *A New System of Sword*

It is all very well to attribute all this to his early rising (five in the morning every morning, and write to midday), but during this time he took off to Bologna, Venice (at least four occasions), Vienna, Rome, Florence and Padua. Meanwhile Isabel prepared a 716-page manuscript of her own, *The Inner Life of Syria, Palestine and the Holy Land. From my Private Journal*, which by the winter of 1876, Messrs King & Co, in London, made a great success of by fetching out two editions for an eager public who were fascinated with Mrs Burton's chatty, inconsequentially middlebrow narrative.

Not until they arrived in Trieste did Dick find a suitable moment to confess to his wife he'd lost a box of jewellery she had put into his safekeeping on the journey out. Dick blamed the loss on appalling freighters and when at last the box did arrive, of course it was empty. How he could have so blithely given up £130 worth of his wife's heirlooms is difficult to understand. Even more peculiar, Isabel puts the entire incident aside as if she'd dropped a tin hair-pin on to the foot lever of her Collier's Silent Sewing Machine.

During this first period in Trieste on £12 a week, Isabel and Richard had an expensive time. Now she is refusing £90 dresses, but *settling* for £30 ones. There they are spending £60 on a week at a hotel in Vienna. Isabel's mother, when she died the year they left for Trieste, settled a substantial sum on her eldest daughter. In most cases such money would go to the senior boy, so it can only be assumed Mrs Arundell took great and kindly pity towards Isabel and made sure the woman would not be left without in foreign parts with her devilish brigand swell of a husband.

As soon as they arrived in Trieste they made very accommodating contact with the permanent Vice-Consul, E. W. Brock. Now, Brock had been there thirty years, and he was such an old hand at Britannic penpushing, it was much to Burton's relief to find out that his junior was all too prepared to take on as many duties as were required. He was no eager young beaver hunting for Dick's post, he wouldn't report

---

Exercise for Infantry, he placed with the publishers Clowes in 1876; the 788-page manuscript of *Ultima Thule; or, A Summer in Iceland* which Nimmo Publications in London produced for him in 1875; a further 616-page manuscript *Two Trips to Gorilla Land and the Cataracts of the Congo* which became a Sampson Low, Marston, Low & Searle publication in 1876; a 275-page manuscript, a mixture of archeological topography and philological inquiry into this newly uncovered pre-Roman society — *Etruscan Bologna* published by Messrs Smith, Elder in 1876; another pamphlet bound for the Anthropological Society — *The Long Wall of Salona, and the Ruined Cities of Pharia, and Gelsa di Lesina*; and a journalistic piece, which was to be printed in two consecutive editions of the 'Journal of the Society of Arts' — *The Port of Trieste, Ancient and Modern.*

back to London nasty descriptions of his superior waltzing halfway across southern Europe, and all he wanted was to keep his head down over his ledger and dream of a pension in a pretty cottage he had bought in anticipation of retirement. These hankypanky smart devils, famous scribblers and the like came and went, but his penpushing went on for ever in its dutiful way. Dick was delighted. Gnarled old scribe at the tall desk. Three maids in the apartment. Isabel's dumb beauty of a girl from Syria. And new inheritances from the Arundell lot. He'd swagger for a couple of years, be bound.

His first thought for comfort was to take rooms in the mountain village of Opçina, more than 300 metres above Trieste where, in the hot summer months, they could enjoy walking and cool days. In the summer of 1873 Charley Tyrwhitt-Drake joined them on a hiking expedition. When he left, the Burtons saw him off all the way to Venice. The following year a cholera epidemic spread through Trieste and Isabel caught the symptoms; back they went to the high fastnesses behind Trieste. Dick came down from the mountain in fine fettle. Then, three days later, inflammation in his groin turned to an alarming tumour. By the time Isabel got him to a surgeon he was in considerable pain. The growth was cut out inexpertly, and the tumour retained its poison. Dick went under chloroform for a second operation. On coming out of the anaesthetic, he read a letter which brought the sad news of Charley's death from malaria in Jordan and he promptly fainted away again. Burton convalesced for seventy-nine days.

Isabel nursed him with devotion. Each day she washed and bandaged the wound. She fed him on a diet of eggs, honey, milk and brandy and cigars. In addition she ordered finest port from London via the Foreign Office. She moved him down to street level rooms in the inn at Opçina, and placed his solid frame in a wheelchair. Isabel was not in very good shape either. At last their own doctor visited them in Opçina, took one look at Dick and ordered him to take to the baths at Battaglia, less than ten miles away; he diagnosed gastric fever in Isabel and he recommended four weeks at Recoaro to drink the purgative waters.

On the grounds that a very distant relative of hers, a Baron Arundell, was awarded the title of Count of the Holy Roman Empire by an Emperor of Germany, Isabel began to refer to herself as the Countess. The award had been originally made in perpetuity, and so if any member of the Arundell clan when abroad chose to, he or she could adopt this spurious designation. No English King or Queen has ever recognised this honour, with the baleful exception of James II. And yet it must be said in Isabel's favour, title conscious as she did become in later years, she had, in Trieste, a perfectly honourable reason for assuming this ghastly bum handle. She had taken over a religious society called the Apostleship of Prayer, in addition to her pet Society for the Prevention of Cruelty to Animals, and it was not much fun signing her name plain 'Mrs Burton' when she was appealing for funds from minor aristocrats. No erstwhile fund-raiser in history can be expected to survive long without a decent appellation atop the headed notepaper. After all, a self-respecting good woman like Isabel had had her fill of asking choleric nobles for pennies at consular bazaars, with a potty husband upstairs determined to frighten donors by leaving unfinished manuscript pages titled *A History of Farting* in obvious places, as he once did. In future, she announced, as long as she remained on the continent, she would be addressed as the Countess Isabel of Arundell (or Wardour), a claimant Countess of the Holy Roman Empire. It certainly worked wonders for the membership of the Apostleship of Prayer. Isabel rounded up 20,000 fully paid subscriptions during the course of her Presidency.

Khamoor, the cloth-brained Syrian maid, was now twenty-two, and Isabel made up her mind to send the girl back home to get married. Pretty as she was Khamoor stood little chance of keeping her *amour-propre*, with three other maids in the Trieste apartment and a shortage of eligible suitors. Isabel wrote to the girl's family in Syria and packed Khamoor off on a boat bound for Beirut.

Dick had recovered from his sickness. He progressed from a wheel-chair to the even more humbling apparatus of an upright sedan chair, suspended on two poles and held in mid-air by four sturdy porters. The operation in his groin made walking an intolerable business. For weeks he had held himself stiffly doubled-up, and only with guts and grimaces and shots of brandy did he manage to lift himself upright. It was a case of waiting until the body healed itself. And it must have been slow indeed. For every time he tried to haul himself up the actual surface tissue of the wound gaped wide once more. By October 1874, he could walk unaided. Isabel, in her diaries, duly records the fact he had to undergo gas at a Trieste dentist for teeth trouble the next month. Unfortunately, he was under the impression the gas had no effect on him at all. He pushed the apparatus away and insisted on Isabel taking the gas to demonstrate its efficiency. With obliging good humour Isabel floated unconscious long enough to convince the irritated consul of the merits of nitrous oxide.

In her quiet way Isabel proved a dab hand at graffiti. On behalf of the Prevention of Cruelty to Animals Society she daubed walls in Trieste with peculiar half-mocking bills addressed at all manner of society, and written as it were in the person of a badly treated domestic animal. No doubt she intended these comments to raise shamed blushes on bullock herders and cab drivers who thrashed their animals into the dirt. By association the anthropomorphic halloos go a long way to invite suspicion about her own married life. A poster announced: '*Man! God made me for your benefit, but He also recommended me to your mercy. The only wish that I have is to love and serve and obey your will. Do not, therefore, break my heart with ill-treatment. I have intelligence, memory, affection, and gratitude, only I do not know how to speak. I want to understand you, but I am often so terrified by you that I no longer know what it is that you want me to do. My head throbs from the blows you give me on my tender nose . . .*'

Within a couple of weeks, Richard ordered Isabel to take all their manuscripts to London and told her he would follow shortly. It was abrupt. He slammed his foot down, and she obeyed. She picked up her bull-terrier, packed the papers, and boarded the train to Paris. Along the route a French worker took umbrage at certain words she muttered in German; he was under the impression Isabel had insulted his sister. Somehow all the blame fell on the bull-terrier which lay at her knee, and the baggage attendant insisted on shoving the pet into the appropriate dog pokey on the freight wagon much to the Countess of Arundell's disgust. She had already bought a ticket for the dog to be allowed on her knee. Far more likely the dog did something unhygienic to the man's sister. Isabel put on airs and mumbled the ten German words she knew, and finally resorted to the action she knew best — opening her blue eyes and bursting into hearty British tears in a carriage awash with garlic Gallic 'old contemptibles' who last saw action in Napoleon's Fourth Army.

She spent the next five months alone in London. To some extent life was improved when the publishers, King & Co jumped at the opportunity to publish her chattering two-volume *The Inner Life of Syria, Palestine and the Holy Land*. But much sympathy is due to her for carrying out paltry and boring jobs for her man, such as accosting the anonymous mining speculator for that £2,000. Once again it wasn't available. She blundered on from supper to dinner-dance, and from cocktail to tea-tattle. She dug up an old letter she had written eight years before beseeching the Royal Geographical Society for greater honours for Richard. This time she made a round-robin of all Dick's old pals, collected thirty signatures and raced into the

Foreign Office with this same letter, slightly updated, and presented it to Lord Granville with the audacity of a puppy. Granville nervously opened the letter. It was a demand for the recommendation of a KCB. Granville pulled himself together and informed the lady he knew of a number of employees in the Foreign Office, besides that of a lowly consul, who might better deserve a knighthood. Isabel carried on regardless. She knew people were guffawing into their gin fizzes – an orful cheek the drone got. Fellah never went to our skools. Pissed about orl over the continent. Skittled orf in the John Company stinkin Indian Garrisons. Slouched about African jungly jingles doin disgustin things to the woggies . . .

On the 1st of March, 1875, a relative rushed to Isabel's hotel room to show her the announcement in the *Scotsman*. The paper had picked up a garbled account of Dick's ten-week tumour agony, and formally declared Captain R. F. Burton dead. Isabel was only marginally relieved to see no other report to the same effect that day. She hurried to the cable office and sent off a shocked message to Dick's Vice-Consul E. W. Brock, in the Trieste office. The next day she received the following telegram from her very much alive husband – 'I AM EATING A GOOD DINNER AT TABLE D'HOTE'. It took him all of seven weeks to arrive in London after that. And, as ever, without a word of explanation. All he was concerned about was whether she had managed to squeeze any advance money from the various publishers. Had she collected that £2,000 from that bounder of a mining speculator? Had she made contact with all his friends? Had she informed *his* family how he was? What had Granville said to the KCB letter? Was Algie Swinburne in town? Where was Monckton Milnes? Where was that quinine? Did she forget to buy the Brand's Essences?

More than anything else, it was a fascination with get-rich-quick which he brooded over so continuously. As soon as he was in town he set about patenting a concoction under the name of 'Captain Burton's Tonic Bitters'. It was a restorative after a heavy night's bout of booze. A single spoonful could be diluted into a glass of sherry first thing in the morning and according to Isabel it 'completely took away the consequences of drinking overnight'. Both she and her spouse went to some trouble to market the tonic in the shape of a pretty bottle bearing his delightfully reassuring visage. It might well have stood a chance, but for the ever-increasing popularity of Angostura Bitters which, since 1824, had successfully sold under Royal Approval its own strange concoction of Venezuelian tree bark and raw alcohol. As ever, Dick arrived pellmell and fresh as last summer's dandelion far, far too late.

The Foreign Office was alerted to the Tonic Bitters pick-me-up campaign; and the relevance of a newly honoured KCB on thousands of tiny bottles promising relief from the previous night's intake of liquor could not have escaped Lord Granville.

Dick gave four lectures to various societies, and managed a suitable number of social handshakes at a Crystal Palace party given by a duchess for the Sultan of Zanzibar. This sort of gadding about reached its climax at one of many evenings given by a Lady Derby, a Lady Salisbury, a Lady Egerton or a Lady Holland: the Burtons were introduced to the Queen of Holland who expressed her wish to Isabel that she'd like to read Dick's most recent publication. Isabel rushed a copy round to the royal door the following morning. It is at a moment like this one yearns for the old Ruffian Dick to pull his moustaches and direct the royal personage to the nearest bookshop. Alas, his confrontations with a public increasingly disinclined to buy his books took away all too much of his confidence. We catch a glimpse of the sartorial ape lounging beside an open doorway at a grand ball one evening. A silly young masher in white waistcoat, his hair smothered in a sweet smelling pomatum, mistook Richard for another:

'Aw . . . are you one of the waitahs?' inquired this D'Orsayed and macassared *beau*.

'No—are you?' said Dick, priming his Chinese mutton-chop whiskers, 'for you look a damned sight more like a waiter than I do, and I was in hopes you were, because I might have got something to drink!'

It must have irked him. This Toffee took one glance at Dick's pocked face with a sabre thrust down one cheek, the hair unfashionable cropped, the eyebrows unplucked, and the shoulders squared and rigid with the authority of bumper book ends. Burton had always prided himself on his startling appearance and in the more recent past it had unfailingly seen him right; now, the evident quaintness of his looks branded him amusingly *déclassé*. Thirty years earlier nobody would have dared such cheek. The sabres would be drawn and they'd both be in the bushes, beneath the French window and the violin quartet, hacking away at each other.

After a six-week trip to Iceland, Burton returned in September with a severe attack of 'gout'. One can perhaps assume he did not make as much use of the patent 'Captain Burton's Tonic Bitters' as he once envisaged for a clamouring eager public of rueful drunks.

Meanwhile he studied the progress of Colonel Charles Gordon, who was in the central lake region of East Africa on an ambitious exploration to map all the lakes which acted as feeders to the great Nile. But Gordon's soldiers were at loggerheads with the Chief Mutesa, and he could not get his steamers up the river past the Murchison Falls. 'Chinese' Gordon managed to map the Nile to within sixty miles of its source. Burton was well aware of this famous Victorian's soldier's route. And it must have haunted him. On a number of occasions Gordon had corresponded with Dick in Trieste. And now he was the forty-two-year-old Governor of Sudan, one of the most famed soldiers in the British Army; he had recovered Nanking with the aid of British and American staff officers and a vagrant army, in the name of the Manchu dynasty; he had gone on to secure Taiping against forces considerably greater than his own. He was a diminutive figure with startling blue eyes, an ascetic soldier hero, and he could quote from the Bible with the familiarity of an addict. Between the two men there lay a bond of mutual esteem. Gordon was twelve years Dick's junior. Gordon's age and career produced just the right distance between them for the younger man to recognise with considerable sympathy Burton's astonishing qualities, which had been so neglected by the powers-that-be. Isabel, in later days when the two men became companions in London, remembered how Gordon would often finish a remark to Dick: 'Dick, there are only two men in the world who can do such and such a thing, I am one and you are the other.' Gordon and Burton, on the surface, seemed very much of the same clay. And soon the younger man's esteem would be put to the test.

Whatever he was feeling about Gordon and the latest Nile expedition, Dick was in a hurry to leave England, what with his gout and Isabel's infatuation with the endless social round. Dick applied to the Foreign Office for an extension of leave. He had already taken seven months off from Trieste, but it appears that the authorities were ready to oblige him with a further six months. It was too late in life now to start quibbling with Burton. He'd take the leave, whether granted or not. Isabel stayed behind in London to pack. Dick decided on a health tour through gastronomic France. By December both Burtons were staying in Paris. They travelled through Turin, Milan, and Venice, to reach Trieste on Christmas Eve 1875. When they were broke they stayed in one place and hugged their knees. But when they had money, they savoured every last port of call. The indications were that once again, Isabel had collected a new legacy. Dick rubbed his hands.

In Isabel's words, 'My husband, finding he had still six months' leave, asked me what I should like to do. I consulted my heart, and it answered "India" . . .' Far more likely, she said to him, 'Let us go back for six months and explore Goa and Bombay, and all those places of your youth I never shared with you. I have enough money for the six months, for the return boat fare, clothes, cab hires and what-have-you, we will be well equipped.' To which he might have made prompt reply, 'Topping scheme, Zookins. You pay and pack. This time I'll be your guide.'

Isabel and Richard were aboard a boat bound for Port Said by December 31, and no doubt the able Vice-Consul Mr Brock meanwhile entertained the English residents to a Consular New Year party from the balcony of his offices which overlooked Trieste harbour. He had often done it before, he would do it many times over in the future. Isabel and Richard sipped lemon tea on a sun deck and shared a leather bag of books. They had a clutch of English novels to read, and at long last Dick announced his plan to write an autobiography. He was in his fifty-fifth year, he had the time at his disposal, and Isabel was beside him ready to take the dictation. To every Burton reader's mortification, he got no further than a roughly dictated draft of about 40,000 words which barely took him beyond his twenties, and history has left no more of such a marvellous confessional than Isabel's jottings during the thirty-three-day cruise to Bombay. On board he had little else in mind to write down, and it is unlike Burton to leave aside such an incomplete piece. After all, he never failed to dot the last 'i' and cross the final 't' of those other windy books of the last six years. Inevitably suspicion must fall on Isabel's head. From her own writings, after Dick's death, we discover almost every page is littered with his quotations, and she kept the remnants of the autobiography purely for her own purposes. She never accounted for the random quotations, and whatever pages they were culled from, these manuscript sources never came to light after her death.

They sailed on to Jidda, Aden, and then Bombay, where they stayed with Dick's old friend, (Foster) Fitzgerald Arbuthnot. They underwent smallpox injections, Isabel caught a mild form of eye disease, and then her pet dog fell ill on her. She found almost everything about Bombay uncomfortable and filthy. From all accounts she had a habit of physically attacking any wretched serf she caught whipping a donkey or kicking a dog, much to Burton's embarrassment. At one stage, so distraught was Isabel, that she fetched six doctors to observe her own pet's plight. Finally, the dog was put to good use, sick as it was, for it attacked and bit another coachman Isabel had berated for his animal cruelty. The six doctors in Bombay, more used to the common sight of human bodies floating about in the tidal wharf beneath their windows, made a confused submission to the pet's mistress that its sight was rapidly failing and the heat was doing something awful to the animal's hydration. She thanked them and paid them off. The dog from then on followed her everywhere in a small basket lined with satin and sweet biscuits. Many a starved corpse floating out to sea must have risen from the wave to glance back in awe at the domestic foibles of the *Englaysie* Consul's wife.

Dick spent his time exploring his old ground. The Indian Army Barracks. His past haunts along the wharfs. The dark alleyways which led to shuttered brothels and officers' drinking parlours. His haunt was melancholic. By the harbour wall, up to his nose roared the smell of effluence. The community suffered from the same sewage problem as thirty years ago when he was here. Little had changed. Some of the buildings. A few of the streets. He was standing on the ruins of his own promise, not Bombay's. He let his heart sicken at the picture of the past. All the dreams of conquest he had nurtured here in his twenties. All the explorations and discoveries his young mind had once promised himself. He commented:

Some twenty-five natives, mostly negresses, haunt the houses which lodged our corps. The Mess-house, to which many recollections attach, still stands, thanks to its foundation of baked brick, but the front is converted to an open stable for human beings. There lived the actors in the famous Phuleli Regatta; there W . . . hatched all the troubles which prevented us from feeling too happy. There is the house which fell down; nearly crushing me and my *moonshee*; the fireplaces are half filled up; the floor is grown with camel thorn. How small and mean are the dimensions, which loom so large in the picture stored within the brain. There I temporarily buried the *young person* when the police-master gave orders to search the house. There T . . . played Peeping Tom upon his father and mother-in-law. How strange are the tricks of memory, which, often hazy as a dream about the most important events of a man's life, religiously preserves the merest trifles. And how very unpleasant to meet one's self, one's *dead self thirty years younger*. Adieu, old home. I shall not perhaps see you again, but it is not in my power ever to forget you.

They travelled to Hyderabad, where, among the English community, Dick enjoyed cockfighting and Isabel watched ostrich races; they were fêted at dinner parties, a military dance and a regatta; Dick inspected all manner of sights from new-laid railway lines to small mining concessions; both Burtons attended a marvellous four-day wedding, and later, a magnificent Shi'ite ceremony in honour of one of the two sons of Fatima, the daughter of the Prophet Mohammad.

They hastened back to Bombay for a grand ceremony to send off the Prince of Wales after his official royal tour of India. It was one of these determined sallies of Isabel to keep any royal personage in view. If they squeezed through the Bombay Consular red tape they could slide into the inner circle of halloos and God Bless yous as the over-weight German heir to the British throne ducked his head below the Royal Yacht bridge. Of course they hurried to see him off. The jolly Prince of Wales might just remember this strange couple. Weren't they the humorous pair who dressed up in all sorts of Arab tunics and flesh paint and with a maidgirl doing a wriggly dance with her bum? Chap who spoke no end of esoteric langwidges no one else got the time to read up?

Isabel and Richard then took a boat to Goa. She had long wanted to see this Portuguese settlement, and in particular the remarkable Jesuit architecture of the majestic cathedral of Bom Jesus which contains the tomb of St Francis Xavier. Dick recovered his usual biting style once on board. He found himself propping up a deck rail alongside a Catholic bishop. In the course of their exchange, Dick was quick to demarcate the creeds in his domestic life:

'My wife is the Jesuit of the family,' he said.

'What a capital thing for you!' exclaimed the dignified frock.

Either the conversation progressed to the current intellectual arguments of the day over Charles Darwin, or Dick made an accurate assessment of his own family lineage, because suddenly the priest drew Burton's attention to some monkeys shinning loose up the mast at the main deck.

'Well, Captain Burton, there are some of your ancestors.'

'Well, my Lord, I at least have made some progress,' Dick replied, 'but what about your lordship, who is descended from the angels?'

The couple were certainly travelling in great style. On board, they took advantage of the very best service the boat had to offer; there was plenty of wine at each meal, the cabins were airy and splendid. Isabel herself remarked that £10 a head for a thirty-six-hour cruise was very steep indeed, and it was unusual for her to detail the cost of travelling best bib-and-tucker class.

They spent the next two months on any number of boats belonging to the Austrian-Lloyds Shipping Company. From Goa they steamed on to Suez, from there to Cairo, then Alexandria, and then Ramleh. At each port of call they stayed a few days. And in July they sailed slowly across the Greek Isles back to Trieste. Isabel observed, during these interchangeable voyages from place to place:

the average English people, if not made comfortable at sea, are as trouble-some as a mustard plaster—nothing was right. They wanted their huge lumps of beef and mutton four times a day; they ate up all the provisions like locusts, and drank the cellar dry. What would last Italians and Greeks six weeks, does not last an Englishman one.

Do we observe Dick here at ship's table, white cotton napkin at his throat, bellowing for wine, and hammering the cloth table top with the wedge ends of his knife and fork demanding more slices of roast, and chump chops of lamb with best redcurrent jelly? Burton displays in this luxurious passage of months an almost overwhelming desire to splurge himself. The year had always belonged to Isabel. The London publishers of King and Co had wired her to the effect that they were shoving out another edition of her two-volume *The Inner Life of Syria, Palestine and the Holy Land*.

There did come a moment when she compared the success of her own writing to his, and in particular when she quite knowingly emphasised the reasons for his ever-dwindling public: his disregard for the reader's appetite, the manic arrogance of his endless marginalia, the shock tactics of his rich and multilingual vocabulary. She was speaking to him as the author of a human and chatty bestseller which the critics had praised for its built-in middlebrow recognitions, the wife abroad, the lady in danger, Faith and Righteousness in foreign parts, an easy and familiar narrative.

'You are like an iron machine, and I do all the wit and sparkle.'

'Oh I dare say,' replied Dick, 'the sparkle of a superannuated glow-worm!'

They were back in Trieste the second week of July, 1876, after a bibulous exploration of every comfort a traveller could wish for, interlaced with certain sad memory hunts of Dick's own, and Isabel had precious small change from £500 for the glorious voyage. In no time, her dog rasped its final breath, and the ever obedient Vice-Consul, Mr Brock, was made responsible for the pet's burial ground. The dog was buried in Mr Brock's own backyard for want of a better resting place, and Isabel ordered a white marble tombstone with engraved messages of devotion, which was exactly a suitable epitaph from a prominent patron of the Society for the Protection of Cruelty to Animals. Isabel wrapped the body in a seal-skin coat, and she designed an intricate burial cradle made up of miniature mattressing, pillows, sheets and blankets, with a curtain on a wire runner just in case the nosy earthworm might peep. The contraption was lowered into the ground, and Isabel uttered a formal Catholic prayer for the departed. The villagers along Brock's street, the Via St Vito, were less enthusiastic about the doggy proceedings. But Dick was not going to interfere. What was it he capitulated to, her new sense of authority? A fragile fiscal independence from him? Was it her Church? Had the *Haji* relented at last? Had he become addicted to the domestic nonsense she afflicted on him?

Richard attended the pet's funeral in the company of Mr Brock. They stood together in the backyard, temporarily cleared of cats and fowl, and listened to Isabel's prayer for the dead. Afterwards, Brock made sure the grave was deep enough to deter midnight seal-skin snatchers.

That very week, Charles Gordon was steaming to the north end of Lake Albert in search of yet another river outlet. He could not find it, and so he moved on east as far as the Murchison Falls. Gordon wanted to map the Nile from Gondokoro to its source, but constantly he was trumped; a tributary fed inwards instead of out, an alternative flow of water led to a falls he could not circumnavigate. It was a far stretch from the little backyard with the marble headstone where Richard stood. He had begun to sleep.

XVII

Not that his light failed, nor enough
swallows aimed south justified winter,
ichance an unfocussed gloom and the
feeding hesitancy of 'tswit tswit',
on the timber sill.

A FASHIONABLE LONDON MAGAZINE, THE *WORLD*, PRINTED A
description of the consul at Trieste over five years after the Burtons
had settled in. The author was keen to detail the 'bohemian and
eccentric' life of his subjects. The piece was called *Celebrity at Home,
Captain R. F. Burton at Trieste*:

> Captain and Mrs Burton are well, if airily, lodged in a flat composed of
> ten rooms, separated by a corridor adorned with a picture of our Saviour,
> a statuette of St. Joseph with a lamp, and a Madonna with another lamp
> burning before it. Thus far the belongings are all of the Cross; but no
> sooner are we landed in the little drawing-rooms, than signs of the
> Crescent appear. Small but artistically arranged, the rooms, opening into
> one another, are bright with Oriental hangings, with trays and dishes of
> gold and silver, brass trays and goblets, chibouques with great amber
> mouthpieces, and all kinds of Eastern treasures mingled with family
> souvenirs. There is no carpet, but a Bedouin rug occupies the middle of
> the floor, and vies in brilliancy of colour with Persian enamels and bits of
> good old china. There are no sofas, but plenty of divans covered with
> Damascus stuffs. Thus far the interior is as Musselman as the exterior is
> Christian; but a curious effect is produced among the Oriental *mise en
> scene* by the presence of a pianoforte and a compact library of well-
> chosen books. There is, too, another library here, greatly treasured by Mrs

Burton, to wit, a collection of her husband's works in about fifty volumes. On the walls are many interesting relics, models, and diplomas of honour, one of which is especially prized by Captain Burton. It is the *brevet de pointe* earned in France for swordsmanship. Near this hangs a picture of the Damascus home of the Burtons, by Frederick Leighton.

As the guest is inspecting this bright bit of colour, he will be roused by the full strident tones of a voice skilled in many languages, but never so full and hearty as when bidding a friend welcome. The speaker, Richard Burton, is a living proof that intensive work, mental and physical, sojourn in torrid and frozen climes, danger from dagger and pestilence, 'age' a person of good sound constitution far less than may be supposed. A Hertfordshire man, a soldier and the son of a soldier, of mingled Scotch, Irish, and French descent, his iron frame shows in its twelfth lustre no sign of decay. *Arme blanche* and more insidious fever have neither dimmed his eye nor wasted his sinews.

Standing about five feet eleven, his broad deep chest and square shoulders reduce his apparent height very considerably, and the illusion is intensified by hands and feet of Oriental smallness. The Eastern, and indeed distinctly Arabic, look of the man is made more pronounced by prominent cheek-bones (across one of which is the scar of a sabre-cut), by closely cropped black hair just tinged with grey, and a pair of piercing black, gipsy-looking eyes. A short straight nose, a determined mouth partly hidden by a black moustache, and a deeply bronzed complexion, complete the remarkable physiognomy so wonderfully rendered on canvas by Leighton only a couple of seasons ago. It is not to be wondered at that this stern Arab face, and a tongue marvellously rich in Oriental idiom and Mohammedan lore, should have deceived the doctors learned in the Koran, among whom Richard Burton risked his life during that memorable pilgrimage to Mecca and Medinah, on which the slightest gesture or accent betraying the Frank would have unsheathed a hundred *khanjars*.

Leading the way from the drawing-rooms or divans, he takes us through bedrooms and dressing-rooms, furnished in Spartan simplicity with little iron bedsteads covered with bearskins, and supplied with reading-tables and lamps, beside which repose the Bible, the Shakespeare, and Euclid, and the Breviary, which go with Captain and Mrs Burton on all their wanderings. His gifted wife, one of the Arundells of Wardour, is, as becomes a scion of an ancient Anglo-Saxon and Norman Catholic house, strongly attached to the Church of Rome; but religious opinion is never allowed to disturb the peace of the Burton household, the head of which is laughingly accused of Mohammedanism by his friends. The little rooms are completely lined with rough deal shelves, containing, perhaps, eight thousand or more volumes in every Western language, as well as in Arabic, Persian, and Hindustani. Every odd corner is piled with weapons, guns, pistols, boar-spears, swords of every shape and make, foils and masks, chronometers, barometers, and all kinds of scientific instruments. One cupboard is full of medicines necessary for Oriental expeditions or for Mrs Burton's Trieste poor, and on it is written, 'The Pharmacy'. Idols are not wanting, for elephant-nosed Gunpati is there cheek by jowl with Vishnu.

The most remarkable objects in the rooms just alluded to are the rough deal tables, which occupy most of the floor-space. They are almost like kitchen or ironing tables. There may be eleven of them, each covered with writing materials. At one of them sits Mrs Burton, in morning *néglige*, a grey *choga*—the long loose Indian dressing-gown of soft camel's hair—topped by a smoking-cap of the same material. She rises and greets her husband's old friend with the cheeriest voice in the world. 'I see you are looking at our tables. Every one does. Dick likes a separate table for every book, and when he is tired of one he goes to another. There are no tables of any size in Trieste, so I had these made as soon as I came. They are so nice. We may upset the ink-bottle as often as we like without anybody being put out of the way. These three little rooms are our "den", where we live, work, and receive our *intimes*, and we leave the doors open that we may consult over our work. Look at our view!' From the windows, looking landward, one may see an expanse of country extending for thirty or forty miles, the hills covered with foliage, through which peep trim villas, and beyond the hills higher mountains dotted with villages, a bit of the wild Karso peering from above. On the other side lies spread the Adriatic, with Miramar, poor Maximilian's home and hobby, lying on a rock projecting into the blue water, and on the opposite coast are the Carnian Alps capped with snow.

'Why we live so high up', explains Captain Burton, 'is easily explained. To begin with, we are in good condition, and run up and down the stairs like squirrels. We live on the fourth storey because there is no fifth. If I had a *campagna* and gardens and servants, horses and carriages, I should feel tied, weighted down, in fact. With a flat and two or three maid-servants, one has only to lock the door and go . . .'

In spite of all this, and perhaps because of it—for the famous Oriental traveller, whose quarter of a hundred languages are hardly needed for the entry of cargoes at a third rate seaport, seems to protest too much—one is impelled to ask what anybody can find to do at Trieste, an inquiry simply answered by a 'stay and see' with a slap on the shoulder to enforce the invitation. The *ménage Burton* is conducted on the early-rising principle. About four or five o'clock our hosts are astir, and already in their 'den', drinking tea made over a spirit-lamp, and eating bread and fruit, reading and studying languages. By noon the morning's work is got over, includ-ing the consumption of a cup of soup, the ablution without which no true believer is happy, and the obligations of Frankish toilette. Then comes a stroll to the fencing-school, kept by an excellent broadswordsman, an old German trooper. For an hour Captain and Mrs Burton fence in the school, if the weather be cold; if it is warm, they make for the water, and often swim for a couple of hours.

Then comes a spell of work at the Consulate. 'I have my Consulate', the Chief explains, 'in the heart of the town. I don't want my Jack-tar in my sanctum; and when he wants *me*, he has usually been on the spree and got into trouble'. While the husband is engaged in his official duties, his wife is abroad promoting a Society for the Prevention of Cruelty to Animals, a necessary institution in Southern countries, where — on the purely gratuitous hypothesis that the so-called lower animals have no souls — the uppermost brutality is shown in the treatment of them. 'You see', remarks our host, 'that my wife and I are like an elder and younger brother living *en garçon.*'

A cosy scene indeed.

For the next eight months Burton shirtily resigned himself to the consular desk, pushing the more boring Britannic items in the direction of the efficient Mr Brock, and finding time to swim and meet with friends on the balcony of the nearby hotel, or put the finishing touches to a 674-page two-volume narrative on his return voyage to India, *Scind Revisited; With Notices of the Anglo-Indian Army.* An up-to-date version of his 1851 *Scinde, or the Unhappy Valley*, the manuscript was bundled off in the diplomatic postbag to Messrs Richard Bentley & Co, the London publishers who first issued his Scinde book.

Ismail Pasha, the Khedive of Egypt, was a forty-six-year-old spendthrift. Since 1863, when he wrestled the country away from Turkish domination, Ismail had borrowed on the international money markets sums approaching one hundred million pounds sterling. He was an extraordinary example of demagogic munificence, constantly opening schools for children under the age of ten, and unable to resist the blandishments of any hustling French or German financier. Ismail took it upon himself to build an opera-house and commission Giuseppe Verdi to write for its grand opening his immortal *Aida.* Ismail built himself two luxurious palaces, one beside the sea and the other up in the hills. He also built a number of sugar refineries, and, by 1876, found himself so short of money he was forced to offer the British his remaining asset, his shares in the Suez Canal. By the time Dick and Isabel returned to Trieste the Khedive's Treasury had reached rock bottom, and the government's printers were churning out sackfuls of paper currency with the industry of an all-night lavatory roll factory. The Khedive was earnestly searching around his bankrupt nation for something to calm the international bankers who were on the verge of a spondulick-type nervous breakdown. In the summer of 1876 Richard Burton had taken it into his head to write somewhat crackpot letters to the Khedive assuring the Pasha of untold gold in the Midian, a large territory which spreads from the peninsula of Sinai, east of the Gulf of Akhaba, beyond the Euphrates and as far south as the great deserts of Hijaz and Nafud, all of which the Khedive laid claim to. Dick's letters referred to an old friend of his, an Alexandrian merchant, Haji Wali, who, twenty years earlier, had ridden with Burton on the famous pilgrimage into Mecca. Burton recalled a trip Haji Wali had made into the north-eastern hills of the Hijaz desert where he had found gold in various rockfaces. The gullible Khedive replied to Burton and encouraged him to send more details on the possibility of gold in the Midian.

Dick was ecstatic. In no time he drafted another letter mentioning Egyptian and Roman gold mines in Jebel Zubara and Jebel-el-Fatira, the haematite iron mines in Sinai and the carbonate substances extracted from the natron lakes of Egypt. He was obviously on the right track because this time the Khedive promptly invited the imaginative Englishman to Cairo. Dick was beside himself with enthusiasm. He referred to himself as 'the new Pharaoh's new Joseph' and he convinced his wife they now had an opportunity to make themselves rich beyond their dreams. Before Richard embarked for Egypt, Isabel's godfather Lord Arundell had been approached for funds to help Burton. It must have been Isabel who applied to her kinsman for the money. Meanwhile, Burton warned the Foreign Office that Trieste was in for a 'hellish cold winter' which would do his gout no good. The Foreign Office, weary to the core of these excuses, caved in to his demand for a month's furlough. All that really remained was to find Haji Wali, if he was yet alive.

Dick sailed for Egypt on the steamer *Espero* on March 3, 1877. Isabel recorded bitterly, 'There was not money enough for us both to go, so I had to make the sacrifice and stay behind.' Eight months earlier she had swanned and wined and fed her man on a nostalgic tour of India. Glumly, she turned back from the port-side, and found a retreat in a Dalmatian Jesuit asylum for the deaf and dumb up in the hills behind Trieste.

Dick spent two weeks in Cairo before he could gain an audience with the Khedive. Fortunately for Burton there was much to do in town. His first priority was to locate the elusive Haji Wali who would now be at least eighty. Dick cabled two friends of his in Zagazig,

J. Charles J. Clarke and Hugh Thurburn, and these two were instrumental in fetching Haji Wali, aged and cantankerous and deaf, back to Cairo.

The Khedive was agreeably surprised to discover Dick Burton had funds of his own, and this swayed the scheme the right way. Ismail Pasha placed three engineers from the Egyptian army under a French mining technician George Marie, and ordered the steamship *Sinnar* loaded up for a month's tour of the hills behind the eastern shore of El-Muwaylih. Dick was forced to take tough measures with Haji Wali. Haji Wali had left his many children at home, he didn't want to be taken on this voyage, he wouldn't draw a map of the area where he last thought he saw gold, he complained about his back, he complained about his front, and Dick was almost in despair when he discovered that two pints of best bitter first thing in the morning could keep the old man relatively acquiescent. While Haji Wali quaffed back the bitter, Burton persuaded the old fellow to think back twenty years to the good days of that exciting pilgrimage to Mecca and Medina. The object of all this consideration pulled his beard and shook his not too reliable ears at Burton. 'You are resolved to be the death of me,' he growled.

Haji Wali led them to all kinds of strange places. For twenty days Dick collected box after box of mineral stones; they were continually rowing ashore to climb up into the range of hills, the Sharmah hills behind As Sawrah, to follow inexact directions from the old one. Eventually, at a point known as Jebel Abyad, twenty miles from the coastline of the Red Sea, the exhausted Haji Wali, much to his own relief, found Burton and George Marie exulting over a series of veined rocks and dust particles. They had in their opinion discovered the richest gold mine in the Middle East.

In all, eight wooden crates of stones were returned to Cairo on the steamer *Sinnar*. Dick had a brief audience with the Khedive. The samples would be sent to London for metallurgical tests. It would take several months. Meanwhile, Dick should return to Trieste. The Khedive said he would call for him when he knew the results of the assay. Dick left the palace and was promptly set upon by Haji Wali who wanted his 'just reward' for discovering these fabulous gold mines. Dick frowned and muttered to the effect that a couple of pints of best bitter a day and a free steam trip around the Gulf of Akhaba were about all the old man could expect. A frightful scene ensued. With typical Arabic bluster the two sat on the pavement cross-legged and hammered and tonged away at each other. 'All those stones in the eight boxes are my property, you infidel thief and fork-toothed crop-haired rogue' spluttered Haji Wali. To which Dick rejoindered, 'You lying and ungrateful son of a thrice born darkness of an impenetrable gloom, who was it who led you and fed you and clothed you on the pilgrimage to Mecca?' Haji Wali was promised a hefty percentage of the next expedition. This first try, Dick assured him, was merely a dress-rehearsal. In a few months they would meet again, and become so rich they could call each other 'Dukes of Midian'.

Cairo was in a state of upheaval. Russia had declared war on Turkey. The Khedive was running wild in the palace courtyard like a headless chicken, unable to decide which country he'd benefit with a gift of Egypt's virtually bankrupt armed forces. If he supported Turkey, England and France would refuse to buy any more shares in the Suez Canal. If he supported Russia, and Russia won, he could forget about his hundred-million-pound international debt. But then Russia might rule the Middle East from Constantinople, and place her enormous fleet in the basin of the Red Sea like a marine gobstopper in the throat of the Pasha's only real money-maker, the Suez Canal.

Dick sailed back to Trieste in May, 1877, to write a 398-page study of his three-week search: *The Gold Mines of Midian and the Ruined Midianite Cities*. At the end of the year he'd post it off to Messrs Kegan Paul, in London, and it would be printed the following spring.

Vice-Consul Brock must have been surprised to find Burton back in Trieste only four weeks late. But that was an *hors-d'oeuvre*. Almost before Isabel could collect her own bags and descend from the Jesuit hide-away up in the hills, Burton was off again. He was two weeks in Verona, then took a pleasure cruise for ten days around the Adriatic coast; there was a ride across the mountains to Austria; there was an excursion through the wooded glades and narrow valleys of Styria; and sometimes his wife caught up with him, sometimes not.

The other unlikely employee of the Khedive in Cairo was the illustrious Colonel Charles Gordon. He had been made Governor of Sudan, a territory the Khedive had annexed for himself in between hiring dancing girls from Paris for his new Music Hall; Gordon was merely the white *Englaysie* nominal chief of the Sudan, for the Khedive had the good sense to provide him with an immediate superior – the Egyptian Governor-General of Sudan. Gordon had accepted the post at Khartoum in good faith. The British authorities were not prepared to offer him a better job. And, in keeping with his scrupulousness, Gordon would not take more than a fifth of the £10,000 a year salary which went with his post.

Gordon had a handful of trained Egyptian soldiers, and with road-builders on slave wages and at least one full-scale tribal war at either elbow, he was expected both to keep the vast Sudan under control, and to maintain the Khedive in his accustomed luxury on the sale of ivory, Sudan's principal export. Darfur, a province in the West Sudan, consisted of a four-million-strong community of Arabs and a black tribe known as the Fur. The 170,000-square-mile of desert and undulating plateau produced tamarinds, white melons and cattle. Its capital was El Fasher. It was the most unruly of all Gordon's dominions, and he had the notion to write to the one man who could control this territory, Richard Francis Burton, because—in Gordon's appalling estimation—Dick was the very man for Darfur. Gordon cannot have read Speke's account of Dick's leadership, nor could he have seen the Bombay Infantry reports to the East India Company noting Burton's military genius at Berbera, in Somaliland. If ever there was a retired junior officer from the Indian ranks who could not control other people it was Burton. Gordon fired off a wonderful letter to Trieste in June 1877, filled with his own admiration for Burton (Gordon never once retracted his enthusiasm for Dick's military ability):

> . . . I have no doubt that you are comfortable, but I cannot think entirely satisfied with your present small sphere. I have therefor written to the Khedive to ask him to give you Darfur as Governor-General, with £1600 a year, and a couple of secretaries at £300 . . . Now is the time for you to make your indelible mark in the world and in these countries. You will be remembered in Egypt as having made Darfur . . .

Dick received this offer with frosty silence. It was a month before he even considered replying to Gordon. Privately, he was disturbed over the Khedive issue. He didn't want Bible-bashing hard life intoxicated army creatures like Charles Gordon putting ideas into Ismail Pasha's soft skull. He had his own peculiar relationship with the Khedive, and the last kind of official audience in Cairo Dick wanted was one where he'd be congratulated on his acceptance of the Darfur job. An adventurer seeking a mining commission in the Midian desert from Egypt was one thing; it was quite another to be a member of the Khedive's army.

It was a bad omen for Burton to discover yet another letter on his door-step, in mid July, with the stamp of the Khartoum office of Gordon on its envelope. Colonel Gordon's tone was one of seduction and temptation.

. . . You will find much interest here, for the Ulemas are well-read people, and know the old history. I found a lot of chain armour here, just like the armour of Saladin's people, time of the Crusades, with old helmets, some embossed with gold . . . The people would delight in the interest you would take in them . . . On the border are Niam-Niam, who circumcise. I suppose they took it from these Arab tribes. I only hope you will come up . . .

One cannot tempt an old fox like Burton with any more naked and bleeding circumcision. As for the people being delighted, Dick had never given a brass monkey's thought in the past to what did or did not delight the native humour. He wasn't going to start now. In addition, Dick knew a great deal more about the growing dangers of Darfur than 'Chinese' Gordon. The most recent 'Mahdi', a certain Mohammed Ahmed, was a young Shi'ite warrior determined to take the Sudan for himself. A 'Mahdi' in the strictest terms is a Messiah, and within the Muslim faith, Shi'ites and Fatimites consider themselves direct descendants of Mohammad. Since the 10th century there had been at least five fanatics who had claimed the title of God's Caliph. Richard Burton was aware of the 'Mahdi' in Darfur. And the painful prospect of defending a bankrupt Khedive from a horde of selfless Shi'ite fanatics, armed with a troop of incompetent Cairo-trained infantrymen was a fate Dick could well do without.

Dick replied to Gordon in Khartoum, 'You and I are too much alike. I could not serve under you, nor you under me. I do not look upon the Soudan as a lasting thing. I have nothing to depend upon but my salary, and I have a wife, and you have not.' Two months later, Gordon cracked off a further letter. '£1,600, or indeed £16,000 would never compensate a man for a year spent actively in Darfur. But I considered you, from your independence, one of Nature's nobility, who did not serve for money. Excuse the mistake—if such it is.' Dick Burton could hardly conceal from himself the indirect insult in Gordon's remarks. In October, Burton replied to Gordon, telling him that the Khedive had ordered him back to Cairo for a second expedition to the Midian. In December, Gordon resignedly wrote back,

I am glad you are with the Khedive, he is most kind, and there are few men for whom I would do for, as I would do for him, for he has not been at all well treated. I am here for some time, for affairs are much complicated, and I want to finish off once for all with the two great questions here, when these are finished then I hope never to come back to these parts alone.

Six years hence the 'Mahdi' and his united forces took El Fasher in Darfur, and then Khartoum in the Sudan, and Charles 'Chinese' Gordon was savagely cut down on the steps of the Governor-General's palace.

Between December 1877 and April 1878, Burton embarked on his penultimate mission of any importance. The Khedive had enough confidence in him to grant two thousand napoleons' worth of credit, in exchange for signed receipts (at sixteen shillings a napoleon). The complement consisted of forty Sudanese soldiers, two engineers, an artist Emile Lacaze, and a blacksmith Jean Philipin. The same steamer was acquired and loaded, and in due course, somebody obligingly rounded up the ubiquitous Haji Wali, as ever complaining bitterly, and after a minor explosion in the boiler, the expedition sailed down the Gulf of Suez.

When the boat reached the shores to the west of the Hijaz hills, Burton led the expedition for six days back to Jebel Abyad. For the next three months, with the manual assistance of troops, Burton and Haji Wali instructed the diggers to pile together anything which remotely resembled extracts of sulphur, basalt, copper, silver or gold. The soldiers were none too willing diggers, and frequently they erupted into mutinous arguments with Burton. Dick used an old military fort, El-Muwaylih, as a general meeting point and a place to retreat to when the going got too much for him. In all, they explored over a hundred miles of desert plateau and inland hillside in this part of the Midian. They were kept going by a perpetual hazy promise from Haji Wali that the really great vein he once discovered was just over the next hill. Of course it wasn't. Burton constantly talked to them of 'black diamonds', 'new California goldrushes', 'turquoises in babbling runnels'; he was sublimely confident. He rattled away with metallurgical and lithological assurances. According to Dick's rarefied account there was free gold in those micaceous schists, and ore in the chalcedony which parts the granite from the gneiss.

Nobody had a clue what he was looking for, and the soldiers had no intention of digging more than a couple of feet through this hard rock. 'I must regret,' wrote Dick later, 'that there, as indeed throughout the exploration, all our specimens were taken from the surface.'

At the end of March, Dick led a caravan of sixty to Umm el Karayat, and left the soldiers to get on with the digging. Meanwhile, he rode on to another place, Umm Harb, where he announced rather hastily, that he had no doubt 'these are gold mines' as he stood over a spot which undeniably showed ancient diggings. Meanwhile the men left behind obediently holding their shovels, had barely cracked the stony ground. For the sake of expediency, they had collected as many surface samples as they could find. And nothing more.

In mid-April, twenty-five tons of specimens were boxed and lifted aboard the *Sinnar* steamship. The expedition returned to Cairo. At the port of Suez Dick saw Isabel waving to him as the *Sinnar* hailed into view. And at Suez he received a tremendous and unexpected ovation from a crowd which had gathered to catch a glimpse of this once famous traveller. The crowd knew him as *Haji* Abdullah of old, the infidel rascal who crept into Mecca. And there standing beside him on the sun-deck was the half-demented Haji Wali. For a few moments Dick received a heady smell of popularity and public adulation. As he acknowledged the crowd he felt great pride, but a pride tinged with ruefulness. This crowd, though modest, was balm to his soul — crumbs of devotion he had long lost sight of. There they were, the smelly, shouting, half-naked dears, 'niggers' and nomads, Islamic cripples and urchins with fingers deft enough to steal your pockets and their contents, scarred and ugly, old and tremulous, a motley echo indeed. Had he the heart he would have cried. He hadn't. He jerked Isabel's arm beside his, and marched her dispiteously through the avid throng, with not a glance in appreciation, or a wink of revelry.

Isabel and Dick sailed on to Cairo. He had spent her money. He had also spent her godfather's money. There was nothing left to promise the soldiers, servants and crew but the two thousand napoleons the Khedive had assured him of. At Cairo docks, the rail freight van broke down three times. The crew walked off in disgust. The soldiers put down their weapons and refused to take on these common labouring tasks in the siding. Burton was embroiled in the familiar activity of promising sixty men they would be paid tomorrow. He was an old hand at that. And Haji Wali, watching from the deck of the *Sinnar* groaned with weary recognition.

In the morning Dick had an audience with the Khedive. He did not know how much gold or silver he had struck, but he assured Ismail Pasha that once these samples were packed off to London, scientific analysis would prove his thesis right. They were on the verge of a great discovery. The Khedive caught the same gold rash as Burton. They believed each other's dreams. Dick wrote out a contract claiming five per cent royalty on all diggings in the Midian. The Khedive delightedly agreed. It only speeded up the crackpot illusion.

Dick's haggling *Haji* Abdullah attitude towards money was almost shrewish. Dick loved money. And he never joked about anything he loved.

Isabel was highly optimistic about the Midian gold mines. She bumped into Colonel Charles Gordon her first week in Cairo. She was alone. Almost at once, Gordon notched up steam and barged into his old offer of Darfur. This time, he'd give Dick £3,000 to come to West Sudan. Laughing, Isabel made a joke to the effect that £3,000 wouldn't buy them a pair of gloves if fortune came through with their Midian gold.

Dick and his engineers drew up hasty maps for Ismail Pasha. The most important item on the agenda was to pack the samples back to London. Dick's friend J. Charles J. Clarke, who was Director of Telegraphs, volunteered to take the crates with him. Clarke was in London by June 20. Dick and Isabel spent a week in Trieste, and boarded a ship bound for London on July 20. He suffered a bad dose of gout, which gave him some sort of excuse for his absenteeism to offer the Foreign Office. In London a few of the English newspapers had devoted space to the romantic exploration of unknown Midian lands by the traveller, Captain Richard F. Burton. But, in a trice Burton was on holiday in Dublin, back again to our shores only to stay with Isabel's godfather, Lord Arundell. Perhaps to explain just where all that money had gone to?

It was fifteen years before Isabel could write publicly on the cost of this expedition. And she has made it more than apparent whose was the greater blame. According to her, both Lord Arundell and Richard were personally out of pocket. But she suffered the heaviest loss – £728. It was the last of those delightful legacies. As for the Khedive, not only was the promise of two thousand napoleons merely on tick, but when they reached Cairo and tapped the ambitious Pasha for the funds, the royal exchequer couldn't oblige. It was a dreadful financial bungle, but the Burtons held their heads high because if only a tenth of their Midian dreams came true they would spend the remainder of their lives awash with a bounty fit for Midas.

Back in London, Dick held his breath and waited for the assay results from the specimen stones. How many dreams filled his hours? How many imaginary times did he resign with a flourish from the Trieste job, slamming the Foreign Office door behind him at long last in Lord Granville's or Lord Russell's face?

He was sitting in his hotel bedroom with Isabel, when a knock came at the door. A messenger from the Foreign Office had brought him a letter via the diplomatic bag. It was another of Charles Gordon's appeals: 'I will give you £5,000 if you'll throw up Trieste!' Nobody before had ever offered him £5,000. But he was determined to refuse. He had the smell of gold in his nostrils.

And that, alas, was just about all he had. The report from the assaying office was not good. There were minute portions of gold in the stones, but they were nothing of the kind which might justify a full scale mining assault on the Hijaz Hills, behind the desert shores of the Red Sea, in the land of Midian. Richard Burton was shattered. He promptly retreated to those Grub Street clubs he once enjoyed so much, and devoted most of his waking hours to port and brandy.

Shortly after, he took himself to Germany for a three-week holiday. Gruffly he told Isabel to catch up with him the following month in Trieste. And he was off.

When she found her consul, he was in a very sorry state. He had drunk himself toxic in Germany, and reached Trieste nigh crippled with lumbago and gout.

It was 1879 and winter was fast approaching. Dick mentioned in passing how the swallows had already begun their annual voyage south to Africa. Isabel maintained a brave face, insisting they went to delightful places up in the hills where there were 'plain and ground mountains all around, the night air was perfectly delightful, with a beautiful starlight', and where 'the woods are lovely, the forest full of squirrels, come and play with you. We had delightful walks . . .' Sometimes she dared not speak to him. His silence was so angry. His brandy breath such a slight to her. She had pains in her stomach she could not understand. Her leg and ankle gave her considerable pain after a recent bad fall. In the morning, on a high terrace wall where they often had early coffee and Dick puffed his Havana cheroot, it was especially bad for him, as well. He would lean tightly back into the cane wicker chair and gasp at a dagger-like sharpness in the base of his spine. Isabel talked to him of a 'bone-setter' she had heard about. She would like to travel to Voslau where this specialist lived, that is – if Dick would come, too. Richard, not to be outdone in the illness stakes, informed her he knew of a very fine man, a Professor Benedict, in Vienna, who was adept at stimulating lumbago with an electrical machine which charged the nerves; that was where he would like to go. Isabel hobbled indoors to pack their cases. She gently prompted Richard to drop a line to Mr Brock. Brock was sure to inform London of Her Britannic Majesty's somewhat reduced consul, and his request for sick leave would not be refused. Dick rolled the cigar butt in his teeth. It had grown cold, and he wasn't going to light up again. Yes, the swallows were turning south towards Africa. Perhaps over Cairo or Aden, above the central lake region, and Somalia, and further still, where it was warm. Every morning he felt cold like this. It was the intake of alcohol. It was the cool of the mountains. And that dull incessant ache, that longing for the life to be another life that it assuredly was not. He stood to his feet and waited for the stab of pain to pass.

XVIII

Oh, what if he still rode on, the old
Contemptible Dick his dander gone;
would they tell him ride, ride, ride,
aunt gunboat sallies by his side?

RICHARD GROWLED AROUND THE ROOMS IN THE UPPER-FLOOR
apartment in Trieste. He could not concentrate on his writing. The
tension was abominable. He'd barely speak. His mind, a closed circuit
to the outside, was in a ferment. And Isabel suffered greatly with her
legs. She could not climb the steep flights of stairs.

Dick and Isabel developed a very peculiar form of communication.
He would leave a note for her. It might be placed in a table drawer she
was sure to open. The note, for example, might say nothing more than
'soup, bacon and two veg, and jam topped suet *Spotted Dog* pudding for
afters, please'. And Isabel silently complied. She was treading on eggs,
all the time. But her nerve would not give way. Some other rum
things were happening inside the apartment, and they centred around
those dispassionate daily messages. In her own words, she suspected a
divine intervention:

> We suddenly began to be inundated by anonymous letters; then our
> private papers and writings would disappear; a great fuss of finding them
> was made, and when all fuss and hope of recovery was over, they would
> reappear. There was always some mystery hanging about, and once we
> found on the floor a copy-book with some very good imitations of my
> hand-writing, or what my hand-writing *would* be if I tried to disguise it a
> little backwards, and some very bad and easily recognisable attempts at

my husband's very peculiar hand. The anonymous letters generally tried to set us against each other, if possible, and I was always finding love-letters thrust into his pockets, whenever I cleaned or brushed his clothes, which I generally did . . .

She never generally cleaned or brushed his clothes. They weren't inundated by anonymous letters. She was in the habit of peeping into his jacket pockets, and he, with a degree of humour, provided her with some juicy bait. It was a mildly cruel practical joke. And he relished it: 'You must be quite sure not to make yourself uncomfortable about any of this sort of thing,' he told her, 'and to tell me everything that occurs, because I am *sure* this is an intrigue, and a woman's intrigue, which has something to do with money.'

She knew he knew. And he knew she knew and would never show. He enjoyed that. Dick *plain*.

His own health improved. He grew careless of his official obligations. It seemed he could get away with whatever he liked as far as the Foreign Office was concerned. One day in the autumn of 1879, he asked Isabel to pack his bags, and he left Trieste for Egypt. He stayed alone for six months in and around Cairo. The dutiful Mr Brock shoved his Vice-consular pen with even greater diligence. Burton spent some exhausting days trying to get inside the Vice-Regal Lodge in Cairo for an audience. Unfortunately for him, all his hopes were ruined. The Khedive was making an undignified sprint for his yacht moored one hundred yards off-shore where a crate of gold conservatively valued at four million pounds was stashed away in the lower hold. It was the State Treasury.

The new Pasha, Tewfik, slammed the door in Burton's face. Dick had no one else to appeal to for reimbursement, and so, by early May 1880, he was ready to return to Trieste. A wicked stroke of fate over-took him one evening when he was returning to his hotel from supper with friends. Nine shadowy thieves assaulted him. Even had he his youth, his cudgel, his pistols, or sword-stick, he would not have stood a chance. After a violent onslaught he was left in the gutter with a battered skull. His gold signet ring was taken, but luckily the thieves did not find his chain vest-pocket time-piece, nor his wallet.

He promptly sailed home. Isabel was shocked at his condition when he disembarked. Recovering some of his spirit, he announced the serious risk of meningitis and ordered himself to be put to bed. In due course a local doctor attended and prescribed a concentrated course of salicin treatment. Isabel blithely recalled: 'I can never remember a more peaceful and happy time with Richard than in Opçina, where we led a Darby and Joan life, principally 1880 . . .'

He returned to Austria, visiting Vienna and Salzburg, and travelling to the tiny alpine village of Oberammergau to observe the 'Mystery Plays' (he came away none too delighted — 'lack of chronological truth revolts the traveller . . . the scourging is altogether without realism'); the archangel's part was performed without the usual wings, and Dick suggested to Isabel that perhaps the archangel might recently have had a moulting problem.

Dick kept his spirits up with more eccentric schemes which he churned out in the direction of the Foreign Office. He sent half a dozen letters to Lord Granville in London. He wanted £2,000 a year, freedom from the Cairo Consul-General, his Trieste post retained on the customary half-salary, and a furlough of two years. He fancied himself as a kind of pirate of the Red Sea, stamping out the slave trade. He saw himself as a sea-going counterpart to Gordon, and as a remorseless crusader for this issue. Granville could hardly have ignored the painful description Burton gave of various forms of mutilation the slavers indulged in. Nor could he have circumnavigated the consul's commonsense advice to, (1) register existing slaves; (2) proclaim that non-registered slaves were free; and (3) forbid itinerant Arabs travelling without passports or identifications from buying slaves. In particular, Dick railed against the trade in eunuchs. As many as eight thousand boys a year were transported to Arabia, Egypt and Turkey. There was an average price of forty dollars per head. Burton, at pains to soften the horror these children endured, put his case forward with the utmost diplomacy.

> The nature of the subject forbids details in pages intended for the public eye; but, in communicating with my Government, I have been as explicit as decency permits, and my description makes the blood run cold. The subjects range between four and ten; if the operation be performed on older boys, they seldom survive. At the age of ten the loss may be seventy percent; and even in the case of younger children about one-fourth, to state a low figure, die from the razor.

This report was presented to Granville, and the Foreign Office decided it was not sensible to place Dick somewhere in the Midian, from where he could operate his gold quest side-line. Above all, the report ended with a peculiar additional recommendation. After he had fulminated long and correctly over the dreadful sales of human beings, their mutilations, and their fates, Burton was not satisfied to confine his indignation to the slavers' 'league with death and covenant with hell', and added:

> And when humanity is satisfied by setting men free, it is to be hoped that Egypt will do something towards the prevention of cruelty to animals. The Egyptian is not brutal; his is the thoughtless cruelty of the child, who cannot realise the fact that beasts suffer like himself. Such is the force of custom that a donkey boy rarely passes a donkey in the street without dealing a cut of the *jerid*, or palm stick.

Isabel had got into the habit of writing out in copper-hand his first draft of a letter. It was not too difficult to slip the extra humble appeal into the text.

These months brought with them the crop of deaths a man in his early sixties must learn to face. It was the start of a ghostly harvest which Burton assiduously took note of in his day-books. Like the swallows retreating from his window-sill the names of newly departed friends and contemporaries were buoys alight in the dark channel of his years. Thomas Carlyle died in February, mountebank 'sinner' friend who awarded Dick the title all those years ago of 'Perpetual President of the Heaven and Hell Amalgamation Society'. Then, Benjamin Disraeli, created Earl of Beaconsfield, died in April, 1881. Each death Dick pencilled in with care.

In September, Richard met the young explorer, Captain Verney Lovett Cameron, in Venice. Born in 1844, Cameron joined the navy at thirteen, and led the RGS expedition. to aid Livingstone in 1873. Cameron was an old admirer of Burton. Some twenty-three years Dick's junior, like 'Chinese' Gordon he held considerable respect for the consul from Trieste. That year an International Geographical Congress was held in Venice, and it was left to Isabel, in her notes, to ask indignantly why such a notable and distinguished traveller and cartographer as Burton, was excluded. She rightly felt no official function such as this could afford to ignore the proximity of the consul. Meanwhile Dick attended a few of the social evenings given by the Venetian Society, and wrote a witty article for the *Academy* magazine in London, in which he emphasised the lack of British participation in the Congress. It amused Isabel greatly when, just as the most illustrious geographers attending the Congress passed by the Lido one afternoon, Dick and Verney rolled up their trousers, kicked their boots and socks off, and began to make a collection of mud pies.

'Look nurse,' cried Burton to his wife, 'we have made such a beautiful pie.'

'Please tell Dick,' Verney complained petulantly, 'not to touch my spade!'

Burton had found a new 'younger brother'. Edward was still a vegetable in an asylum where he'd stay all his life. The shadow hung over Burton, and throughout his career there are many instances of his keenness for a companion to whom he could wax happily in his role of tutor, guide and seer

Once again in Venice, Dick met up with a shadowy character, half entrepreneur, half romancer, James Irvine. He was similar to the anonymous benefactor who set Dick plunging off into Iceland. Dick was reduced to putting himself up for hire to any mining company or speculator willing to offer him money and equipment for a fact-finding expedition. Henry Stanley had the gigantic resources of his American newspaper proprietor to finance him. David Livingstone had merely required the noble sanctions of the Bible Society and the adulation of an adoring public to continue his explorations. And in 1873 at the time of Livingstone's death, European nations still hesitated to use individual explorers as unwitting agents for colonial expansion. By the 1880s, all this had changed. Belgium, Germany, France and Britain were prepared to use any means at their disposal from the Bible to anti-slavery humbug to achieve their ends. Dick Burton and his junior ally, Verney Cameron, were obliged to seek backers in a more dubious quarter than the machinations of land-hungry governments. There was something disreputable about businessmen like Irvine, as far as the austere Royal Geographical Society was concerned. And yet, how else could Ruffian Dick seek further horizons? Irvine wanted Burton and Cameron to explore what was then called the Gold Coast, in West Africa, for his Guinea Coast Gold Mining Company. Our mud-pie builders jumped at the task.

Dick informed the Foreign Office his health was none too good, and he planned a *healthy recuperation* in the swamp-ridden fever-plagued resorts of the west African coastline. Obligingly, the London office concurred. He and Verney reached the Gold Coast in January 1882, and spent four months exploring for gold and diamonds in Axim, the Nanwa Valley, and along the shore of the Ancobra river as far as Kitza. Burton and Cameron sent in an ecstatic report to the mining company; there was far more gold to be panned out of the land than at present was realised. Too few natives were employed from neighbouring tribes. The labour was by no means productive enough. And Burton recommended a greater dependency on mechanised water sluicing. He even went so far as to recommend importing 'Chinese coolies' for the job. He wanted the engineers to design sluiced rapids which made falls of up to thirty feet, in order to wash the valuable dust from the hillsides. Cameron attested to the same scheme of water-borne hydraulics, but their hopes were dashed by the company's engineers who would not replace their creek operations with a costlier sluice manipulation. The work force might not be up to the more stringent demands of mechanised water courses. An awful lot of shallow surface dust would be lost. Time, as it happened, was to prove Burton correct. But Irvine's Guinea Coast Gold Mining Company was not very impressed, and by May Dick and Verney were on board a ship bound for Madeira to meet up with Irvine. Both men had fevers, and Irvine's lack of enthusiasm did nothing to alleviate their condition. Dick carried with him enough notes from their expedition to make up a patchy narrative, only too closely resembling his earlier *Wanderings in West Africa*, notes filled with random excesses and frequent references to the egotism of a Christian Church. He would compile all this into the two volume, 735-page, *To the Gold Coast for Gold*. He had plans to foist this manuscript on Messrs Chatto and Windus, as soon as he got back to London.

Isabel had gone to meet Richard and Verney off the American mail ship *Loanda* in Liverpool docks, on the 20th of May. She made light of her personal problems, and presented a cheerful mothering self when the ship docked. Dick was still very low with fever, and she packed him off to bed for several days once they reached their London hotel. A month before, Isabel's specialist, Professor Liebman, had advised her of a growth on the wall of her womb. She had noted a curious loss of energy these past months. She couldn't take fencing lessons with her usual gusto. Climbing stairs was a difficulty she put down to the bad fall when her legs were almost broken in 1879. It is a measure of the seriousness with which she took her problems that the specialist was allowed such a detailed inspection. Although she could feel no pain in her lower abdomen, the general weakness was an ill-omen. In those days, horrifyingly emotive and terminal words such as 'cancer', 'inoperable', or 'malignant' were not as feared as now. There was justifiable reason to disbelieve one's own medical practitioner. It was a time when bleeding was still recommended for an astonishing variety of ills. A time when many pains, no matter how excruciating, were put down to generalities such as lumbago or indigestion or the weather.

Isabel told Dick nothing of this. He sat up in his hotel bed and asked her to call his doctor to him. This she did with obedience. He sniffed at the port she had decanted for him on the side-table. He'd need those special black cheroots, and she must fetch them from Allen & Ginters, in the Holborn Viaduct. And a set of twenty Star Safety Razors, plus an unshined leather strop, in one of those tall enamelled boxes. Thank you, Zookins.

She was rather shocked when he tried to explain the contractual ramifications of his deal with James Irvine. Dick and Verney had allowed Irvine to procrastinate in Madeira. Once his engineers had collected the naive explorers' information, Irvine instructed his men to dismiss the carefully devised scheme for hydraulic sluices. When Irvine met with Dick and Verney in Madeira he announced he would have to abort the whole mission. It was not clear until after both men had set sail for England that Irvine had no intention of reimbursing them for their four months' work. Isabel was distraught. Dick would never learn. He must, she insisted, pursue Irvine through the courts. But all the legalities were on the side of the Guinea Coast Gold Mining Company. Dick had signed a contract which, if his expedition proved a waste of funds, held himself and Verney liable to refund even their original commission money. Irvine dazzled them with a smokescreen of scornful engineers; they were victims of trust and optimism; somewhere in London, in the corner of a club's splendidly ornate smoking-room, a gaggle of Pompous People recounted the story with glee, their fat laughter danced around the sliver thin smoked glass and red gauze bulbs of the newly installed gas chandeliers.

Isabel managed to sneak a glance into his day-book. Usually he kept it close by him, but on this occasion habit had given him the slip. He was in the next room, upright in bed, quaffing that medicinal port. Her eyes were accustomed to the steeply angled handwriting, close-cropped, vowels blurred with ink pools, dashed down in haste and ill-temper. She particularly observed two heavily underlined entries.

The previous month he had been sitting on the front stoep of the Hotel English in the port of Bathurst, on the west African Gold Coast. An urchin black scruff had brought him the *Graphic* and *The Times* from the quayside. Only two items interested him. One was a lengthy obituary. The other was a letter which confirmed another death the week before. He carefully wrote down the details, and drew broad black lines beneath the names.

Isabel wondered why, as she leafed through his day-book, he had so vigorously marked in the death of Dante Gabriel Rossetti on April 10, and then that of Charles Darwin on April 19. He was watching his contemporaries with considerable interest: they did indeed seem to be dying with increasing frequency. Men he had spoken with on numerous occasions, whose promise he had always respectfully noted, but whose accomplishments he had rarely mentioned. And yet, close as they were to him in years, they seemed on their deaths a long way from him in achievement. The heroes were falling, the obituaries were recording, but Dick did not want to believe these final years were an inevitable pulling down of the shades. He was making a comparison in his mind when he chalked up each famous departure with the Holy Rower. Something inside him would not allow him to admit the idea of eclipse. By nature the fox had to dip and skulk, then harry the prey with that curious slippy hip sidle step, always searching out a territorial marker. But the abyss lay as close as his port in the bedside glass.

The Burtons had been away from Trieste a long time indeed. Dick had spent twenty months between Africa, London and Trieste. He arrived there in September 1882. He returned to his large workroom where a piled manuscript beckoned him from its upright school desk surface. For some years he had been working on a project called *The Book of the Sword*. He had intended the work to become a definitive study of the subject. He had three headings for the proposed volumes: *The Birth, Parentage, and early Career of the Sword; The Sword Fully Grown*; and lastly, *Memoirs of the Sword, Which After Long Declining Revives Once More in Our Day*. It was an enormous undertaking. In Trieste he steadily put together the first book. The others were never completed.

All these years, whenever Richard flew the consular nest in Trieste, he had reimbursed his Vice-Consul with half his own salary. Now Brock had celebrated his fortieth year in the consular service and retired, with £170 which Isabel had gallantly collected as a mark of appreciation from the British in Trieste.

The Foreign Office sent the new Vice-Consul to Trieste. He was a P. P. Cautley. He had been warned beforehand about the notorious 'amateur consul' he was to serve under, but Cautley's job was to obey Burton, if and when he ever found him, and Cautley was by no means averse to taking half Dick's pay if the explorer wished to travel to other parts. The Vice-Consul did not have to wait six weeks before his roving master received a dramatic cable from the London office:

H.M. GOVERNMENT WISHES TO AVAIL THEMSELVES OF YOUR KNOW-
LEDGE OF BEDOUINS AND THE SINAI COUNTRY TO ASSIST IN SEARCH
FOR PROFESSOR PALMER. THERE IS A CHANCE OF HIS BEING STILL
ALIVE, THOUGH BODIES OF HIS COMPANIONS, CHARRINGTON AND
GILL, HAVE BEEN FOUND. PROCEED AT ONCE TO GHAZZEH: PLACE

Richard was galvanized into action. His gout flew over the window-sill, his lumbago was but a figment of his wife's imagination. For Palmer was the same linguist and archaeologist he had explored the deserts around Damascus with—Edward Henry Palmer. Edward, like the late Charley Tyrhwitt-Drake, was another of Dick's 'younger brothers'. With two junior officers, William Gill and Harold Charrington, Edward Palmer had led an absurdly dangerous mission into the Sinai with bags of gold bullion slung over his camel saddle to bribe various Bedouin tribes. It was rumoured they carried £20,000's worth of gold sovereigns, and they were in the capacity of 'official couriers' for HMG riding rough across unknown desert. The gold was a bribe. The British and the French and the Egyptian governments did not want the Bedouin to attack the Suez Canal. Somewhere in Whitehall, a quite numbingly stupid civil servant had recommended that three daring chappies should be given buckets of gold coins, and a few decent elephant guns, and packed off into the desert.

Edward Palmer had promised the Cairo authorities he'd reach a point between Kantara and El Arish, in the desert, and with the assistance of his two officers they'd disconnect a major telegraph wire. As soon as Cairo realised the wire was not cut, and they heard no more from the valiant three, an alarm was sent to London. And so the cable arrived for Dick. He promptly dispatched a reply which did little to calm the nerves of his superiors in London:

READY TO START BY FIRST STEAMER. WILL DRAW £100. WANT GUNBOAT FROM ALEXANDRIA TO GHAZZEH OR SINAI. LETTER FOLLOWS.

R. F. BURTON: CONSUL.

As far as Whitehall was concerned a gunboat was out of the question. All they'd asked him to do was to take a reasonable second-class boat ticket to Ghazzeh and present himself to the Consul Moore who *might* have further information on the missing three. Richard, to their horror, had got the wrong end of the stick. He was strapping on his Turkish cutlasses, lacing his belt with long-case pistols, thrusting knives in all sorts of strange corners of his clothing, drawing a hundred pounds from Vice-Consul Cautley's emergency petty cash box, and, without as much as a by-your-leave, he was making plans to assume command of a gunboat and ignite war with the Arabian tribes by his salvoes top deck as he steamed up the Gulf of Akhaba. And before London could draw breath to answer, Isabel followed him down to the quay where, as he leaped aboard the first steamer he could find, she called out—

'Mind, if they are really dead, don't be put like a ferret into a hole to bring out the dead bodies.'

Notwithstanding the almost impenetrable opaqueness of her meaning, Richard chomped the cold remains of a morning cheroot and gingerly tapped his buttoned-down inside flask pocket for reassurance. Sailors shouted, wives hallooed, and the hawsers snaked from the iron bollards.

'If they are dead, no,' he hailed her from the poop-rail, 'but if there is a chance of saving dear old Palmer, I will go anywhere, and do anything!'

Panic set into Whitehall. The Foreign Office ordered two hundred troops into Sinai under a youthful soldier-explorer, Charles Warren, to make contact with the lost men. The picture of mad old Burton armed to his knee-caps at the helm of a gunboat toting a couple of recoilless four-inchers galvanized the authorities. It forcibly struck home to someone just what sort of a diplomatic rout in the Suez Canal area could engulf a decade of good intentions if a man as volatile as Dick was let loose.

The country had, at last, made its appeal to him. What more could he do but offer up his services? He was a leader again. Where's the army? Fetch the troops. Raise the flag.

Dick was allowed no further afield than Cairo. Rumours were everywhere—Charrington and Gill had been cornered by tribesmen and when they stood their ground to face the bullets, the energetic Palmer leapt over a precipice and escaped. Warren had already discovered their bones, picked hideously clean and strewn across the sand. Eventually, much to Burton's chagrin, Warren sent word back. He had found some remains. A sock with a foot inside sliced at the heel. As for Palmer's fate—it was anybody's guess.

The expedition to bribe the tribes was a disaster. Who could take the plans of the Foreign Office seriously after that? It was such a remarkable waste—to send three good men and true with camel-loads of gold into a village of a desert like the Sinai. As soon as one tribe learned these white lunatics were handing out bullion with manic abandon, the desert grapevine was a babel.

Dick presented his compliments to the various consular dignitaries in Cairo. They were kindly and obliging, and they did nothing to discourage him from his tales of the past, his adventures, his languages, his old enemies; but they were merely detaining him an extra day or two. They did not know quite what to do with such a man. He made them feel on edge. He told them they must tighten the defences of the Suez Canal, and he had umpteen schemes to secure the land from Port Said to Ras Mohamed at the all-important peninsula gulf to the Red Sea. Perhaps they listened to him patiently, those white-jacketed satin-waistcoated *Englaysie Shaytans*, tippling back their gin fizzes on the verandah of Shepheard's Hotel. But they knew he'd have to go back soon to his consular corner in Trieste, and he was still the rank outsider, almost a spy a *jussu*, in their midst; he had no purpose now; buy him a drink, let him gab the night, beckon dewy morn in a cloud of mosquitoes and whisky-skies; it was only Dick Burton, the ruffian neck of him, and a little scrawny at that.

He wrote a detailed account of his plans for the security of the Suez Canal and its environs. He envisaged a Chelsea Barracks' load of Peeler-blue policemen, funny pointy helmets and HMG truncheons at the ready, and iron-studded regulation issue boots to step lightly upon the gossamer sand. *Tant mieux* — nobody in Cairo wanted to print it. He was lucky. He could have made himself look a lot sillier with:

Far better to raise a brigade of three thousand 'Bobbies', officered, drilled, and dressed after our London fashion. These men, who would not speak a word of any language but English, should be stationed in the port and capital, with detachments, relieved every quarter, at the six important towns . . .

He was in Trieste harbour on December 10. There would be no more official missions. His world had properly shrunk; now there was only Isabel, and her Church, and her cats, the brandy, the port, and the upstairs rooms in Trieste. He allowed his gout to return, and he took to his bed for a time. She fussed and concerted all her energies to his well-being, telling him nothing of her own ills. He was dismayed when his favourite fencing instructor died. He heard that the artist Gustave Doré had passed away in January, 1883, and he carefully noted the fact in his day-book. He found the energy to attend a masked ball in Opçina, behind Trieste, and Isabel rigged him up as a twelfth-century crusading King Richard Coeur-de-Lion, his beamy chest in mock mail and a broadsword clattering on the marble steps behind him. He looked splendid.

Afterwards he was back to bed complaining of gout, and he noticed an announcement in the *Graphic* of the publication date for John

Payne's nine-volume translation of *The Book of the Thousand Nights and a Night*. The publishers, the Villon Society, had limited the edition to 500 sets. He had exchanged letters with Payne two years earlier. Now he wrote again to tell him that there was a plan afoot to start a Kama Shastra Society. He and his old friend Foster Fitzgerald Arbuthnot needed allies in this new Society. They intended to translate and print limited editions of oriental erotica. He admitted that John Steinhaeuser had encouraged him those years ago in Aden to make a similar translation from the famous epic of Baghdad. Burton went as far as to suggest that he and Steinhaeuser had already written out versions of some of the legendary tales. And furthermore, Dick wrote, he saw no reason why, should he complete Steinhaeuser's task, there could not be room for another interpretation of the *Arabian Nights*. His old friend John Steinhaeuser, linguist and orientalist, had died in 1865, bequeathing Dick a number of papers which included certain translations from eastern erotica; and Burton may have made use of this material in the first three chapters of his own *Arabian Nights*.

The rooms the Burtons kept in Trieste were twenty-seven in number, and it took a hundred and twenty steps to reach their sleeping quarters. Dick suddenly announced he could not abide this any more. He wanted to live in a proper house with a garden. He didn't like the drains here. He worried incessantly about his heart. The breathlessness which came to him with greater frequency had little to do with gout or lumbago. He could feel his body weakening. He was angry and cold; the Trieste wind knifed the shutters when he tried to sleep. At three and four o'clock in the morning he'd sit up and ring the hand-bell. He wanted hot tea and biscuits and conversation. How soon would it be dawn? Had the light broken on the sea's grey curve?

It took Isabel five months to secure a lease on a vast house, set in woods high above Trieste. It had more than forty rooms, a ballroom which could squeeze a thousand bustles within it, a carriage entrance for horses which was covered and which opened on to a wide marble staircase, and below the pillared portico a large garden and an orchard or *campagna*. The day Isabel signed the contract Dick left Trieste for Krapina-Teplitz. He was gone seven days. For days the heavily laden donkey carts mounted a steep lane. Although they had lived frugally in Trieste, and all Dick's consular socialising was paid for by HMG, they were setting themselves up in style like a wealthy Trieste merchant once they settled inside their forty rooms, and their *campagna* and ornamental garden which overlooked forest and rooftops to the warm Adriatic waters.

Dick took the largest drawing room in the mansion, naturally. He wanted it to perform three tasks—that of bedroom, workshop and library. He installed all his books, his lamps, his maps, rugs and photographic mementoes, and virtually cut himself away from prying eyes. He had all kinds of schemes whirling about inside his head.

He locked the door, drew the curtains, tossed logs into the wide grate, and jiggled with the oil lamps. He laid out eight separate tables piled with manuscripts. Each table held pen and ink trays; there was a box of books neatly placed beside every work-top. Outside in the echoing hallway his wife sweetly called for him. Did he want his usual supper tonight? She dared not knock to enter. If he said nothing in reply, through the closed doorway, it was their private code and meant 'yes, tell those wretched girls to scrape the potatoes and clean the fish'. (His favourite delicacy was a reeking plate of cod and vinegar, mashed spuds, and cold wet wringing nazi guts *sauerkraut*, topped with a cream cheese relish.) After the menu for the evening was settled, he wrote steadily under the soft beacon of the desk oil lamp. The warmth from the glow drove the moths towards the flame. Dick could faintly hear his wife's illiterate Italian bawling at the girls down below in their cavernous kitchen quarters. There rose a howl of anger. A righteous cry. Then, the rattle of scoured pans. An odour noxious in vegetable oil and thrice heated potato water wafted into the shadowy drawing room-cum-library-cum-bedchamber. He reached out for a small medicine cabinet he kept at his feet. Inside, neatly fitted, lay a cut-glass misted *bidon*, decanted with port to the brim.

XIX

The man with the promising past.

THAT SUMMER OF 1883, LATE PART OF THE INDUSTRIALLY fattened Western progress, bore strange comparisons to Dick's plight. Walt Whitman, half dead from old malaria waste and paralysed, took to his cottage and his soul invocative, never to be cured from his love for Democracy, dreaming fabulous praises, and banner lust for boys: oh, not Dick Burton's way. That same summer, Leo Tolstoy, it would appear, did his damnedest to push all the copyrights for *Anna Karenina* and *War and Peace* on to his wife Sonya, and ordered the first of many hand-stitched rough calico hair-shirts. He had taken to poverty, sandals and the scythe around the perimeter fields of the house at Yasnaya Polyana, and defended his sexual abstinence from what he called 'the sham of cement kisses'. He had become the renouncer: oh, not the way of Dick Burton with his forty mansion rooms and a port bottle for a wife.

The old fox's light at last had a focus in his Kama Shastra Society. He wanted to talk to Arbuthnot when he arrived in Trieste from London about their printing plans, and he did not know how much he ought to explain to Isabel. It was important for Arbuthnot to explore the commercial opportunities in this rather innovative form of publishing. Dick had had enough of the normal author-publisher relations. He was sickened by the London book world. Arbuthnot had a friend in H. S. Ashbee, the Paris based printer and collector of erotica. Arbuthnot, a curiously reserved and scholarly linguist, was just as excited by the financial motives as was Burton. Arbuthnot would have already primed Ashbee before he reached Trieste. Dick kept his eyes glued to the newspapers. He was a beady watchful chaperon of the legal columns, this consul impersonated; for, if the twenty-six-year-old Obscene Publications Act did not encourage a prosecution against Payne, and his *Nights*, and the Villon Society, there lay ahead enormous opportunities for printings of similar fruity ephemera. Ever since Lord Campbell's Obscene Publications Act of 1857, almost every conceivable form of published scribble was at the mercy of this legal assault on common sense. It defined obscenity as 'something offensive to modesty or decency, or expressing or suggesting unchaste or lustful ideas or being impure, indecent or lewd'. Payne was undisturbed. And happy in this knowledge, without which he could not possibly have considered proceeding with the plans for the Kama Shastra printings, Dick felt a floodgate of opportunities had opened up. If nobody prosecuted Payne, who would bother with Burton? True enough, Lord Campbell became Chief Justice of the Queen's Bench and did his best to ban divorce proceedings from the national newspapers; but it was Sir Alexander Cockburn (a wintry legal buffoon who prosecuted transvestites and relied with curious relish upon police evidence of anal penetration) who laid down the dubious definition which has until recently remained the guiding definition for the world's bigots: 'The tendency of the matter charged as obscenity is to deprave and corrupt those whose minds are open to corruption and into whose hands a publication of this sort may fall.'

Cause and purpose had come together as never before in Dick's life, and in a form which entirely suited his secretive nature. He would share the laughter and the nubile to the knuckle camaraderie with only Arbuthnot, or Henry Ashbee, the erotologist. Burton relished the secrecy of his printing and translating plans. It was a way of achieving Byronic fame, a little *farouche*, but in the main acceptable. It was a sneakingly curt operation he could exclude Isabel from. She would not want to share the plans of an Ashbee or an Arbuthnot. He knew she would demur at the task of writing out the scribbled translations in that hasty ink blot vowel hand of his. And how it suited the old fox. It was yet possible to be fox who went to ground, boy who never told, and man who never gave himself. An epitasis in the *Lear* dotage of his days.

These years were going to be his pornographic investment. His old friend Fred Hankey, the porn purveyor who made his money by concealing those Miss Floggem and Master Lickem plain-bound soft-cloth volumes inside a cripple's false hump when he wanted to export across the British Channel, Fred, the very pal he'd promised a black pudenda to, now, alas, was dead. 'What of Hankey,' wrote Dick, 'what of poor old Hankey?' Dick needed Arbuthnot, and the resourceful Henry Ashbee, and Leonard Smithers an artistic porn publisher, and H. S. Nichols, printer extraordinary, ever willing to take on anything of an exotic nature; and Burton fully intended to indulge his cerebral follies in his Trieste mansion bed-sitting-room, with the door firmly closed on Isabel.

Isabel maintained he shared every page of the project with her. It is not too onerous to seek out the root of her fib. She was not trying to conceal the real Dick from public knowledge. She merely wanted to assuage the pitiless abandon into which he had cast her. There never was anything very wicked about her later remarks. After his death, what she wrote concealed her hurt, but it did not distract those who knew him well enough. Isabel's champions and friends have not helped her cause by pinning these fibs to a popish flag. Isabel's enemies have served her better than her allies. Those who have tried to exalt Dick Burton have worked jolly hard to denigrate his clumsy stumble-footed wife. There was a sweet sadness in Burton's Isabel, his 'Zookins' or his 'Puss', or whatever else he was in the habit of calling her; she stood by him, and yet received more kicks than cement kisses.

By 1883, Burton had allowed too many anecdotes to drivel from gossipy lips. The common whisper accused him of not playing straight with the FO. He already had many enemies in London. The next seven years, his last, would see many more added to the list. His books were not being reprinted, and what public he had left now thought of him as the explorer-cum-consul who knew thirty-six languages and dialects, as the Byronic shadow who had married a plain and plump mediocre thing and bullied the life out of her, and as an arrogant bad hat who relished these dark anecdotes. There was tiny Algie Swinburne fluttering Walter Pater's eyebrows with the umpteenth version of Dick and the case of the black girl's infibulated trophy, or the account of the pet monkey who cherished Dick's affections. Ho, haw, hum, it had become something of a yawn, he appeared to have outlasted his true time, and he looked rather boring. Once a writer has lost that quality of being dangerous, one might as well stick him on the remainder shelf.

Somehow Burton could not resist stoking up more fury. The

destructive element in him tricked him into going too far. He had already huffed and puffed and waved two fingers at the academic establishment with his many exotic languages. And what good did it do him? Backs merely turned. Hackles were raised. Burton was quick to broadside William Palgrave's *Narrative of a Year's Journey through Central and East Arabia*. He suggested the author's scholarship was greatly lacking. And on one occasion, when the two met over supper, Burton's hothouse animosity wrecked the evening. Years later he could not resist a final wound at the expense of his own integrity. William Palgrave was a professional diplomat all his life. Of greater interest, he was one of four talented brothers, Francis, Reginald, Robert being the others. The family name was Cohen, the brothers assumed the surname Palgrave, and it was common low Clubland lavatory knowledge that the very Anglican Palgraves were not quite the pure Mayfair strain. And Dick, as was his bent, just went too far.

He could not resist detecting a degree of depreciation of the Muslim faith in William Palgrave's book. Nor could be resist a description of Palgrave's peculiar loss of religious identity: 'The author has had ample opportunities of comparing creeds: of Jewish blood and born a Protestant, he became a Catholic and a Jesuit ('Père Michel Cohen') in a Syrian convent; he crossed Arabia as a good Muslim and he finally returned to his premier amour, Anglicanism.' Dick flayed Palgrave with racist sarcasm. He wrote of 'Father Cohen', and provokingly malicious, he constrained Palgrave to ponder on the Muslim attitude towards the Written Laws of the Hebrews, which he called 'the Inadmissible Grace'.

William Palgrave held his breath. He took no court proceedings. Burton had done himself more harm than good, and his low pre-dilections were noted. He had overcooked the zeal. It was bad enough as far as the academic world was concerned to be too clever with his damned languages by half, but this time he had brought the lavatorial sniggers on to the Club supper-room table.

All those Palgrave brothers had teething pains in this cultured English society. Francis, for one, felt that tell-tale sting of dirty dog humour once his anthology of poetry, the *Golden Treasury*, became a bestseller in the early 1860s. It first became known as *Palgrave's Golden Treasury of Songs and Lyrics in the English Language*. Those who, like Burton, shared the same short-trousered laughter, were quick to call it *Cohen's Golden Treasury*. Indeed, it is hard to imagine the Oxford University Press in the 1860s saddling a pastoral bestseller with a title like that. That this ambitious family found it so important to adopt the genteel and mellifluous tone of 'Palgrave' reflects more upon the hypocrisy of the English way of life than on any confusion or choice between creeds.

There is more than merely the embarrassed mnemonic in Burton's last years in Trieste. The walls of insularity began to close in on him. He could barely conceal his desire to be singular in life, achieve a bachelorhood of the mind. And yet all his actions, though self-punitive, were calm and ordered on the surface. Richard Burton could have stepped out from Hermann Broch's novel *The Sleepwalkers*, dressed to the last button of panic in retreat from the public's disdain, as if Broch's prose was tailor-made—

> Great is the anguish of the man who becomes aware of his isolation and seeks to escape from his own memory; he is obsessed and outcast, flung back into the deepest *animal* anguish, into the anguish of the creature that suffers violence and inflicts violence, flung back into an overwhelming loneliness in which his flight and his despair and his stupor may become so great that he cannot help thinking of inflicting violence upon himself so as to escape the immutable law of events.

He had sealed off the cuts and shut away from sight the bruises. It was the fox, run to cover, bearing all the indignities of an emotional plague. His was a state of resolved stasis. That dice-thrower of firstnesses would only reward himself with the banality of fabulism. Every day of his life he retreated from his past. He could only blame and be slow to forgive. A closing for always of the natural standpoint, the outside deceived.

Having locked out Isabel from his library door, Dick now devoted his energies to his translations. It was an erotic search through a com-pendium of Arabic folk-humour. He had chosen with care his partners in the Kama Shastra Society. He had Henry Ashbee, the fiery anti-Catholic who under the name of Pisanus Fraxi had published in 1868 a wicked confessional entitled *The Confessional Unmasked: Showing the Depravity of the Romish Priesthood, the Iniquity of the Confessional and the Question put to Females in Confession*. Ashbee, not unnaturally, appears but once in all Isabel Burton's memoirs—she attended a brief supper with him in London in Dick's company. Ashbee had a curious scholastic penchant. He compiled three indices of banned books— *Index Librorum Prohibitorum* (1877), *Centuria Librorum Absconditorum* (1879), and *Catena Librorum Tacendorum* (1885); and contributed a considerable amount of pasty titillation to any number of publications.

He was adept at taking a Rowlandson print, for example, and penning a suitable piece of nonsense beneath the engraving in a volume entitled — *With Pictures of Good Old English Sports and Pastimes*:

> A meanly furnished room with a small window at the back, into which an ugly old man is peeping. On a low bed is seated a naked girl; and between her legs stands an old man, dressed in a hat and long cloak, with his breeches down. The girl with her left hand clasps the old fellow round the buttocks, and with her right handles his member, which is unnaturally large, and its shape quite *à la* Rowlandson; the girl is bald about her parts.

There was Leonard Smithers, a printer, and friend of Beardsley and Wilde who, by all accounts, dressed like an undertaker and, according to Oscar Wilde 'loves first editions, especially of women; little girls are his passion'. Smithers started life in a solicitor's office, clean-shaven and sporting a monocle; legend has it he was in the habit of having himself photographed whilst buggering his lady wife in a basement printing-works on the west side of Shepherd's Bush. Always there is something faintly ludicrous about the 19th-century titillators, and Smithers was no exception. At one point in his career he acquired a large house on the River Thames and tried to adopt the prosperous guise of a bohemian. Alas, his days were numbered. His wife became an alcoholic. He went bankrupt at the turn of the century, and from his deathbed Aubrey Beardsley begged Smithers to destroy the remaining obscene drawings of his which the philanthropic printer possessed. Smithers corresponded with Burton, but no evidence exists that they ever met.

It was Smithers who introduced Burton to the printer H. S. Nichols; and Nichols was the key figure for all his adventures in the world of privately printed erotica. The man was a none too scrupulous adherent to the laws of obscenity. But being fairly harmless as an underground printer (he was quite apolitical), Nichols managed to survive in London for many years. If, at times, he would not take all the risks involved with a certain publication, say for example a coy illustrated yarn extolling the delights of tribadic chastisement, Nichols would share out his load. He knew any number of basement printers willing to take on a portion of the trade. He was in weekly contact with such varied printing firms as Ellis Spear and Philip Justice, even the notorious William Dugdale, and it was his duty to procure the cheapest and safest route to getting the job done.

Foster Arbuthnot had already introduced a young Arabic scholar Edward Rehatsek to Burton; essentially what all these contacts had in common was Isabel Burton's barely concealed distaste. If years earlier she had enjoyed meeting Arbuthnot in India, and even claimed him then to be a firm friend, by the 1880s Arbuthnot's name was barely mentioned by her. In future she was to be confined to her quarters in the Trieste mansions whilst Dick worked. And she played very little part in the plans to publish a number of erotic works under the name of the 'Kama Shastra* Society of London and Benares'. Benares was not an ancient Hindu city on the banks of the River Ganges, but a cloudily humorous synonym for Stoke Newington, a rather murky London borough famous according to the British Tourist Board for its reservoirs, its waterworks, and an inordinately high percentage of Saturday-night pub brawl fatalities between Irish dockers and Chinese merchant seamen. H. S. Nichols agreed to tender some of the planned publications to a firm called Miller and Richard in Stoke Newington, and thereafter the name Benares stuck.

Between 1883 and 1890, Dick Burton maintained close contact with Henry Ashbee, Leonard Smithers, H. S. Nichols, Edward Rehatsek; and the Arabic scholars M. O. Houdas, J. F. Blumhardt, W. A. Clouston and E. J. W. Gibb. The Persian dictionarian Dr F. Steingass contributed an account of Arabic prosody and metre in Burton's Terminal Essay (vol X), of the *Thousand Nights and a Night*. Although John Steinhaeuser was dead, Burton still maintained intermittent meet-

---

* The Kama Shastra printing company lasted until Richard Burton's death. Including a number of reprints, the following publications complete the seven-year existence of this private printing enterprise:

The Kāma Sūtra of Vatsyayana. London and Benares, printed for the Hindoo Kama Shastra Society, 1883. (in seven parts).

Ananga-Ranga: (Stage of the Bodiless One) or, the Hindu Art of Love . . . annotated by A. F. F. & B. F. R. Cosmopoli, for the Kama Shastra Society, 1885.

The Perfumed Garden of the Cheikh Nefzaoui. A manual of Arabian Erotology. (XVI century.) Cosmopoli, for the Kama Shastra Society, 1886.

The Behāristān (Abode of Spring) by Jâmi, a Literal Translation from the Persian, printed by the Kama Shastra Society, 1887.

The Gulistān, or Rose Garden of Sa'di, faithfully translated into English, for the Kama Shastra Society, 1888.

A Plain and Literal Translation of the Arabian Nights' Entertainments, now entituled The Book of the *Thousand Nights and a Night*, with introduction, explanatory notes on the manners and customs of Muslim men and a terminal essay upon the history of The Nights by Richard F. Burton. Benares, MDCCCLXXXV: printed by the Kama Shastra Society, Volume I. 1885. (This volume appeared on September 12, 1885, along with nine other volumes which made up the initial set.)

Supplemental Nights to the book of the Thousand Nights and a Night, with notes anthropological and explanatory by Richard F. Burton. Benares, 1886. (Six volumes which appeared in the order of vols I and II, 1886. Vols III and IV, 1887. Vols V and VI, 1888).

ings and exchange of letters with Foster Arbuthnot and J. J. Aubertin, and though Monckton Milnes was soon to die, he had Swinburne to confide in. Isabel concealed as best she could the humiliation heaped on her. She claimed Burton wouldn't allow her to read these manuscripts, as if he did not dare besmirch her Catholic soul. She had to protect her own fear of isolation. Once he had chosen business partners like Ashbee, that virulent anti-Catholic, domestic war was declared. In her own accounts of these last years there is a paucity of names and friends involved in the Kama Shastra programme. In their place she contrives an appalling list of social occasions and splendidly titled chance acquaintances she has made. It must have been grisly. Suffering the first symptoms of cancer, locked out of her husband's workrooms, the ever conciliatory plump blue-eyed woman never showed her tears; always that chum-faced, infuriating optimism. Her Church, and her fierce forum against cruelty to animals, were her ultimate supports. She tells us she hugged his arm as they promenaded together, and he smoked his cigars and counted the Jews on the grand hotel balcony, and the sword stick he carried sparked the pavement with its steel tip. She asked for nothing because nothing was exactly what she would get. She wanted to tell him such underhand publications might jeopardise his chances of greater honours from Her Majesty's Government. She'd have liked to warn him against the risk of prosecution, for she was thinking of his pension rights by 1891, and the spendthrift future of their final days. Instead, she counted her own pennies and did everything in her power to keep him less than four months out of every year in Trieste, and made no bones about his formal allocation of half salary to his first clerk.

But the glimpses of Burton from his own private accounts in the 1880s are rare indeed. Where was that diary he kept all his married life? What about those day-books he filled so assiduously every morning? Norman M. Penzer, who compiled the remarkable annotated bibliography of Burton in 1923, despaired as much as any Burton reader over this great loss of narrative detail in the life of the man. Penzer from his conversations with Burton's last doctor, Grenfell Baker, who travelled with his patient from October 1887 to October 1890, gleaned a picture of the old traveller still searching out new material for his various Kama Shastra publications. There is some indication that Richard planned to use considerable extracts from a great German erotologist and Latinist, Karl Ulrichs, who was known in Leipzig as *Numa Numantius* for a number of studies of sexual inversion. Ulrichs now lived in Naples, where Burton frequently stayed. And it is as likely that Dick sought out the notorious German in that city as it is that Isabel would not mention the name Ulrichs in her account of their journeys. If she could dismiss Henry Ashbee in a line, and refuse to mention the letters she exchanged with Leonard Smithers, what chance did *Numa Numantius* have? Burton intended to use Ulrichs' research into pederasty, and to transcribe some of the German's studies into a much extended version of *The Perfumed Garden*, which would include an entire missing chapter on homosexuality by the Cheikh Nefzaoui.

Apart from trekking for four months around London society with Isabel in 1882, and venturing alone to Paris for a week to meet Ashbee, it is fairly difficult to pinpoint just exactly when Burton actually got down with Foster Arbuthnot to their 198-page translation of *The Kama Sutra*, by the 6th century AD poet and scholar Vatsyayana. More than likely, it was during the early months of the year in Trieste. Isabel does not give the subject a mention. She does, nevertheless, tell us that in that final quarter of that year Dick started *The Book of the Sword*, which he planned on an exhaustive scale, and in which he hoped to stretch the subject in its entirety from philosophy to iron smelting and gymnastics through three successive volumes.

The first edition of *The Kama Sutra* in seven pamphlet parts was quickly sold up. The second edition was hardbound, and slipped inside the first reprint of this hardbound version was an announcement of further volumes from the Kama Shastra Press. Translations of *Ananga-Ranga* and *The Perfumed Garden* were promised. Clearly Burton and Arbuthnot had made enough money to cover all the costs and they felt emboldened to publish two more examples of eastern erotica. It enabled Burton to return to Trieste for the first four months of 1883 with the glad jingle of coins in his pocket. He felt quite elated. Never before had he published a book to such instant profit. It was a remarkably unfamiliar feeling. He had, after all these years, at last discovered the public's taste. He made up his mind to satiate his public.

There were all types of Indian manuals of erotica to pick out for translation. Burton could have gone to the *Smara Pradipa* or the *Ratirahasya*, perhaps settled for the *Rasmanjari* or the *Panchasakya*: *The Kama Sutra*, of all these ancient works, was classified as the most notorious by the western world. It included the famous list of sixty-four ways of making love, some of which have always seemed capable of causing more physical damage than a stroll across to the Arc de Triomphe in Paris on an early Friday evening. Arbuthnot and Burton contrived to preserve the style of the original in their translation, for

Vatsyayana wrote in a concise, technical style, as if he was compiling legal notes. In effect, the book is a gentle ironic essay in the belief that, though pleasure is not an adequate goal by itself, no life can be complete without it. Burton had made a wise choice in bringing out this particular Hindu classic. It would have been difficult for a prosecution to be taken out against the publishers for this manual of love. The style and the chronological structure of the book, its *shastra*, and very formal language, could not be condemned as material which might corrupt. Vatsyayana intended the manual to be a text for the third of the traditional three disciplines relating to human behaviour — *kama*, or pleasure (the first two categories being *dharma*, religious law; and *artha*, material advantage). Burton and Arbuthnot guessed well, when they presumed the English public would lap up this first imprint from a secret publishing house. Even now, there are few similar publications in any language which have been so plagiarised.

As love manuals go, the *Ananga-Ranga*, in its original Sanskrit, was a fairly run-of-the-mill compendium of delights. It was unlikely that Burton alone would have bothered with its publication. Foster Arbuthnot probably translated this and Burton merely tidied up the manuscript. Certainly, Arbuthnot had attempted a translation of the *Ananga-Ranga* in India as early as 1872, and made an effort to have it published, only to withdraw the scheme from the anonymous printer after less than half a dozen copies had rolled off the machines. But with the success of *The Kama Sutra*, Arbuthnot put forward his *Ananga-Ranga*, and Burton and he felt confident enough to print their initials backwards on the title page — 'annotated by A.F.F. and B.F.R.' The 144-page manual of Kalyana Malla, or, as he is sometimes referred to, Kullianmull, was a compendium of instruction in how to maintain a true marriage of practised variety in all matters carnal. The original text of this 16th-century manual was in a bluff, no-nonsense style, part medicinal and part hortatory, and they captured this well in their translation:

> The chief reason for the separation between the married couple, and the cause which drives the husband to the embraces of strange women, and the wife to the arms of strange men, is the want of varied pleasures, and the monotony which follows possession . . .
>
> And thus all you who read this book shall know how delicate an instrument is woman, when artfully played upon, how capable she is of producing the most exquisite harmony; of executing the most complicated variations and of giving divinest pleasures . . .
>
> Fully understanding the way in which such quarrels arise, I have shown

how the husband by varying the enjoyment of his wife, may live with her as with thirty-two different women, ever varying the enjoyment of her, and rendering satiety impossible . . .

There is nothing to be found in either the *Ananga-Ranga* or *The Kama Sutra* which lifts the writing to the level of the books to come, *The Perfumed Garden* and the sixteen volumes of the grand *Arabian Nights*. Burton himself made a sharp reference to the origin of the translator of *Ananga-Ranga*, in one of his footnotes. He calls the reader's attention to *Ananga-Ranga* translated by one 'Reverend Koka Pandit'; this curious name was a vulgarism for a very obscure Wazir of the 'great' Rajah Bhoj. One can see the sweet and kindly natured Foster *Koka Pandit* Arbuthnot wriggling with the wit of it; Dick could make 'em smile. He could erect a smoke-screen of joke historicisms, and only the few, those members of the Kama Shastra in particular, would realise the kindly dig. He'd keep the *Koka* anecdote for Smithers, and Smithers would tell it to Ashbee in Paris, and they'd all refer to Arbuthnot as 'Koka' in private. But nobody ever told Isabel.

The Kama Shastra Society was doing well. Neither Foster Arbuthnot nor Burton had lost a farthing in the various projects. Nobody had come forth with legal proceedings. Nichols hadn't yet come across a nervous printer who baulked at the last minute over a saucy page.

The *Ananga-Ranga* went into a third printing, and this was enough to persuade Foster to publish two further love manuals translated from the Persian by Edward Rehatsek: *The Behāristān*, or Abode of Spring, and *The Gulistān*, or Rose Garden of Sa'di. Neither work achieved the popularity of the earlier printings from the Kama Shastra Society of Benares (or, if you prefer, Stoke Newington).

In 1886 during the first three months Burton was in Tangier, then Gibraltar, and then Naples. He spent March to June in Trieste. It was there he was sent (by Ashbee?) the so newly published French translation of that panegyric of love, *The Perfumed Garden* by Cheikh Nefzaoui, a three-hundred-year-old book of bawdiness and sensual advice. (The particular translation from the Arabic was an incomplete version of the original: *Le Jardin Parfume du Cheikh Nefzaoui*, Manuel d'Erotologie Arabe: XVI Siècle. Traduction revue et corrigé. Paris, Isidore Lisseux, 1886.)

In this period, publishers were careful to keep the town magistrates, the smut hunters or 'prurient prudes' as Charles Reade called them, at a safe distance. Already editors had expurgated St Augustine's *City of God* and Robert Burton's *Anatomy of Melancholy*. The Church took upon itself to lead this heaving monster of public righteousness, and all publishers in England were held at gunpoint by the Society for the Promotion of Christian Knowledge and the Religious Tract Society. Publishers were deftly caught between commerce and liberty, and it is no exaggeration to say there was a higher percentage of cash buying book readers in the market for new publications than exist today. Of the four million literate members of the British public there were over half a million book buyers among this number. It was routine for an ardent reader to collect the issues of a magazine in which a novel was serialised, and buy the bound volume on publication day. As for poetry, Coventry Patmore sold 250,000 copies of *The Angel in the House* (1877), a feat barely equalled by the most popular poets in hardback editions today—Rod McKuen or John Betjeman or Minou Drouet. Publishers and printers alike had to keep their eyes skinned for the sudden invocation of the law. The importance of Burton's bold translation of *The Perfumed Garden* must be seen against the reigning vigilante Acts of the time: the Vagrancy Act, amended 1838, the Metropolitan Police Act, the Town Police Clauses Act and the more recent Obscene Publications Act. Printers' shops, publishers' display counters, bookstalls and individuals could be brought to court for a book's title alone, without it being opened.

If Dick had been successfully prosecuted, it would have meant the end of his career as a Consul, and the loss of his pension of £300 a year. And he certainly needed far more than that to maintain the mad grandeur they had settled for in Trieste.

Although he never ceased from natural curiosity, and was prone at the drop of a trouser-leg to take a close look at various forms of mutilation, it has been a common mistake to assume this natural zeal made Burton into a pioneer physiologist. In too many of his observations, he has hardly stepped outside the rut of base prejudicial thinking of his own time, particularly in regard to the supposed mysteries of female 'sperm'. This is noticeable in his edition of *The Perfumed Garden*, where he blithely translated: 'The female sperm may penetrate into his urethra, and grave malady may ensue therefrom'. Elsewhere in *The Perfumed Garden*, Burton translated 'Do not leave the vulva directly after emission, as this may cause canker', and added his own footnote to the effect that canker, or *sefia*, a form of putrefaction, was nothing less than '. . . simply gonorrhea'. A major fallacy of the middle 19th century was this curious male dominated belief in vaginal ejaculation. As if, at this juncture, he had capitulated to uninformed general knowledge. But a mere cursory read of the gynaecologist Edward Tilt's *Uterine and Ovarian Inflammation* (1862) would have assured him that gonorrhea cannot be contacted unless one of the two parties concerned already carries the disease. For that matter, if Burton had bothered to glance at his own doctor's bookshelf he might well have come upon a popular home-help manual, J. M'Gregor-Robertson's *The Household Physician* which contained fairly exacting descriptions of membranous lubrication, vaginal catarrh, and 'the whites' or leucorrhea.

The Cheikh Nefzaoui's erotic manual and moral tales did nothing to emancipate the female sex from the habitual political and economic yoke it has suffered for centuries long before the day of Abraham. It was hardly likely Dick Burton would take up the cudgel for womanhood.

Dick had achieved, in high literary fashion, a form of erotic stylised writing, which was acceptable to the public nerve. Nobody, with the exception of the Paris-based pornographers, had reached at that time such a degree of frankness. *The Perfumed Garden* was privately printed, but its legendary nature and tone of scholarship brought it much closer to the realm of art, or *acceptable* art, than sundry texts such as John Cleland's *Fanny Hill* or 'Colonel Spanker's' *Experimental Lectures*. Dick had made a gamble. He had indeed thrown the first dice.

There was a strange innocence about the book world. How, for example, can the publishers in Burton's day justify many of the titles they gave to their most respectable and genteel minded books? The euphemistic bawd in the Club smoking-room was in stitches of laughter when Lady Colvile published her delicate narrative *Round a Black Man's Garden*, and when Mrs Lynn Linton produced her sober piece of fiction titled *Grasp your Nettle*, for *The Englishwoman's Domestic Magazine*. One can only assume, to Burton's good fortune, that the enemy was a naive and blinkered pooterpuffball.

The Perfumed Garden is an extremely witty compendium ranging from advice on how to recognise an unworthy woman to the recipe for a concoction of egg yolk, onions, asparagus, and rancid butter fat with the help of which the casual reader might deflower at least eighty virgins; men's various members are identified as *crowbars, tailors* and *housebreakers*, and women's organs assume quite remarkable identities disguised as *hedgehogs, crushers, gluttons, biters, starlings* and *wasps*; and to the miserably equipped imagination of Western Man the mind blitzes somewhat at the possible explosions and painful collisions when the vulva *crusher* encounters the member known as *the flabby one*, according to Burton, 'the one who can never get in because it is too soft, and which is therefore content to rub its head against the entrance until it ejaculates, it gives no pleasure to women', or when the vulva *hedgehog* meets the member *rummager* — 'it is named thus because as soon as it penetrates it begins to rummage about vigorously until it has appeased its passion'. There is charm and humour in the variations of congress, albeit written from an emphatically male approach. As when the member *stumbler* trips at the very gate of love, and the vulva gently enquires, 'What has happened to you that made you stumble about so?' the clumsy member replies, 'Oh my love it was a stone lying in the road.'

But beneath all this disarming analysis of our most delicious physical responses, there lurks something more sinister. And neither the Cheikh Nefzaoui nor Richard Burton makes any apology for it. One notes with resignation, how the negroes and the Jews ever receive the brunt of savage insults. And women become fornicating harlots the moment an honest man's back is turned. And the harlots jump into bed with black men whose titanic doodles take on the proportions of croquet mallets. Men appear to be honest and hard working and when a young thing is easily seduced it is all part and parcel of the day's labour. But when a wife seeks elsewhere for a love and locks him up with her for seven days 'and completely drains him', she instantly becomes deceitful. According to *The Perfumed Garden*, a man who must be held in contempt is the solitary weakling who ejaculates prematurely. But when it comes to women who are held in contempt, the list is quite endless. It includes every poor creature whose tongue is —

> garrulous, whose hair is woolly, her forehead projecting, her lips are small and blear, her nose is enormous, the lips lead-coloured, the mouth large, the cheeks wrinkled and she shows gaps in her teeth; her cheekbones shine purple, and she sports bristle on her chin; her head sits on a meagre neck, with very much developed tendons; her shoulders are contracted and her chest is narrow, with flabby pendulous breasts, and her belly is like an empty leather-bottle, with the naval standing out like a heap of stones; her flanks are shaped like arcades ...

and on and on. Even then Burton doesn't let up; aside from his obvious relish in the translation of this piece, he has to add a footnote when he comes to the poor creature's feet; he quotes Rabelais' 'feet like a guitar'. As if any more insult was needed to pile up on the lot of being an 'unattractive' woman.

Dick loved to use heteronyms. He could hide himself behind a neat curtain of fiction. He had by now got into the habit of tinting his black and grey Tartar hair-style. The grey was sneaking through with more haste than his vanity could allow. Dutifully he translated Chapter 18, entitled *Of Things that take away the Bad Smell from the Armpits and Sexual Parts of Women and Contract the Latter*. Burton pounces on the Cheikh's mention of antimony, and informs us, 'the subject in question, *hadida*, by which name goes the oxide of copper of commeric, which, exposed to the action of fire, pulverised, and mixed with gallnut, is used for dying the hair black'. There appears, increasingly frequently, the shadow of the heteronym in all his translations. He lowers his head and produces another disguise out of the bag. The sage in the chapter *On Men Who are to be Held in Contempt* puts an answer to a young male plaintiff in the form of a rhetorical question: 'If you had a fine member you might dispose of her fortune. Do you not know that women's religion is in their vulvas?' (It would have taken the Host of the angelic Heavens to convince Isabel Burton of that.)

In taking up the translation of *The Perfumed Garden*, Burton made it amply clear he wished to contain his sense of curiosity on a distant shore made up of sands and shallows highly contemptuous of womankind. No strictures accosted him, he saw no reason to redress the Cheikh's harsh usury of the common flesh and its congress. And his footnotes take on the shape of barbed and snarked whispers, quick and cruel, where women's feet become guitars and seminal fluids disgust as if vaginas are indigenous carriers of diseases. A guilty dark, penetrable but shameful. A decoy for infantile gratification.

From early 1884 to his death in 1890 it is possible to follow the course of Burton's various ills. Isabel carefully recorded every new attack he had. It is now apparent that Burton suffered from a heart condition. Whenever Dick ached, whenever his toe took a twinge, it seems a band of dreadful helpers stood by to assure him it was another devious form of gout, and they promptly took away his bottles of port, poured rhubarb medicines down him, and doused him twice a day in skin-wrinkling hot sulphur baths, followed immediately by an ice-cold sponge-down, and with hot water bottles applied to his feet and cold wet pillows tied around his ears. It was a humiliating charade, but Dick allowed them this liberty. Gout in itself can, of course, be very painful. Its more obvious signs are joints swelling, reddish urine, and a severe increase in uric acid body content. Burton exhibited all the signs of heart embolism, or perhaps a weakness in the valves of his heart, and here clearly lay the root of his pains. The ghastly round of money-hungry Doctor Bleedems produced nothing but a variety of prescriptions and reckless theories which, though they could not cure the patient, produced a mental catharsis in Isabel.

Richard had a stroke in February 1884, in Trieste, and temporarily lost the use of both legs. He lay in his huge bed-sitting-room overlooking the gardens and suffered Isabel to fetch him daily doses of digitalis. He filled his day book with notes, avidly recording the latest deaths of old contemporaries. An Admiral Glyn died on Feburuary 16, and on April 10 the novelist Charles Reade died. His mind was not in the present, these newly cut tombstones were metaphors for a past filled with promise. In John Berryman's lines he had commended himself to—

> Advance into the past!
> Henry made lists of his surviving friends
> & of the vanished on their uncanny errands
> and took a deep breath.

But soon he seemed fit enough to sit by his desk at the tall open windows which overlooked the wide bay of water, and he pursued his translation of the exotic folk epic of tales *The Arabian Nights*. He possessed copies of the earlier British orientalist's, Hereford born scholar Edward Lane's *The Thousand and One Nights, or Arabian Nights Entertainments*. He had the latest John Payne translation with him in Trieste, and in addition worked from an 18th-century version by Antoine Galland, who published *Mille et Une Nuits, Contes Arabes Traduits en Francais*, in Paris. Burton did not own a copy of the most complete edition of Galland's work, which came in twelve volumes. He acquired a six-volume edition dated 1726, and from all these sources he was prepared to commence a definitive epic version of the famous and anonymous collection of Arabic folklore.*

Burton intended his *Nights* to become the unrivalled classic. Above

* Burton's *Nights* consist of 262 tales, accompanied by 233 variations and continuations of particular tales. Burton does not hesitate to explain his debt to Payne in many instances; he also pronounces 23 of the tales as spurious off-spring in a compendium of folklore which had no standard text until the 15th century. The *Nights* have a basis in the 10th century translation into Arabic of the ancient Persian book *Hazar Afsana*. The *Nights*, nevertheless, include Indian fragments from the books of early fables, stories from the Baghdad court poet Abu Nuwas, and various additions made during the Mamluk period in Egypt. Burton willingly concedes his own adaptation, in certain cases, from among the twenty-one versions of past *Nights* which he records. In the main, Burton and/or Steinhaeuser worked from the Bulak text of Abd al-Rahman al-Safati (Cairo 1835); and after Steinhaeuser's death, Burton expanded his search for the definite tales by working from, and in frequent tales, borrowing from the 12-volume Breslau edition, edited by Max Habicht (1825–1843) which was Payne's main source, the 4-volume (later Sir) William Hay Macnaghten's Calcutta edition (1839–1842), Jonathan Scott's *Tales, Anecdotes, and Letters, translated from the Arabic and Persian* (London 1800), and the 6-volume *The Arabian Nights' Entertainments*, from the ms. of Edward Wortley Montagu (1811).

all it was a perfect vehicle for his secretive soul. He could tell a tale about himself, and call it ancient folklore. He could hide all his prejudices and all his secret innuendoes behind a cataract of footnotes, all on the surface purporting to illuminate the fictional text. The translation, or compilation, or at times plain bowdlerisation, would take him three years. He was, in his own mind, far away again at last, just as in the old days, when he took off on expeditions without a word to Isabel. It was a chance to explore the 10th-century world of the despotic monarch Shahriyar and his nightly seduction (from tales both profane and witty) by the girl Shahrazad (Scheherezade), who saved her neck each night by telling him a new story, bore the king children, married him, and lived at least five years in his bed-chamber. This cerebral voyage was the last great expedition the Gods allowed Dick. It was a final search among the ruins of memory and anecdote and his store-house of fragmented lives. All his days had he not glimpsed shards and broken pot lids of achievement and success? All his years had he not admitted before how his enormous energies were so often shredded and left without focus? The *Nights* were to be his forest. He'd hide there. He'd dig deep and bury and lie in wait, and if the armchair traveller truly cared enough to seek him out, there he could be found, this man who never gave of himself completely, this boy who never told, the decoy rider laughing amongst sentinel stars. He felt safe.

He acquired a permanent secretary, and Isabel was allotted the task of writing out envelopes to Kama Shastra Society subscribers. And when, after barely two months work on the *Nights*, his wife took him at her expense on a seven-month orgy of social frivolities which would not return him to Trieste until January, 1885, he did not demur. They travelled through Austria and wandered from one expensive hotel to another, taking with them his secretary and her personal maid. It was surely an extravagant voyage. And each new day brought a social en-gagement of stunning triviality. Iasbel has gleefully recorded the Lord Northbrooks, the Lord Wolseleys, Major Wardropps, Marcheses di Guiccioli, Madames Nub Pasha, and itinerant Dukes Saxe-Cobourg of principalities long since hocked in ignominy. Ah, it was unending. When would this woman give up? Didn't she know he was dying? It was as if she wanted to stifle his literary endeavours with an over-load of engagements. Meek as a fox in lamb's clothing he acquiesced. He tightened his collar-stud and blackened his whiskers, and scuttled along to the next rattle of cocktail glasses in the wake of his wife's quite insatiable desire for social standing. He was too clever by half for her. This parade of well-dressed gewgaws could not penetrate his kingdom of wazirs and marmelukes and breathlessly whispered tales of Baghdad plunder and wit. This old fox tinkled glasses in chandeliered halls with the best of them, but his sharp nose had already sniffed the menstrual blood of a Court harem, in that last citadel of Muslim faith and knowledge which lay beneath the zealous shadow of the empire of Constantinople.

Isabel insisted that Burton commenced his *Nights* on April 1, 1884. In his appendix to the Supplemental Volume, no VI (1888), Dick wrote, 'During the autumn of 1882, after my return from the Gold Coast my task began in all possible earnest with ordering the old scraps of translation and collating a vast heterogeneous collection of notes. At first my exertions were but fitful and the scene was mostly a sick bed to which I was bound between October 1883 and June 1884.' Burton meant, of course, the old scraps of Steinhaeuser's translations, and many of his shared attempts at the epic of tales with his friend. It may be that Isabel was referring to the arrival of Mrs Victoria Maylor, the typist he hired in 1884, in Trieste. Bearing in mind Burton's health and Isabel's determination to keep him on the move from one watering place to another, it is doubtful whether he could have written a million and a half words between the spring of 1884 and late summer of 1885, by which time at least seven volumes of the epic were in hand. He no longer possessed that kind of energy. Isabel simply did not know what he was doing behind the closed door. By early 1885, Burton realised the extent of the public response to the projected epic. He had already decided upon an edition of 1,000 sets, but he had received firm orders for twice that number. It meant that, at a guinea a copy, the ten volumes plus the six supplemental volumes would gross £16,000 for the Kama Shastra Society. It was a fortune he had never dreamed, hitherto, of making from his pen. Stubbornly, he would not enlarge the first print beyond 1,000.

Dick set sail for London, stopping off at Naples, Venice and Lisbon. Isabel took a roundabout route via Italy and France and arrived in England twelve days before him. On board he carefully noted the death of Victor Hugo. Once in London, Burton had one main task ahead of him. It was quite obvious he personally couldn't afford to pay the printers for the sixteen-volume edition. And printers always asked for the cash in advance. Dick could not deal with the money issue without the assistance of Arbuthnot and Smithers, and Henry Ashbee. Dick had on his person a thousand promissory notes from the subscribers to the Kama Shastra Society. This was enough to guarantee themselves the £5,000 necessary for the printers' costs. Though

£5,000 was an enormous gamble to put up for the printing of material which might at any time be open to prosecution. It is not known exactly how Arbuthnot, Burton, Smithers and Ashbee shared out the potential £11,000 profit from the *Nights*, but by 1887, Isabel was moaning over the necessity to put aside £2,000 for Dick's failing health when he was in Cannes, and by 1890, on Dick's death, the Burtons were penniless once more.

During these last years Dick attended many suppers and lectures alone. There were times when he had to attend a fuctional evening with the Prince of Wales, or Bernard Quaritch gave a dinner in Burton's honour, and, sad as it may seem, and much to Isabel's social dismay, she found herself excluded. But as always she stood waiting in the wings for Jemmy to return in the early hours of the morning, and she would announce some piddling teacup escapade they would both take part in the following day, perhaps a fund-raising charity do for Christian dogs and cats in the Countess of Puke's front parlour. Jemmy dear, it is *very* important you attend. And he did. Isabel had taken to a curious habit of dressing in the style of the Catholic martyr Mary Stuart. During the day she wore a clumsy flowing garment, half sack, half cloak, which was decorated, according to one witness 'with a crucifix and a sort of ruff'. Desperate and alone, Isabel was a sad, wilted, yet defiant creature. She was driven to even more eccentric devices to announce her presence. And, of course, they were directed always at Burton. And, of course, he never looked her way. It was the unconcealed affrontedness of a naif turned penitent-outcast.

The Burtons stayed in England long enough to see the first five volumes of the *Nights* through the binders and dispatched to sub-scribers. In due course a number of journals received copies, and to Dick's frank delight there was nigh universal praise for his work. *The Morning Advertiser*, the *St James' Gazette*, and the *Whitehall Review* were fulsome with congratulations. But the *Edinburgh Review*, in an article of acute bile, let loose an invective: 'Galland is for the nursery, Lane for the library, Payne for the study, and Burton for the sewers.' Dick could not have taken this too seriously for it took him two years to reply. The shock of his newly acquired riches numbed his critical faculties. Finally, in the tradition of good clean fun he suggested his Scots critic 'must be prurient and lecherous as a dog-faced baboon in rut'. At the end of the year, Dick had almost prepared a further two volumes for the printers, and he set sail for Tangier alone in the hope he might at last pick up the vacant consulship in Morocco. It was a weedy enough excuse, but it allowed him two months' respite from his wifelet. But Isabel would not allow him to miss their wedding anniversary on January 22, 1886, and he grudgingly met her at the dockside in Gibraltar. She seemed remarkably chipper, and he was quick to learn she had inherited yet another of those delicious £500 legacies from a dead relative. The couple spent their time energetically travelling back and forth from the mainland. They toured behind Algeciras and Malaga in the hills beyond.

The Burtons had returned to Gibraltar, and were sitting in their hotel room, when a bell-hop brought a cable. It was addressed 'Sir Richard Burton'. Burton refused to open the envelope.

Some fellow is 'playing me a practical joke, or else it is not for me. I shall not open it, so you may as well ring the bell and give it back again.'

Isabel opened the cable and read aloud the information that Her Majesty's Government had seen fit to award him a KCMG in the new year's Honours List. Dick shuffled uncomfortably, and quite rightly declared,

'Oh, I shall not accept it!'

After all, this particular knighthood was pretty low down in the order of stately things, and below such puffs as the Garter, the Thistle, St Patrick, the Bath, the Star of India, his particular award of Knight Commander of St Michael and St George barely had precedence over the measly knighthood of the Indian Empire which was ladled out by the bucketful to any tin-pot commissioner who could demonstrate he had lasted thirty years of his life on the teeming shores of the Indian Ocean. But Isabel upped and burbled with the authority of a seasoned social campaigner. She would no more need to rely on that letter-head rubbish of 'Countess of the Holy Roman Empire'.

'You had better accept it, Jemmy, because it is a certain sign that they are going to give you the place.'

She meant, of course, the place as consul in Morocco. Once more she was wildly wrong. No one was going to offer Dick any new post. He knew what the worth of that KCMG was. It was an ever so genteel kiss-off from Lord Salisbury in London. It was intended to soften the blow of his last years in Trieste. It was a suitable sop for his hungry wife. The title guaranteed him a certain status. If he reached hard times following his pension, he could rely on the knighthood for that extra social credit it still stood for. It was the old old story. Porters saluted a little more smartly, shopkeepers rang up accounts without a murmur, you could be sure of a good seat for a decent show in town when you called at the box office. He could already see the swallows on the wing.

The dark winter nights which would herald the long silence of the grave.

In March, 1886, the Burtons set sail in foul weather for Trieste. The storms never let up, and there came a moment when Dick looked out from his deck to see what appeared to be a baggy fat feather pillow somebody had tossed on the lower deck. Within moments, fellow passengers rushed to pick up the unconscious Isabel who had stepped off the deck, expecting to find the ladder beneath her, and tumbled fifteen feet to the deck below. Burton waited until the ship reached Naples. He bundled her off the boat and insisted she took the train on to Trieste. 'I made her continue her journey by land,' he wrote, 'whilst I, who thoroughly enjoyed the sea, rejoined the ship.' By this time she had developed rising tumours in the wall of her womb and in her right ovary. Dick's lack of concern would have won him the commendation Shit of the Year, 1886.

In Trieste, Dick laboured for six months on volumes VIII and IX of the *Nights*. He was back in London with Isabel for the latter half of the year, and quarrelling with the curators of the Bodleian Library, Oxford, who wouldn't allow him to take out of the building a particular manuscript he needed for Vol. X of the *Nights*. Burton huffed and puffed to no avail, and finally his wife with considerable foresight advised him to have the pages photographed. Burton growled dismally, admitted it was a good idea, and stumped back to Oxford. Suddenly he came down with something quite painful, but he just managed to fire off a telegram to Isabel in London—'GOUT IN BOTH FEET. COME DIRECTLY'. Isabel, valiant as ever, trundled down to Oxford with a 'gout doctor', Dr Foakes, and arranged for an ambulance to take the broken warrior back to London. He was in a foul mood the whole year. He lay in bed for six weeks and composed a plea to Lord Salisbury to give him a Civil List pension of £300 a year, in addition to his coming retirement pension. Salisbury rejected the idea.

According to Isabel, a publisher offered the Burtons £500 for a Household Edition of the *Nights*. Dick was unwilling to sell the copyright for such a venture, but he did not put up too much fuss when Justin McCarthy was hired to bowdlerise Burton's proofs and inject 'society words' in place of Dick's more expressive narrative. In fact, McCarthy, ripped out more than that. He traduced at least two fairly juicy tales of honest buggery, and blue-pencilled out a large number of Burton's most direct footnotes which concerned Church, Faith and aspects of modern family life.

Dick lay in bed with his gout, and Isabel and McCarthy worked glove in hand on their own interpretation of his epic translation. She often took McCarthy's blue-pencil Grundyisms back to Burton, for, when all was said and done it was his work which lay under the scrutinising hack, and Dick made a few meagre efforts to stet some of the worst examples of McCarthy's frenzy. Isabel worked alongside McCarthy to send the first two volumes to the printers. The cream-coloured cloth bindings were a third of the complete Household Edition. They were entitled *Lady Burton's Edition of her Husband's Arabian Nights. Translated Literally from the Arabic, Prepared for Household Reading by Justin Huntley McCarthy*. The first volume bore a frontispiece portrait of Isabel, the second bore a portrait of Dick.

Burton had no great liking for McCarthy ('a name well known in the annals of contemporary literature'), and made no bones about his contempt. Two years later Burton recalled that of this edition of one thousand copies, barely 500 were sold: 'The public would have none of it; even innocent girlhood tossed aside the chaste volumes in utter contempt.' As for Isabel, she maintained that Dick never allowed her to read the realism his own rendering of the *Nights* was so famous for. She said all the naughty words were excised, and all she had to do was find a few more suitable social words to replace the original. The outcome proved academic. Burton was in haste to leave London. Isabel had to leave McCarthy with the brunt of the social text he had been commissioned to produce, and from Dick's peremptory manner it was obvious he had no more time for Isabel's Household grammar. Later, he did allow—

> Before dismissing the subject of the Household Edition, I would offer a few words of explanation on the part of the Editress. While touching-up and trimming the somewhat hurried work of our friend Mr McCarthy, she was compelled to accompany me abroad, and to nurse me through a dangerous illness, which left but little time for the heavy claims of business. Unable to superintend, with the care required, the issue of her six volumes she entrusted the task to two agents in whose good will and experience she had and still has the fullest confidence; but the results were sundry letters of appeal and indignation from subscribers touching matters wholly unknown and unintelligible to her.

Dick allowed this bowdlerised edition because he had been greedy enough in the first place to be influenced by the £500 for a Household Edition of the *Nights*. Now it had come to a financial disaster, he wanted to get shot of the project. He wanted to leave with all speed, and by January 4, 1887, both he and Isabel were aboard ship for France, and within forty-eight hours they had reached Paris. From Paris they swanned south to Cannes, and Dick embarked on an orgy of social engagements. In Isabel's words – 'One meets with friends without number, and what with breakfasts, lunches, five-o'clock teas, dinners, balls, and suppers, not to speak of picnics, and excursions, time is thoroughly taken up.' It was a non-stop marathon of dressing up for Lady Murray's fancy dress ball, and Mr and Mrs Walker's garden party, and a noble breakfast on the prom with their Imperial Highnesses the Prince Leopold and Princess of Hohenzollern-Sigmaringen, followed by a gout-enlivening ten-course supper with a certain Archduke Mecklenburg-Schwerin, and Dick was eventually 'sent for' to be presented to none other than the Duke and Duchess of Baden. One week ago he was being nursed through a 'dangerous illness', the next moment finds him wolfing down pork cutlets aux Vin de Champagne, Dindon rôti aux Truffes a L'Espagnole, and Fontaine Royale garnie de Pâtisserie à la Génévoise, over breakfast with a pack of Austrian nobles, washing it all down with the choicest Bual Madeira.

Six weeks of this indulgence brought Dick down with a bump. At the close of February he suffered what appeared to have been an epileptic fit. He was unconscious for half an hour, during which time Isabel took it upon herself to baptise the prostrate figure and shower his whitened features with water. Soon enough though, he was on his feet, and Isabel packed him off to Monte Carlo for a further headlong rest. They railed on towards Menton, and then to Asti, and on to Milan, and hence to Venice: in fact, it took Burton, with his remarkable illness, four whole months to get back to Trieste where the Foreign Office suffered him as their consul.

Somewhere along this slow and luxurious route back to Trieste, Isabel persuaded him to sign a document she had drawn up. He definitely put his signature to the articles contained therein; and, if anything, this sheet of paper clearly explained Isabel's frame of mind:

Should my husband, Richard Burton, be on his death-bed unable to speak – perhaps already dead – and that he may wish and have the grace to retract and recant his former errors and join the Catholic Church and also receive the Sacraments of Penance, Extreme Unction and Holy Eucharist, he might perhaps be able to sign this paper or make the sign of the cross to show his need.

Meek as a lamb, Dick signed it. After his death his old allies and chums in underground printing presses and Fleet Street beer parlours could howl as much as they liked, he had signed the thing and that was that. The man didn't care any more. He'd go along with any whim. He was keeping his real self snug to his own dreams. She wouldn't penetrate there.

By June, the British population in Trieste was prepared to celebrate the Queen's Jubilee. Dick, as consul, presided over a supper and read out a piece of grovelling nonsense in front of a large audience:

> We are about to drink the health of the greatest Lady in the land. Tonight is a great night for us, and a proud one. All the world is assembled tonight throughout the globe to do honour to one Woman, the only woman in history who for fifty years' glorious reign, as Wife, as Mother, as Sovereign, as Widow, as Mother of her people, has been a shining light in each of these capacities to the whole world . . .
>
> . . . although she may have been in public all day, perhaps tired, perhaps suffering, perhaps obliged to be in Society a greater part of the night, she never once omitted (so long as her children were little) to go into her nursery every evening at a certain hour to hear them say their prayers at her knee, lest those little prayers should ever become a mockery—just as any homely mother amongst us would do, if she had good sound sense and a womanly heart . . .

That week he was working on the final volume of the *Supplemental Nights*. Dick, with his customary emphasis on the masculine-dominated world of ancient Baghdad, was not slow to point out the most suitable position in life for womankind. 'Throughout Al-Islam in default of a father the eldest brother gives away the sisters, and if there be no brother this is done by the nearest male relation on the *sword* side. The mother has no authority in such matters nor indeed has anyone on the *spindle* side.' One very much doubts any obligation Burton might have held for royalty when it comes to placing any woman anywhere but on the *spindle* side of the correct order of things.

Dick spent a month riding around Austria by train with Isabel, between Vienna, Marienbad and Laibach. He again lost the use of his legs, and employed porters to carry him from hotel to railway carriage upended in a peculiar bath-chair. The consulate at Trieste was informed of the immediate arrival of the Prince of Wales, and a retinue of Anglo-Kraut royals, and much panic was endured when the Burtons were forbidden to attend the famous arrival by their doctor. Dick was back in the hills behind Trieste, and he gave orders for his house to be thrown open for the honoured guests. Food and drink and flowers were laid on every day. Much to the amazement of Isabel, his

Imperial Highness didn't go anywhere near the Burton building. He preferred to stay on the royal yacht, in company with his friends.

The Burtons had been keeping a resident doctor with them for most of the year. Now this man had been offered a better post elsewhere. Isabel remembered a young Dr F. Grenfell Baker whom they had met in Cannes. Baker himself had suffered ill health, and could not continue with his London practice. Isabel cabled him and offered him the post of resident practitioner to the Burtons. Baker accepted the post and arrived in Trieste by October, 1887. Immediately the Burtons whisked him off to Abbazia, in Croatia, where they were continuing a very expensive and leisurely course in the local waters, not forgetting Dick's doses of rhubarb, carbonate of soda, potash, cream-of-tartar water, beef teas and sitz-baths. Baker travelled with the Burtons on their plush round of hotel convalescence until March, 1888, when they all returned to Trieste. On March 19, Dick celebrated his sixty-seventh birthday, laid aside the last volume of the *Nights*, which he had completed, and took to reading *Little Lord Fauntleroy*. Baker was an astute young doctor. He noticed the tiny examples of general disability which were encumbering Dick's daily routine. He could not always remember where he'd put papers. He sometimes lost the use of his fingers for short periods. He complained about noises above his hotel bedroom which didn't exist. He had got into the habit of concealing bottles of port and brandy from Baker. Baker smiled to himself, and allowed the old buffer his idiosyncrasies. Baker's job was not to alarm either Isabel or Richard. But he knew that all this fuss over gout was merely over a symptom, and not the real cause. The heart of this profoundly schizophrenic *haji*, reaper of heteronyms, sore sailor of past desert seas, the heart of the man had stumbled: at last it was clear to Baker just what kind of cruel retort the fates had brought. It wasn't social disgrace, or Foreign Office indifference, or lack of intellectual acclaim, it was a palely pumping ventricular retort, a cheap snub really, what irony that the *haji's* strong body should bend to paltry this. Baker knew all right. The dust beckoned.

There is a natural, but rather insensitive reaction to the picture of this old titan sitting in the sun demolishing *Little Lord Fauntleroy*, with evident pleasure: how would one best put it? The most rebellious farm tup has had itself knuckled? In his *Laocoön*, Gotthold Lessing's quarrel was with the riddle of why it was correct for Virgil to write of the man's stony scream, when all the sculptors (Polydor, Agesander and Athenodor) could only allow Laocoön a sigh. Lessing kept his famous argument strictly between the difference of poetry and the plastic arts.

The priest Laocoön had infuriated his God, Apollo, by handing out too much devious advice to the Greeks, and twin monster serpents were sent to destroy Laocoön and his two sons. But there is an area where the priest's pathos need not be confined to Lessing's hierarchy of signs. If Laocoön had escaped this horrible death, there was nowhere for him to hide. If he accepted the mortal coils as payment for his errors, death would in any case take him to Apollo. There is a concept of binary aesthetics here. The statue's sigh could be no more than a realisation that the death was the greater freedom. It promised him life with his deity. Likewise with Richard Burton, he might have signed and puffed and rough shouldered his domestic coils, but he was not in mortal fear as such, he had another 'life' hidden away; it kept his day-to-day social nonsense at a safe distance, as if he were staring at his wife from the large end of a telescope. Laocoön's sculpted expression is by no means a painful cry for *release*; he would reach the land of the Hyperboreans. It was no further than Baghdad lay from Burton.

We observe how Richard and Isabel travelled as with a frenzy of itchy feet as soon as they possessed ready cash. After a bare six weeks in his consulate, Dick ordered the bags packed, and the faithful Dr Baker followed the Burtons to Milan, Lucerne, Montreux, and Geneva. From Paris they reached London by the middle of July, 1888. It was to be his last visit to England. He stayed with the Stisted family, and they were shocked at his condition. He met Henry Irving and Algie Swinburne in London, and, although a Dr Mortimer Granville gave Burton a clean bill of health, he could not stay on his feet past eight o'clock in the evenings. Burton waited to see the last two volumes of the *Supplemental Nights* through the presses, but by November he had had enough of British weather, and he ordered his caravan back to Trieste via Lausanne. It took him three months to reach Trieste.

Now that the mammoth task of *The Arabian Nights* was completed, Richard planned translations of *Il Pentamerone*, Catullus, Juvenal, and the *Metamorphoses* or *Golden Ass* of Apuleius. In addition, he collaborated with Leonard Smithers on the first English translation of the Latin *Priapeia, or the Sportive Epigrams of Divers Poets on Priapus*. It was intended to be the first of three books, the second being *The Carmina* by Catullus; but, at the last minute, Dick was dissuaded from putting his name to the Roman translation. It is not clear at all how much work he contributed to Smithers' research on the *Priapeia*, but there is much evidence for Dick's hand in the verse. The *Priapeia*, although dated 1888, was not published until the middle of 1890. It is no surprise to learn that Isabel put her foot down over this particular translation. The pension due on his seventieth birthday was now so near, that the least hint of public prosecution over a volume of erotica he hadn't completely written might jeopardise it. She used her full powers of persuasion in this case, and she prevailed.

In November, 1889, Dick was engaged in an oafish correspondence with the Foreign Office in London. Evidently they were disturbed by his constant absenteeism, and the presence of a travelling doctor did little to assuage the powers that reigned. To make amends for this lapse, if not to redeem himself in his own eyes, Burton packed his bags and dragged both wife and doctor on board the Austrian-Lloyd steamer *Ettore*, and sailed for Brindisi where he visited Virgil's house. Not satisfied with that, the consul continued on a four-month tour of Malta and North Africa. He did not return to Trieste until March 19, 1890. It was his sixty-ninth birthday to the very day. So much for the Foreign Office. Dick must have felt he'd made his point. Did he want to dare the Foreign Office to withhold the pension? How long could Isabel rely on these infrequent distant Dame Sib legacies? The Burtons were spending one hundred pounds a week, moving maid and doctor, pets, and baggage from one hotel to another.

The artist Albert Letchford worked in the Burton house for a number of weeks. He had already completed a set of oil paintings, seventy-one in all including a portrait of Burton, for various tales from the *Nights*. Now Letchford had added a set of signed prints based on these pictures for new Library editions of the *Nights* which H. S. Nichols was in the process of reproducing. The prints were to be sold in two different sizes. (There are versions of these prints on Japanese vellum, Plate paper etc in six different printings ranging from *de luxe* to *ordinary*.) These were hand-blocked heliogravure reproductions, and for several years after Burton's death, Smithers and Nichols & Co were churning out a remarkable variety of these etchings. Whether or not Letchford received a fair return for his copyright is not clear. But Smithers and Nichols brought the selling of the *Nights* to a rarefied conclusion when, on marketing an Edition de Grand Luxe of the translation, they produced these Letchford plates bound in polished mahogany caskets, shaded, and with mouldings and lattice-worked glass doors which hung on ornate brass hinges. Letchford was a steadfast friend and admirer of Burton. Between March and July, Letchford and Dr Baker shared the great house on the slope behind Trieste with the Burtons. Isabel was left to her pets and her animal cruelty campaigns, her confessional, and some serious attempts at that most popular sport of the time – extra-sensory perception, table-tapping and the like. Dick and Baker and Letchford had much in common. Meal-times still bore a certain masculine domination and their hearty matters with unvoiced repudiation allowed her less and less space for canine defence or Roman homilies. She complained that Richard had in some way let her down, for he was 'talking more than ever agnostically at the table'.

Almost the last entry from his diary which has come from Isabel's random selection of these day-books and journals, is a tantalising note: 'March 21, 1890. Began or rather resumed Scented Garden.' Before July of that year, the manuscript had reached 1,282 pages. And he told Grenfell Baker –

'I have put my whole life and all my life-blood into that *Scented Garden*; it is my great hope that I shall live by it. It is the crown of my life.'

According to the earlier biography by Thomas Wright, *Life of Sir Richard Burton* (1906), Baker warned Richard that Isabel might destroy this new and extended version of his *Perfumed Garden*. She was aware of his intention to replace the missing chapter on sodomy, coupled with notes from Karl Ulrichs (*Numa Numantius*). And Dick's reaction was naive to say the least –

'Do you really think so?' he replied. 'Then I must write to Arbuthnot at once, and tell him that in the event of my death, the manuscript is to be his.'

We have only Wright's word on it that Dick wrote this letter. It was Wright's opinion that Isabel also knew the contents of the letter.

Bravely, Isabel referred to her tumours as another attack of 'peritonitis'. Grenfell Baker supplied her with laudanum drops and she lay in bed for several days with a dreadfully swollen belly under the influence of the opium tincture. For two months, between July and September, the Burtons took themselves off on what was to be his last little trip. They stayed in Zürich, then Davos, and then in Maloja, on the Engadine plateau, in Switzerland. Dick sat upstairs on his bedroom balcony in the snowy sunlight writing sundry observations on sodomy and the catamites of Tunis according to the words of the Cheikh Nefzaoui, for his *Scented Garden*. Down below on the terrace, Isabel ploughed through the social order of things dressed in her Mary Stuart white ruff, stiffly tweaked cuffs, and billowing gown, until she had made the necessary acquaintanceships of the Duchess of Leinster, a Lord Elcho, the Lady Mabel Fitzgerald, and Mrs Main, who according to Isabel, was shortly to become Mrs Fred Burnaby,

As soon as the beef tea was served in the Alpine Buttery, she'd call Jemmy down to perform a similar round-robin of how-do-you-dos. By coincidence, they were staying at the same hotel as Henry Morton Stanley who was there on his honeymoon. It is impossible to think that Dick did not record this in his day-book. It is left to Dorothy Stanley, editing her husband's *Autobiography*, to pick up the threads of the exchange. Stanley saw Dick's broken health, and he suggested Burton might start work on his reminiscences. Dick replied it was an impossible task, there were too many people in his past, and he didn't want to write about many of them. Stanley told him to be charitable to people, and write only of their best qualities. At this, Dick flared up—

'I don't care a fig for charity; if I write at all, I must write truthfully, all I know.'

It is not surprising that Isabel couldn't bring herself to record this exchange.

They were back in the cold mansion in Trieste on September 7, 1890. Richard came low with a bout of the familiar 'gout'. One day that month, he asked Isabel—

'When the swallows form a dado round the house, when they are crowding on the windows, in thousands, preparatory to flight, call me.'

Dr Grenfell Baker spent much time in the garden taking photographs of them all—'kodacking' it was called in those days. Eventually Isabel the widow would collect all the snaps and have them varnished in a gelatine substance on to lamp-shades. In the evenings, Baker insisted on giving Dick dyspepsia medicine, a ferment of pupain. Baker weighed Burton, and found to his approval that his patient had put on four pounds, and stood at eleven stone six. Isabel was acutely aware of 'bad omens', and a chilly spasm gripped her when he announced that a bird had been tapping at his window all the morning.

That Friday, October 17, on the margin he scribbled in his day-book—

> Swallow, pilgrim swallow,
> Beautiful bird with purple plume,
> That, sitting upon my window-sill,
> Repeating each morn at the dawn of day,
> That mournful ditty so wild and shrill,—
> Swallow, lovely swallow, what would'st thou say,
> On my casement-sill at the break of day?

He complained of lumbago, as well as his liver, and he talked of his plans to retire to England to a small cottage which was to be crammed with his swords, his carpets, his collection of pistols and saddles, and his thousands of books. In five months' time his term of service would be up; he could divest himself of this consulship, and on his seventieth birthday accept that paltry pension. Dick set up his telescope on the verandah outside the study windows. The garden in the evening waltzed with the *chooc chooc chooc* crescendoes of the nightingale, close by the house, awaiting migration.

On Sunday morning, October 19, Dick found a robin half-drowned in a garden tank. He made a great fuss about it, and ordered Dr Baker to revive the nasty little predator, greedy nuisance amongst its feathered kind. The last life he should save was that of the most selfish of all feathered pecker bills one can find in a house garden.

Albert Letchford, Grenfell Baker and Isabel dined early with Burton on the Sunday evening. Dick was in bed by nine-thirty. From midnight on the sickly man woke frequently and called out to the others. Isabel attended him. Grenfell Baker saw Burton at four a.m. and did not express any more alarm than was required for what he assumed to be an attack of gout.

Baker left the large room by the verandah windows and returned to his own bed. Half an hour later Dick was in clear distress. He was gasping for air. Isabel ran in panic to Baker. Burton was in grave danger. Both Isabel and Baker came to the conclusion it was the man's heart which was about to fail. Isabel called it 'a clot of blood to the heart'. Isabel and Baker lifted him to a near-sitting position. She tried to cradle the broad shoulders in her arms. He was growing weaker and consequently heavier in her embrace. He gasped—

'Oh, Puss, chloroform—ether—or I am a dead man!'

'My darling,' she answered, 'the doctor says it will kill you. He is doing all he knows.'

Grenfell Baker set up his somewhat primitive apparatus of electrodes beside the bed. He dampened Burton's chest with salt water, plunged the chamois leather-covered terminals into a beaker of water beside him and steadily bore down on the patient's chest with the moistened shockers. He placed one electrode against the heart, the other he pressed on to Burton's shoulder-bone. During the course of these convulsive vibrations, with half a breath left in his lungs, Richard cried out—

'My God, I am a dead man!'

This *Haji*, lord of distances and master of disguise, now slipped below the conscious surface; not quite dead yet, not totally the victim of their electrodes and tears and shriekings, drowning, but yet waving, close to them, close as a touch but distant as a star in the eye of his verandah telescope; his dream kingdom was a morganatic divorce of the mind, what once he called the 'walling of the horizons' was ever intended to outdistance those too close to him. The *Haji* was not wholly theirs, oh not quite dead, breath of a fox yet remained, a last leap at a brick wall by the boy who never told, not the sum total relinquished . . . not all . . .

The secret wood was in his *Nights*. Richard Burton was tucked away in the hundreds of notes, and in the sixty thousand word Terminal Essay of Volume X of the *Nights*. All his days, that final decade, he allowed the surface of his domestic routine to cloud over and almost obliterate the man *seen plain*. It was his character armour. The pale shell of his near lifeless body remained, but the potential of his inner life was drained out elsewhere. Gramsci's 'possibility is not reality: but it is in itself a reality. Possibility means freedom.' In Burton's case, his freedom always had to be a factor of secrecy.

In the volumes of his *Nights*, one is aware of two voices. Almost every other page of the million word text is annotated. In the first instance, translation and commentary are combined in a running analysis of the ancient tales, and Burton makes many comparisons with previous translations. In the second instance, beside the footnotes, there appears from time to time a number of insertions (euphemisms, callow gags, heteronyms etc), which bear his most personal signature. In the final six volumes of *Supplemental Nights*, these deeply felt remarks dry up. But the very nature of these insertions, their often quite savage assaults, almost stain the pages with what can best be described as tricky bile. Unintrusive marginalia, barbed and imprisoned, half-gagged snarls in a sea of words, sardonic and bitter and cold, these whispers tagged on to profane and witty tales about coyntes and prickles, yards, members and pomegranates (anuses), literally seethe with an uncontrollable contempt.

There is no mistaking the childhood picture of himself when, in the tale of *Ali Nur al-Din and Miriam the Girdle Girl* the father Tajal-Din approached his son and smelt the strong reek of wine. The boy promptly dealt the father a welt over his right eye. For no logical reason, the margentor could not resist declaring 'How true to nature the whole scene is; the fond mother excusing her boy and the practical father putting the excuse aside. European paternity, however, would probably exclaim "The beast's in liquor!" . . .' It was an echo from across sixty years, the words were his father's, Colonel Joseph's, and Dick added them to the text of the *Nights* with the confidence of a Baghdad gossip of the 10th century.

Jamil told the story of his pious wake beside a tomb for three nights and three days in the tale of *The Lovers of the Banu Uzrah*: Burton added a footnote to this on the propriety of paying a fee to modern-day church mourners, and he assumed the title of 'one who shall be nameless'. He wrote scornfully:

> Muslims do not pay for prayers to benefit the dead like the majority of Christendom and, according to Calvinistic Wahhabi-ism [doctrinal fanaticism], their prayers and blessings are of no avail. But the mourner's heart loathes reason and he prays for his dead instinctively like the so-termed 'Protestant'. Amongst the latter, by the bye, I find four great *Sommites*, 1) Paul of Tarsus who protested against the Hebraism of Peter; 2) Mohammed who protested against the perversions of Christianity; 3) Luther who protested against Italian rule in Germany, and lastly 4) one (who shall be nameless) that protests against the whole business . . .

Burton is 'a certain pilgrim' in the anecdote he supplied to the one hundred and twenty-second night, the *Tale of Aziz and Azizah*. He wrote:

> Muslims never stand up at such times [in a reference to male urination], for a spray of urine would make their clothes ceremonially impure: hence the scrupulous will break up with stick or knife the hard ground in front of them. A certain pilgrim was reported to have made this blunder which is hardly possible in Muslim dress.

For it was once rumoured Burton had to kill a man who caught the explorer upstanding in the act on his pilgrimage to Mecca.

Dick could not forget the accusations of pederasty set against him in Bombay; and yet he did little to dispel the rumour when he called himself the Bombay officer in a note he attached to the tale of *Judar and his Brethren* – 'I remember an officer in the Bombay Army who, having learned Hindostani from women, always spoke of himself in the feminine and hugely scandalised the Sepoys.'

But the most slashing heteronyms were reserved for Isabel Burton. At times they reached such a crescendo of bile, it can only be put down to her 'ignorance', as he liked to refer to it, that she never fully understood the violence of these attacks. In a footnote to *The Seventh Voyage of Sinbad the Seaman*, Burton assumes the mantle of a Maltese gentleman. 'I remember an Italian lady being much hurt when a Maltese said to her "Mia moglie—con rispetto parlando" [my wife, saving your presence]. "What!" she cried, "he speaks of his wife as if he would of the sweepings!" . . .' In other words, Burton spoke in Italian to a lovely woman in front of Isabel. Isabel could not follow the conversation. The clumsy man suggested he'd rather think on the woman as his real wife.

Again and again Burton's domestic life penetrated the text of the *Nights*. It can best be observed when he makes a point of congratulating a husband for his lack of ardour. In the *Tale of Kamar al-Zaman*, he described the Princess Budur's passion for Kamar al-Zaman as 'a marvellous touch of nature, love ousting affection' when the woman cannot flint a spark of sexual response from the iron hard man beside her in bed—

Then, Princess Budur shook him with her hands and said 'my life on thee, hearken to me; awake up from thy sleep and look on the narcissus and the tender down thereon, and enjoy the sight of naked waist and navel; and touzle me and tumble me from this moment till break of day! Allah upon thee, O my lord, sit up and prop thee against the pillow and slumber not!' Still Kamar al-Zaman made her no reply but breathed hard in his sleep. Continued she, 'Alas! Alas! Thou art insolent in thy beauty and comeliness and grace and loving looks! But if thou art handsome, so am I handsome; what then is this thou dost? Have they taught thee to flout me or hath my father, the wretched old fellow, made thee swear not to speak to me tonight?' But Kamar al-Zaman opened not his mouth neither awoke, whereat her passion for him redoubled and Allah inflamed her heart with love for him. She stole one glance of eyes that cost her a thousand sighs: her heart fluttered, and her vitals throbbed and her hands and feet quivered; and she said to Kamar al-Zaman 'Talk to me, O my lord! Speak to me, O my friend! Answer me, O my beloved, and tell me thy name, for indeed thou hast ravished my wit!' And during all this time he abode drowned in sleep and answered her not a word . . .

Indeed, Burton provided no better heteronym for his *Haji*, than that of Kamar al-Zaman. He added to the footnotes in this sequence, 'the world shows that while women have more philoprogenitiveness, men have more amativeness; otherwise the latter would not propose and would nurse the doll and baby'. It has been common knowledge since his death that it was Isabel who forced the proposal. So much for Dick's amativeness 'drowned in sleep'; his bed with Isabel right from the start bore all the appearances of cold sheets and empty arms.

And one can recognise his frequent references to the 'ignorant' in his notes. He took the hemistichal couplet in the *Tale of Ali bin Bakkar and of Shams al-Nahur* —

Give me one kiss in gift	Or loan if thou devise:
And if thou crave for more	Take all that satisfies,

and re-addressed the reader in the direction of Isabel. His note read, 'These naive offers in Eastern tales mostly come from the true seducer — Eve. Europe, and England especially, still talks endless absurdity upon the subject. A man of the world may "seduce" an utterly innocent (which means an ignorant) girl.' One is left in no doubt as to who was 'the man of the world', and who the ignorant woman. These slights fall thick and fast throughout the notes. He could not leave a bone unpicked, and in Volume VII he offered up more than four alternatives for a correct interpretation of the sentence, 'Follow me, for I should know her with blue eyes'. With overkill, this obscurantist manic at last re-translated 'blue eyes' into 'blue-eyed, dim-sighted, purblind'. Isabel, of course. And in *The Adventures of Mercury Ali of Cairo*, he barely bothered to disguise his own marriage — 'Many a woman, even of the world, has fallen in love with a man before indifferent to her because he did not take advantage of her when he had the opportunity.'

As far as he was concerned, he had had enough of her simpleminded devotion. He scornfully dreamed of finding a wife who had the honest guts to admit her defects: 'The greatest of all explorers and discoverers of the world will be he who finds a woman confessing inability to keep a secret.' As for the long separations he so carefully contrived in the past, and often when she had already paid and packed for him: 'So the Hindus speak of *the defilement of separation* as if it were an impurity.' He sarcastically drew his own assumption of marital bliss. Sometimes in the text there appears a ghostly figure out of his own experiences. She might be called a hag or a bawd or a witch. In *Ni'amah bin al-Rabi'a and Naomi his Slave-Girl*, an old woman wears woollen clothes of a devotee and hangs around her neck a rosary of beads. Burton hastened to invoke this wraith in his footnote; in his opinion this kind of female was a common lot in the western world — 'She is found in the cities of Southern Europe, ever pious, ever prayerful.'

What with his hair dyes and his more than fifty pairs of polished boots, old age brought him a strangely antiseptic form of dandyism, akin to Baudelaire's *dandyisme* which was a sunset, like the declining daystar, glorious, and without heat and filled with melancholy. He developed absurdly squeamish theories about physical appearances, and there remained a hint of tactile disgust — 'The faces of children who sleep with their grandparents, of a young wife married to an old man and of a young man married to an old woman, show a peculiar wizened appearance, a look of age overlaying youth which cannot be mistaken', and so forth.

In the *Tale of King Omar bin al-Nu'uman and his Sons* Burton tore a phrase out of context: 'but Time passed over him, as though he had never been', and wrote at the bottom of the page 'tender and true'.

All his life, Richard Burton made a point of telling the truth on the surface of things. It was the life itself—half submerged and encumbered with the adroitness of a fox's eye, which gave the lie to his possibilities. 'Man is not what we think he is, he is what he hides,' wrote André Malraux. The great French Catholic Gabriel Marcel asks in *The Mystery of Being*: 'Can I give my life without giving myself?'; in Burton's case the answer was a resounding yes.

By five o'clock in the morning, October 20, the kitchen girls from downstairs had already risen. The houseguest, the artist Albert Letchford, could not sleep either. Gas brackets were lit. Cats and Isabel's collection of stray dogs silently scanned the long stone corridors on the ground floor. A sense of possessive panic emanated from Dick's quarters. There was the sound of a woman's voice half in tears, half in supplication, leaning by a bedside uttering prayer. Occasionally, Grenfell Baker shouted out and one of the kitchen girls came running. South and beneath the verandah windows the water in the bay, now dark and chilled, caught the first white and yellow light shards from the direction of the Capo D'Istria hills as if the sun had tossed at random a fistful of mercury pyrites on to this Adriatic gulf. Isabel, seeking omens, believed she heard a dog commence to bark wildly just as her man's breathlessness reached an extreme. She made the doctor press his chamois leather electrodes on to the crippled heart for the following two hours, without let-up, but the patient had already escaped the bonds of their worldly ministrations. A priest, Father Pietro Martelani, was rushed down the corridor. He took one look at the body on the bed and raised his eyebrows. He had attended as many corpses as the doctor. Is this man alive? he inquired. And, according to Isabel, both she and Baker attested to the fact that he was. Is this man a Catholic? Isabel insisted he was. She said she would provide the evidence later.

There were three other people in the room, beside the priest and Burton's body. The third party was, in all likelihood, the girl Lisa, Isabel's maid. The priest administered the Holy Sacrament for one who was at the point of death, as Isabel insisted, and commenced with the words 'Si vivis . . .' By seven o'clock, Isabel could no longer disguise the fact of his death. Although she ordered a final charge of electricity to be fed to the left ulnar vein there came no response whatsoever. She was a widow. Grenfell Baker folded up his tubes and batteries. He tamped down the body's eyes, and allowed Isabel to bind the chin. According to the laws of Trieste, Richard was to be buried within sixty hours.

Over 100,000 people in Trieste turned out for the funeral. Sailors from a British ship newly arrived in port formed the cortège. Three requiem masses were held in the city. And the Bishop of Trieste led the oration after the pomp of the military formalities. The coffin was shrouded by a Union Jack, and after all the ceremonies of the day, it was placed inside a hastily prepared *chapelle ardente*, in the grounds of the Catholic cemetery, and laid on a catafalque. In four months' time, his widow would have prepared a final resting place for Richard's embalmed body in a tomb shaped like an eastern tent in the Catholic cemetery of Mortlake, West London.

'Rome took formal possession of Richard Burton's corpse, and pretended, moreover, with insufferable insolence, to take under her protection his soul,' wrote Richard's niece, Georgiana Stisted, in high family ire. It came as a great shock to his relatives, and every friend of Burton's who was in any way intimate with his way of thinking, that these Catholic Services were conducted over his *haji* bones: they were, according to Georgiana, 'the excuse for an ecclesiastical triumph of a faith he had always loathed'.

Isabel heard this storm collect around her ears, but she was adamant: 'Let the world rain fire and brimstone on me now!' She consoled herself with waiting to join his Caravan, 'I am waiting for that welcome sound, the tinkling of his camel-bell.' Ever since his final burial plot in Mortlake took on all the characteristics of her Roman zeal, Isabel has been the target of abuse. Her actions were symptomatic, they were not the root cause of the problem. That lay in the man himself, even if he was a corpse. For he had by no means totally given himself up to anyone, friend, foe or widow. He had had plenty of time to make arrangements for his passing. The very presence, all those months, of Grenfell Baker, was nothing less than a black coated shadow of death, a walking (and fully paid) portent; but Dick did nothing about it. He gambled the fate away. It was another of those ambiguous hurls, dice tosses, into the void. The first agony of death he was determined to disregard. Blithe *haji*.

The eight bench-tops in his workroom, each one filled with a manuscript in various forms of completion, and his fifty years and more of day-books, and those piles upon piles of private journals with their familiar green ledger bindings each 3″ × 4½″, plus a ton of papers inside Bombay Army tin trunks and requisitioned Debenham & Freebody, and Army & Navy Stores' lined wicker hampers for shipping brandy and port, were a Balzacian nightmare of uncompleted literary voyages and padlocked confessions. Richard had made no plans for the contents of his verandah quarters in the Trieste mansion, with the exception of the one-thousand-page second version, of *The Scented Garden*, which he likened to his greatest work.

All these years he had acted as his own Boswell. At the last, he appeared content to let the treasure house of words fall into what posthumous hands the gods decreed. That military funeral and beflagged halt on a silken catafalque in the *chapelle ardente* was a temporary resting place for an escaped heart. The rest of this warrior, intrepid burglar of Meccan nights, dreamer of a Koranic kingdom, Baghdad wallings of his horizon filled with beys, harems, perfumed infibulations and succulent untruths, succubus personas of his own sleep, not forgetting his pills and his gout, Burton dead lay still half-alive in those Debenham & Freebody hampers and Army & Navy Stores' export containers and old Bombay Regimental jinnee tin trunks with Her Majesty's Imperial seal embossed on the brass locker . . . Drowned, yet waving . . .

Isabel Burton locked herself in the verandah room which opened on to the terrace where the rows of quaintly upright deal wood desks stood. On her own admission she busied herself in this place sometimes from ten in the morning until four o'clock the following morning, and until her eyes ached with exhaustion from reading the material. For sixteen days she ploughed through every last scribble she could decipher. She put all the papers into a semblance of order. And she made her own list of the various piles she had separated. She put aside for preservation, and possible future publication those which, in the first place, appeared the most complete of the manuscripts — *Uruguay* (preserved today in the Huntington Library, San Marino, Calif.), *Ladislas Magyar's African Travels*, *Il Pentamerone* (587 pps), *A Book on the Jews* (two further essays, *Materials towards a Book on the Gypsies* of 154 pages, and *An Essay on Islam* of 57 pages were edited together with the essay *A Book on the Jews* of 128 pages, by W. H. Wilkins and published as *The Jew, The Gypsy and El Islam*, 1898, with a certain amount of Burton's most repulsive anti-semitism excised). In addition, a one-hundred-page translation of *Pilpay's Fables* and the commenced draft of a translation of the *Metamorphoses* or *Golden Ass* by Lucius Apuleius both seem to have emerged from Burton's quarters, although Isabel herself has never laid claim to their care and protection. Isabel nevertheless put aside *The Carmina of Catullus* (337 pps), *Greek Proverbs* (52 pps), and a fragment, *The Dying Language of Veglia Island* (19 pps). At a later date, the manuscript known as *Ladislas Magyar's African Travels* disappeared from amongst her possessions after she had moved to London.

Isabel ordered a bonfire to be lit on the sloping garden below the verandah wall. With the exception of one or two manuscripts which might have been given additional titles, and already known to the student bibliographer of Burton, she consigned to the flames *More Notes on Paraguay, Personal Experiences in Syria, Lowlands of Brazil, South America, North America, Central America, A Book of Istria-more Castellieri, Materials for Four more Books on Camoens, Slavonic Proverbs, Dr Wetstein's Hauran, Ausonius Epigrams, A Study of the Wali, A Trip up the Congo* (1863), *Ober Ammergau, Vichy, Lectures and Poetry, The Eunuch Trade in Egypt, Akits as Mirza Ali, The Ashantee War, Inscriptions, Sind-Karachi, The Adelsburg Caves, The Neapolitan Muses, Syrian Proverbs,* and *Four Cantos of Ariosto.*

So intense was the fire, all afternoon the sparks soared up against the windows, and all night the flames driven by the harsh *bora* wind could be seen from the belvedere smoking lounge of the Hotel de Ville beside the harbour walls. The heat from the ashes was insatiable. Come the dawn, she'd rise early and begin again.

And she burned twenty-seven years of his private journals (with the exception of just one of those 3″ × 4½″ cloth bindings). And she burned every day-book of Burton's he had kept for as long as he'd known her. And she burned the entire manuscript of his newly revised 1,282-page *The Scented Garden.* And she burned

Bibliography

ASIDE FROM BURTON'S BOOKS, POETRY, AND TRANSLATIONS, NO
study of the man can be complete without recourse to the 163 pages of
autobiography to be found in Isabel's *Life*. Today, half of Burton's letters
remain in the hands of three private collections; the remainder are with
the Huntington library, San Marino, California, and Trinity College
Library, Cambridge. The Royal Anthropological Institute in London
possesses the bulk of Burton's library which survived Isabel's death. Lady
Burton nominated as her literary executors, her secretary Minnie Plowman,
and her sister Elizabeth Fitzgerald. Instructions were left in Isabel's will to
destroy or burn the remaining private manuscripts and letters which were
still in her possession. Accordingly, Elizabeth Fitzgerald announced her
intention of following Isabel's word to the letter. Minnie Plowman hastily
persuaded the Central Library, Kensington, to take the mass of papers and
books, filing boxes and documents; where they stayed for many years until
being transferred to the Royal Anthropological Society. In addition, the
British Museum Manuscript Department and the offices of the Royal
Geographical Society contain a number of manuscript pages and letters.
There have been a number of biographies of Burton since 1880. They
usually fall into three categories: those early enough to contain partial
hearsay such as *A Short Sketch of the Career of Captain Richard F. Burton* by
'An Old Oxonian' (Alfred Bates Richards) and Francis Hitchman's *Richard
F. Burton*; those such as *The Real Sir Richard Burton* by Walter Phelps Dodge
and *Burton* by Byron Farwell which present unbiased chronology; and
there are those which cannot resist an interpretation of the facts and the
available manuscript material such as Fawn Brodie's *The Devil Drives*.
Finally, no work on Burton can do without the incomparable diligence of
Norman M. Penzer's 351-page *An Annotated Bibliography of Sir Richard
Francis Burton*.

A few exceptionally gifted writers have, in their individual ways, also
applied themselves to the Burton legend. Alan Moorehead's *The White Nile*,

273

Frank Harris's *Contemporary Portraits*, Hugh J. Schonfield's *Richard Burton: Explorer*, Jean Burton's (industrious and sympathetic) *Sir Richard Burton's Wife*, and Lesley Blanch's two books *The Wilder Shores of Love*, and, *The Sabres of Paradise*.

Mrs Brodie's imaginative study of Burton at long last brought the subject into the realm of interpretation and comparative historicism: only slightly marred by an attempt to lean over backwards in order to decode Speke's ill-timed death. *The Devil Drives*, though it demonstrates fastidiously researched source material, comes to grief with a superstructure involving images of the Devil and the 'demon-driven'; unfortunately the analysis is all too facilely undertaken, and one is left with no satisfactory evidence for this particular theory. But, Fawn Brodie's method *is* right. With but a glance at the man, his life, and his work, she realised there must be a key somewhere to the many inconsistencies. A man equipped with all those extraordinary talents deserved a better life than the fates allowed him. The life and work of Richard Burton require a form of coda. A plain calendar of the years won't do, any more.

How can a portrait of Burton reconcile this problem? Of late, libraries have become swollen with biographic chronologies of 'What did he have for breakfast, lunch, dinner and tea?' And too much biography has been reduced to gossip dressed up as *received* history. The novel itself hides away in shame when yet another biographed hero, hitherto deemed whiter than white, is triumphantly revealed as 'a syphilitic heroin-jabbing ingrate who shot his father's balls off with a hammerless buffalo gun on his step-mother's wedding day'. And yet, it would appear that the goal of biographer and novelist do intertwine. In as much as *Saturne*, André Malraux' study of Goya as 'the first of the moderns' requires a form of comparative historicism, Hermann Broch's *The Death of Virgil* is undertaken with a scrupulous regard for interpretation through detail. And yet the former is criticism, and the latter a work of fiction. The extraordinary final passage in Broch tries to render Virgil's transition from life into death. Broch has made a portrait based on 'a language which would help the eyes to perceive, heartbreakingly and quick as a heartbeat, the unity of existence'. In both these cases, there appears to be a quality of the sublime. And equally in both cases the writer adopts Goethe's 'He who firmly stands by the inner meaning forms the world to his mind'. After all is said and done, biographer and novelist often link up to share the identical goal of verisimilitude. And all biography remains a form of fiction. And some fiction is a form of biography. In Richard Burton's case—a life filled with enigmatic silences and self-effacing heteronyms, a schema in order to penetrate the mysteries is a required support.

Although there are enough letters by Burton in private hands to make up a complete book, it remains a matter of regret that those who possess all this material appear quite disinclined to advance such a project. From time to time, new and hitherto unknown manuscripts return to the surface. For the moment, it is not without interest to the modern bibliographer to record a number of new manuscripts which have come to the present writer's attention during the course of this book:

A Manuscript in Persian and Urdu. A 105-page octavo manuscript volume. Each sheet opposite a Persian copyplate is faced by an Urdu version. Many of the pages are annotated by Burton. And this is possibly a study book for his tuition in India as early as 1846. Unrecorded anywhere before. And although dated and inscribed 'Richard Burton, 1856', it could well be the earliest manuscript known of Burton's.

A Manuscript of Greek Proverbs. Comprising two quarto note books, in all 52 pages. It looks like the same manuscript Isabel Burton recorded in Trieste just before the burning, and which Penzer assumes disappeared on that bonfire. It belongs to the late 1870s.

Autograph Manuscript of an Unfinished Report on Sayid Barghash of Zanzibar. Consists of eight quarto pages. Between 1857 and 1871, Burton mislaid an entire manuscript of his book on Zanzibar. Eventually, through two intermediaries, and the somewhat covert operations of a bookseller, the larger manuscript was returned to Burton. It is possible that this unfinished essay belongs to the bulk of papers which made up his mislaid narrative. No date attached.

A Blue Notebook of Arabic Proverbs. Five pages with English translations; unknown before, but again it must be one of a number of smaller items somebody recovered from the Trieste flames.

Autographed draft of a projected work — *The Dying Language of Veglia Island.* Nineteen pages with the autographed title. Unknown before, but Burton spent a week on the northern Adriatic island of Veglia in 1873, studying a now abandoned language which possessed Daco-Roman and Macedo-Roman roots.

The Case of Captain Burton, Late H.B.M's Consul at Damascus. A folio pamphlet of 141 pages, printed by Clayton & Co. for circulation within the Foreign Office, 1872. With two inserts, a letter from Rashid Pasha, and Burton's reply. Known to Fawn Brodie; curiously Byron Farewell made no use of this, although he makes a passing reference in his own bibliography under the heading 'Correspondence Respecting Captain Burton's Proceedings at Damascus', which is not at all the same thing as Penzer's entry. Penzer rightly records the correct Clayton & Co., printing of 1872. In the case of the added inserts, these are important, because they almost certainly must be Burton's own copies.

Correspondence with British Agents in Foreign Countries, and with Foreign Ministers in England, relating to the Slave Trade; an official Blue Book, published for the government by Harrison & Sons, 1863. Thirty-three pages on human sacrifice in West Africa by Burton, most likely to have been written whilst consul at Fernando Po, are contained in this 316-page volume. Although unknown to Penzer, Byron Farwell makes reference to an 1864 publication of the same name.

Correspondence with British Agents in Foreign Countries, and with Foreign Ministers in England, relating to the Slave Trade; an official Blue Book published for the government by Harrison & Sons, 1865. A brief four-page account of Burton's mission to Gelele's court at Dahomey is contained in this 319-page volume. Unknown before, it has a curiosity in so much as it is the only printed report in official papers of this mission.

RICHARD BURTON'S BOOKS

Goa, and the Blue Mountains; or, Six Months of Sick Leave by Richard F. Burton, Lieut. Bombay Army. Author of a Grammar of the Mooltanee Language; Critical Remarks on Dr. Dorn's Chrestomathy of the Pushtu, or Affghan Dialect, Etc Etc. Richard Bentley, London. 1851.

Scinde; or, The Unhappy Valley by Richard F. Burton, Lieut. Bombay Army. In two volumes. Richard Bentley, London. 1851.

Sindh, and the Races that Inhabit the Valley of the Indus; with Notices of the Topography and History of the Province. By Richard F. Burton, Lieut. Bombay Army. Wm. H. Allen & Co., London. 1851.

Falconry in the Valley of the Indus by Richard F. Burton, Lieut. Bombay Army. John Van Voorst, London. 1852.

A Complete System of Bayonet Exercise by Richard F. Burton, Lieut. Bombay Army. William Clowes and Sons, London. 1853.

Personal Narrative of a Pilgrimage to El-Medinah and Meccah by Richard F. Burton, Lieut. Bombay Army. Three volumes. Longman, Brown, Green, and Longmans. London. 1855.

First Footsteps in Africa; or, An Exploration of Harar by Richard F. Burton, Bombay Army. Longman, Brown, Green, and Longmans, London. 1856.

The Lake Regions of Central Africa. A Picture of Exploration by Richard F. Burton, Capt. H.M.I. Army: Fellow and Gold Medallist of the Royal Geographical Society. Two volumes. Longman, Green, Longman, and Roberts. 1860.

The City of the Saints and Across the Rocky Mountains to California by Richard F. Burton. Longman, Green, Longman, and Roberts. 1861.

Abeokuta and The Camaroons Mountains. An Exploration by Richard F. Burton, Vice Pres. Anthrop. Soc. of London; Gold Medallist, Geog. Socs.,

Paris and London; F.R.G.S. London; M.A.S.; M.A.S. Bombay; M. Ethno. S. London. Two volumes. Tinsley Brothers, London. 1863.

Wanderings in West Africa From Liverpool to Fernando Po by A.F.R.G.S. with Map and Illustration. Two volumes. Tinsley Brother, London. 1863.

The Prairie Traveller, a Hand-book for Overland Expeditions by Randolph B. Marcy. Edited (with notes) by Richard F. Burton, F.R.G.S. Trubner & Co., London. 1863.

A Mission to Gelele, King of Dahome. With Notices of the So-called 'Amazons', the Grand Customs, the Yearly Customs, the Human Sacrifices, the Present State of the Slave Trade, and, the Negro's Place in Nature. By Richard F. Burton, (Late Commissioner to Dahome). Two volumes. Tinsley Brothers, London. 1864.

The Nile Basin. Part I. Showing Tanganyika to be Ptolemy's Western Lake Reservoir. A Memoir read before the Royal Geographical Society, November 14, 1864. With Prefatory Remarks. By Richard F. Burton, F.R.G.S. Part II. Captain Speke's Discovery of the Source of the Nile. A Review. By James M'Queen, Esq., F.R.G.S. Tinsley Brothers, London. 1864.

Wit and Wisdom from West Africa; or, A Book of Proverbial Philosophy, Idioms, Enigmas, and Laconisms. Compiled by Richard F. Burton (Late) H.M.'s Consul for the Bight of Biafra and Fernando Po. Tinsley Brothers, London. 1865.

The Guide Book. A Pictorial Pilgrimage to Mecca and Medina. Including Some of the More Remarkable Incidents in the Life of Mohammed, the Arab Lawgiver by Richard F. Burton. William Clowes & Sons, London. 1865.

Stone Talk: Being Some of the Marvellous Sayings of a Petral Portion of Fleet Street, London, to One Doctor Polyglott, Ph.D., by Frank Baker, D.O.N. Robert Hardwicke, London. 1865.

The Highlands of the Brazil by Captain Richard F. Burton, F.R.G.S. Two volumes. Tinsley Brothers, London. 1869.

Vikram and the Vampire, or Tales of Hindu Devilry. Adapted by Richard F. Burton, F.R.G.S. Ernest Griset, London. 1869.

Letters from the Battle-fields of Paraguay by Captain Richard F. Burton, F.R.G.S. Tinsley Brothers, London. 1870.

Unexplored Syria, Visits to the Libanus, The Tulúl el Safá, The Anti-Libanus, The Northern Libanus, and The 'Aláh by Richard F. Burton and Charles F. Tyrwhitt Drake. Two volumes. Tinsley Brothers, London. 1971.

Zanzibar; City, Island, and Coast by Richard F. Burton. Two volumes. Tinsley Brothers, London. 1872.

The Lands of Cazembe. Lacerda's Journey to Cazembe in 1798. Translated and Annotated by Captain R. F. Burton, F.R.G.S. Also, *Journey of the*

Pombeiros, P. J. Baptista and Amaro José, across Africa from Angola to Tette on the Zambeze, translated by B. A. Beadle; and, a *Resumé of the Journey of MM Monteiro and Gamitto* by Dr C. T. Beke. Published by the Royal Geographical Society. John Murray, London. 1873.

The Captivity of Hans Stade of Hesse, in a.d. 1547–1555. Among the Wild Tribes of Eastern Brazil. Translated by Albert Tootal, Esq., of Rio de Janeiro, and Annotated by Richard F. Burton. Printed for the Hakluyt Society, London. 1874.

Ultima Thule; or: A Summer in Iceland by Richard F. Burton. Two volumes. William P. Nimmo, London. 1875.

Etruscan Bologna: A Study by Richard F. Burton. Smith, Elder & Co., London. 1876.

A New System of Sword Exercise for Infantry by Richard F. Burton, Author of 'A System of Bayonet Exercise' (1853). William Clowes, London. 1876.

Two Trips to Gorilla Land, and the Cataracts of the Congo by Richard F. Burton. Two volumes. Sampson Low, Marston, Low & Searle, London. 1876.

Scind Revisited: With Notices of the Anglo-Indian Army; Railroads; Past, Present, and Future, Etc. by Richard F. Burton. Two volumes. Richard Bentley and Son, London. 1877.

The Gold-Mines of Midian, and The Ruined Midianite Cities. A Fortnight's Tour in North-western Arabia by Richard F. Burton, Membre de L'Institut Egyptien. C. Kegan Paul & Co., London. 1878.

The Land of Midian (revisited) by Richard F. Burton. Two volumes. C. Kegan Paul & Co., London. 1879.

The Kasîdah of Hâjî Abdû El-Yezdi. A Lay of the Higher Law: Translated and Annotated by his Friend and Pupil F. B. London, privately printed. 1880.

Os Lusiadas (The Lusiads): Englished by Richard Francis Burton: (Edited by His Wife, Isabel Burton). Two volumes. Bernard Quaritch, London. 1880.

Camoens: His Life and His Lusiads. A Commentary by Richard F. Burton. Two volumes. Bernard Quaritch, London. 1881.

A Glance at The 'Passion-Play' by Richard F. Burton. W. H. Harrison, London. 1881.

To the Gold Coast for Gold. A Personal Narrative by Richard F. Burton and Verney Lovett Cameron. Two volumes. Chatto & Windus, London. 1883.

The Book of The Sword by Richard F. Burton, Maitre D'Armes (Breveté). Chatto & Windus, London. 1884.

Camoens, The Lyrics, Part I. Part II, (Sonnets, Canzons, Odes, and Sextines). Englished by Richard F. Burton. Bernard Quaritch, London. 1884.

Iraçéma, The Honey-lips. A Legend of Brazil by J. De Alencar. Translated by Isabel Burton. *Manuel De Moraes, A Chronicle of the Seventeenth Century* by J. M. Pereiera Da Silva. Translated by Richard F. and Isabel Burton. Bickers & Son, London. 1886.

Priapeia or the Sportive Epigrams of divers Poets on Priapus: the Latin Text now for the first time Englished in Verse and Prose (the Metrical Version by 'Outidanos') with Introduction, Notes Explanatory and Illustrative, and Excursus by 'Neaniskos'. Cosmopoli. 1890.

THE KAMA SHASTRA SOCIETY PUBLICATIONS

The Kāma Sūtra of Vatsyayana. With a Preface and Introduction. London: Printed for the Hindoo Kama Shastra Society. 1883.

Ananga-Ranga: (Stage of the Bodiless One), or, The Hindu Art of Love. (Ars Amoris Indica). Translated from the Sanskrit, and Annotated by A.F.F. & B.F.R. Reprint: Cosmopoli. 1885. For the Kama Shastra Society of London, and Benares.

The Perfumed Garden of the Cheikh Nefzaoui: A Manual of Arabian Erotology, (XVI. Century); Revised and Corrected Translation. Cosmopoli. 1886: for the Kama Shastra Society of London and Benares.

A Plain and Literal Translation of the Arabian Nights' Entertainments, Now Entituled The Book of The Thousand Nights and a Night; With Introduction Explanatory Notes on the Manners and Customs of Moslem Men and a Terminal Essay upon the History of the Nights by Richard F. Burton. Printed by the Kama Shastra Society in ten volumes, 1885 to 1886.

Supplemental Nights to the Book of The Thousand Nights and a Night, With Notes Anthropological and Explanatory by Richard F. Burton. Printed by the Kama Shastra Society in six volumes. Vols I and II, 1886. Vols III and IV, 1887. Vols V and VI, 1888.

The Behāristān (Abode of Spring) by Jâmi, A Literal Translation from the Persian. Printed by the Kama Shastra Society. Benares. 1887.

The Gulistān or Rose Garden of Sa'di. Faithfully Translated into English. Printed by the Kama Shastra Society. Benares. 1888.

POSTHUMOUS PUBLICATIONS

Marocco and the Moors: Being An Account of Travels, with a General Description of the Country and its People by Arthur Leared, M.D. Oxon., F.R.C.P.

Second Edition. Revised and Edited by Sir Richard Burton, K.C.M.G. Sampson Low, Marston, Searle and Rivington, Ltd., London. 1891. (Burton did not contribute to the first edition.)

Il Pentamerone; or, the Tale of Tales. Being a translation by the late Sir Richard Burton, K.C.M.G. of Il Pentamerone; Overo Lo Cunto de li Cunte, Trattenemiento de li Peccerille, of Giovanni Battista Basile, Count of Torone (Gian Alessio Abbattutis). Two volumes. Henry and Co., London. 1893.

The Carmina of Caius Valerius Catullus. Now first completely Englished into Verse and Prose, the Metrical Part by Capt. Sir Richard F. Burton, K.C.M.G., F.R.G.S., etc., etc., etc., and the Prose Portion, Introduction, and Notes Explanatory and Illustrative by Leonard C. Smithers, London. 1894.

The Jew, The Gypsy and El Islam by the Late Captain Sir Richard F. Burton, K.C.M.G., F.R.G.S. Edited with a Preface and Brief Notes by W. H. Wilkins. Hutchinson & Co., London. 1898.

Wanderings in Three Continents by the Late Captain Sir Richard F. Burton, K.C.M.G. Edited with a Preface by W. H. Wilkins, M.A., F.S.A. Hutchinson & Co., London. 1901.

Selected Papers on Anthropology, Travel & Exploration by Sir Richard Burton. Edited with an Introduction by N. M. Penzer. A. M. Philpot, London. 1924.

Between the years 1849 to 1888, Burton wrote approximately one hundred and twenty letters, articles and abridged sections of longer narratives, which he contributed to a number of journals. These range from his earliest contribution, 1849, *Notes and Remarks on Dr. Dorn's Chrestomathy of the Pushtu or Affghan Language* printed in the Journal of the Bombay Branch of the Royal Asiatic Society, to a long letter describing *Three Months at Abbazia* signed by himself and Isabel in the Vienna Weekly News, 1888.

PREVIOUS BIOGRAPHIES OF RICHARD BURTON

A Short Sketch of the Career of Captain Richard F. Burton by 'An Old Oxonian'. (Alfred Bates Richards.) William Mullan & Son, London. 1880.

Richard F. Burton by Francis Hitchman. Two volumes. Sampson, Low, Searle & Rivington, London. 1887.

The Life of Captain Sir Richard F. Burton by Isabel Burton. Two volumes. Chapman & Hall, London. 1893.

The True Life of Capt. Sir Richard F. Burton by Georgiana M. Stisted. With the authority and approval of the Burton family. H. S. Nichols, London. 1896.

The Life of Sir Richard Burton by Thomas Wright. Two volumes. Everett & Co., London. 1906.

The Real Sir Richard Burton by Walter Phelps Dodge. T. Fisher Unwin, London. 1907.

Burton: Arabian Nights Adventurer by Fairfax Downey. Charles Scribner's Sons, New York and London. 1931.

Richard Burton: Explorer by Hugh J. Schonfield. Herbert Joseph, London. 1936.

The Arabian Knight: A Study of Sir Richard Burton. Arthur Barker, London. 1936.

Burton by Byron Farwell. Longmans, Green & Co. Ltd., London. 1963.

The Devil Drives by Fawn M. Brodie. Eyre & Spottiswoode Ltd., London. 1967.

REQUIRED BURTON READING

'Burton as I Knew Him' by Verney Lovett Cameron. *Fortnightly Review*, December, 1890.

The Romance of Isabel, Lady Burton by W. H. Wilkins. Two volumes. Chapman & Hall, London. 1897.

'Richard Burton' by Ouida. *Fortnightly Review*, June, 1906.

Contemporary Portraits by Frank Harris. Methuen, London. 1915.

My Diaries by Wilfrid Scawen Blunt. Two volumes. Martin Secker, London, 1919 and 1920.

'Sir Richard Burton as I Knew Him' by F. Grenfell Baker. *Cornhill Magazine*, October, 1921.

An Annotated Bibliography of Sir Richard Francis Burton by Norman M. Penzer. Preface by F. Grenfell Baker. A. M. Philpot, London. 1923.

'Memories of Richard Burton' by Luke Ionides. *The Transatlantic Review*, March, 1924.

Dramatis Personae by Arthur Symons. Faber & Dwyer, London. 1925.

Monckton Milnes: The Years of Promise by James Pope Hennessy. Constable, London. 1940.

Monckton Milnes: The Flight of Youth by James Pope Hennessy. Constable, London. 1951.

Index

284

285

286